MW00413406

Getting
Started with
Neurofeedback

JOHN N. DEMOS, MA, LCMHC, BCIA-EEG

W. W. Norton & Company
New York • London

For information about permission to reproduce
selections from this book, write to
Permissions, W. W. Norton & Company, Inc.,
500 Fifth Avenue, New York, NY 10110

Production Manager: Leeann Graham
Manufacturing by Quebecor World Fairfield Graphics

Library of Congress Cataloging-in-Publication Data

Demos, John N.
Getting started with neurofeedback / John N. Demos.
        p.   cm.—(A Norton professional book)
Includes bibliographical references and index.
ISBN 0-393-70450-5
1. Biofeedback training.   I. Title.   II. Series.

RC489.B53D45   2004
616.89′16—dc22   2004049254

W. W. Norton & Company, Inc., 500 Fifth Avenue, New York, NY 10110
www.wwnorton.com

W. W. Norton & Company, Ltd., Castle House, 75/76 Wells St., London W1T 3QT

3 5 7 9 0 8 6 4 2

Dedicated to the designer of the brain who made this book possible

Contents

Figures and Tables

Note: A lowercase letter "c" after a figure number (e.g., Figure 5.5c) indicates that the figure appears in the color insert.

FIGURES

TABLES

Abbreviations

A/T	alpha/theta
AAPB	Association for Applied Psychophysiology and Biofeedback
ADD	attention deficit disorder
ADHD	attention deficit/hyperactivity disorder
ANS	autonomic nervous system
APA	American Psychological Association
AQ	attention quotient
AVS	audiovisual stimulation
BAI	Burns Anxiety Inventory
BASK	behavior, affect, sensation, knowledge
BCIA	Biofeedback Certification Institute of America
BDI	Beck Depression Inventory
BPD	borderline personality disorder
BWE	brain wave entrainment
CBF	cerebral blood flow
CEU	continuing education unit
CNS	central nervous system
CPT	current procedural terminology
CPU	central processing unit (microprocessor)
CSA	compressed spectral array
CSF	cerebral spinal fluid
DBT	dialectic behavior therapy
DES	Dissociative Experiences Scale

| DID | dissociative identity disorder |
| DOS | disk operating system |

EDA	electrodermal activity
EEG	electroencephalograph (electroencephalogram)
EKG	electrocardiogram
EMDR	eye movement desensitization and reprocessing
EMG	electromyogram (electromyograph, electromyography)
EMI	electromagnetic interference
EPSP	excitatory postsynaptic potential

FDA	Food and Drug Administration (United States)
5HTP	5-hydroxy L-tryptophan
fMRI	functional magnetic resonance imaging

| GABA | gamma-aminobutyric acid |
| GSR | galvanic skin response |

HEG	hemoencephalography
HMO	health management organization
HMR	holographic memory resolution
HRV	heart rate variability

IPSP	inhibitory postsynaptic potential
IQ	intelligence quotient
ISNR	International Society for Neuronal Regulation
IVA	intermediate visual and auditory

L&S	light and sound
LCMHC	licensed clinical mental health counselor
LD	learning disorder
LED	light-emitting diode
LH	left hemisphere

| ND | naturopathic doctor |

OCD	obsessive-compulsive disorder
OS	operating system
OTC	over-the-counter

PDR	posterior dominant rhythm
PET	positron emission tomography
PMS	premenstrual syndrome

PNS   peripheral nervous system
PPO   preferred provider organization
PTSD   posttraumatic stress disorder

QEEG   quantitative electroencephalograph

RAS   reticular activating system
rCBF   regional cerebral blood flow
RCQ   response control quotient
RFI   radio frequency interference
RH   right hemisphere
RMS   root mean square

SAD   seasonal affective disorder
SEMG   surface electromyography
SMR   sensorimotor rhythm
SPECT   single photon emission computed tomography
SSRI   selective serotonin reuptake inhibitor
ST   skin temperature

TBI   traumatic brain injury
MTBI   minor traumatic brain injury
TMJ   temporomandibular joint pain
TOVA   Test of Variables of Attention

Preface

GETTING STARTED WITH NEUROFEEDBACK is written for the professional health care provider who wishes to add neurotherapy to his or her practice as well as the experienced clinician who is looking for a concise treatment guide. Please read this book in the order it was written. Each chapter builds upon the concepts contained in previous chapters. Having a basic understanding of neurofeedback will transform your first seminar from one of confusion to one of illumination. Having a basic understanding of neurology will empower you to isolate specific regions of the cerebral cortex that likely contribute to your client's distress. My review of neurology is organized specifically for neurotherapists. Later chapters will provide you with a step-by-step assessment process that will boost your confidence when you diagnose and train your first client. Furthermore, the color insert demonstrates the rationale for electrocephalography (EEG) assessments and the power of neurotherapy. It can be used as a teaching aid during the initial consultation.

Getting Started with Neurofeedback guides the reader through the process of diagnosing and treating clients. The following is a summary of the entire neurotherapy process that will be expanded upon in this book:

1. The initial consultation: Prospective clients need as much as 1 hr of your time before they are ready to commence neurotherapy. You must be ready to educate the clients and answer their questions.
2. The clinical evaluation: Computer-driven performance tests as well as behavioral checklists form a clinical baseline. Psychiatric interviewing adds to the diagnostic process. EEG equipment takes electrical measurements from the scalp. Those measurements may be used to create topographical brain maps akin to the ones shown in

the color insert. The goal is to isolate specific regions of the cerebral cortex that function outside of normative limits. Each region of the brain is known to contribute to specific neurological functions. For example, clients who are mathematically challenged will likely present with abnormal electrical activity in the specific regions of the cerebral cortex known to govern the ability to calculate and solve mathematical problems. The initial evaluation takes from 2 to 4 hrs to complete.

3. Treatment plans: Clients need to know what you intend to do and what is expected of them. They can be informed verbally or in writing.

4. Neurofeedback training: There is more than one way to improve brain metabolism, and the reader will be presented with various treatment options. Clients require 20 to 60 training sessions to achieve their goals. Some conditions require even more than 60 sessions. Homework may be assigned to enhance treatment goals. About every 10 to 15 sessions the client retakes one or more of the original tests to ensure the efficacy of neurofeedback training. Once the original goals of treatment have been met, the client continues to train for an additional 5 to 10 sessions to prevent relapse.

This book is written to smooth the way for the next generation of neurofeedback providers. The likely candidate for neurofeedback training is a licensed health care professional who has received graduate school training. However, graduate school programs teach students to use *standard* diagnostic and intervention methods. Rarely do they show students how to apply neurology and EEG in the clinical setting. My first 5-day training seminar was difficult because so many new ideas and concepts were presented. There was insufficient time to reflect upon and absorb manifold precepts of science, technology, diagnosis, and treatment, as well as a brief review of major historical characters. To make matters worse, there were no books dedicated to teaching the fundamentals of this exciting but new process. Consequently, I did not learn how to accurately diagnose and confidently train new clients because my foundation of knowledge was faulty and personal theory was missing. My unfortunate experience need not be repeated. This book answers essential questions: How does neurotherapy work? What is the rationale for treatment? When is neurotherapy the treatment of choice? Most important, why should I add it to my already existing health care practice?

The book introduces the reader to the world of neurofeedback, its history and scientific basis. Case studies help the reader to apply what they are learning. Charts and examples of topographical brain maps serve as teaching aids. My goal is to take the mystery out of the whole assessment process. Advanced techniques will be explained and demonstrated by additional case studies. The reader will be shown how to use biofeedback for the body to augment neurofeedback training. Learning to work with the body and having a basic knowledge of complementary medicine is a plus. I conclude the book with practical suggestions on marketing, purchasing equipment, finding appropriate training and supervision, and keeping up with the ever-growing profession of neurofeedback. It is my fondest hope that all providers will strive to become certified in neurotherapy. The credibility of neurotherapy and its providers depends upon the existence of a major certifying body. To date, the largest certifying body is the Biofeedback Certification Institute of America (BCIA). This organization has created a professional model for practice that includes a code of ethics, minimum education requirements, supervision and internship requirements, as well as the acquisition of continuing education units (CEUs).

The health care system in the 21st century has already seen the development of computer-assisted assessment tools. Neurofeedback is founded upon computer technology joined with auxiliary equipment that can measure the metabolic activity of the cerebral cortex. It empowers the client to use his or her mind as a tool for personal healing. It is client-centered therapy at its technological best. Neurofeedback training combines the principles of complementary medicine with the power of electronics. The small child can master it. However, it is also appealing to the intellectual who makes up this computer-savvy generation. Many health care professionals are more than ready to add brain imaging technology and neurofeedback training to their practice. *Getting Started with Neurofeedback* will help you to decide if neurotherapy is for you. Even if you do not wish to pursue neurotherapy, you will find this publication useful because it contains many nonequipment clinical intervention skills.

John N. Demos, MA, LCMHC, BCIA-EEG, can be contacted at www.eegvermont.com.

Acknowledgments

I WISH TO EXPRESS APPRECIATION for the time and attention afforded me by many instructors, lectureres, writers, and researchers in the field of neurotherapy. I would like to thank Bob Gurnee for his personal attention that added to my overall understanding of quantitative electroencephalography (QEEG). I would like to thank Hershel Toomim for sharing some of his wisdom in the application of hemoencephalography (HEG) neurofeedback. My thanks to Richard Soutar for introducing me to the article written by Montgomery and colleagues (1998) which was the basis for Table 5.1 in Chapter 5. My thanks to Peter Van Deusen for providing me with dominant frequency training software for BioExplorer (© Cyber Evolution, Inc.) which was the basis for Appendix Figure 2.2. My thanks to Doug Youngberg for his insights on the FDA. Other clinicians who also took time to discuss important matters included Mary Jo Sabo, Robert Thatcher, Jay Gunkelman, Mike Doohan, Margaret Ayers, and Joel Lubar. Fortunately, I also had the support of peers who agreed to proofread and offer suggestions on my original manuscript. I would like to express many thanks to Leslie Sherlin whose advice and critique greatly added to the accuracy of this publication. Leslie's expertise in QEEG theory and application will no doubt continue to add to the quality of this ever-evolving field of neurotherapy. I would also like to thank Tom Collura who took time out of his busy schedule to read and review my manuscript. Tom's philosophy of wellness and growth through neurotherapy is an inspiration. I would like to thank my editor Deborah Malmud whose wisdom guided much of the overall organization of the book. I would also like to thank Robert Crowson of Athens, Vermont, for the production of all of the freehand drawings in this publication. Last but in no ways least, I would like to thank my wife, Marge, who supported me in two ways during this writing project. First, she put up with my late hours and many absences from her side. Second, her comments on my writing presentation and style improved the overall quality of the book. My wife is a prolific reader in the field of complementary alternative medicine. She is a certified reflexologist and polarity therapist.

Getting
Started with
Neurofeedback

Introduction

NEUROFEEDBACK IS A COMPREHENSIVE TRAINING SYSTEM that promotes growth and change at the cellular level of the brain. It takes science out of the laboratory and into the hands of private health professionals. Neurofeedback is technology's answer to psychotherapy, cognitive rehabilitation, and poor cerebral functioning; it has been successfully applied in the treatment of depression, anxiety, posttraumatic stress disorder (PTSD), personality disorders, addictions, and unresolved emotional issues. It is an effective treatment for the disorders of early childhood such as attention-deficit/hyperactivity disorder (ADHD), pervasive developmental/disorders (PDD), reactive attachment disorder, Asperger's disorder, learning disorders, and obsessive-compulsive disorder (OCD). For over 30 years neurotherapy has transformed the lives of those with seizure disorder and epilepsy. Victims of closed-head injuries and headaches, as well as those with age-related cognitive decline, have found neurotherapy to be an effective tool for symptom reduction and cognitive enhancement. Neurofeedback providers also offer peak-performance training for business executives, athletes, performers, and many others.

With so many applications, it is no wonder that professionals from various disciplines have added neurotherapy to their practice. Mental health professionals, educators, occupational therapists, rehabilitation counselors, and doctors are among those using neurotherapy to augment the healing and personal growth of their clients. Some have made neurotherapy their primary treatment modality; others have made it a part of a larger clinical practice. Until now, there has not been a single comprehensive yet easy-to-understand guide for the practitioner interested in exploring neurotherapy, adding neurotherapy to their practice, or starting a practice devoted entirely to this modality.

High-tech brain imaging has opened a large window of understanding of the brain, and we now know that the functional brain does more than just serve as a center of cognition and memory. Numerous studies have revealed the brain's role in emotional processing, the development of the conscious self, and various personality traits that are central to our ways of being. Scientists have concluded that ethical decision-making and behaviors are not always rooted in psychological processes or early childhood learning. Severe head injuries may cause characterological disturbances and breaches in personal integrity, and we know that dysfunctional brains make dysfunctional decisions (Damasio, 1994). Research has shown that "the brain of the violent patient is clearly different from that of the nonviolent person" (Amen, 1998, p. 212). Brain imaging has allowed scientists to observe metabolic activity within specific regions of the brain during cognitive and emotional activities. This knowledge is key to understanding how neurotherapy can effectively help clients.

Getting Started with Neurofeedback covers the entire process of becoming a neurofeedback provider. It offers advice about buying equipment, choosing a good training program, and setting up an office. Moreover, it has been designed to help you get the most out of your first training experience. Pictures and illustrations will facilitate your learning experience. Pictures can also be shown to prospective clients to help them understand the neurotherapy process. Once in practice, you can use this book to help in the diagnostic and treatment process. This book will give you an overview of several biofeedback and neurofeedback modalities. It will also show the connection between the history of neurotherapy and present-day clinical practice.

TRADITIONAL PSYCHOTHERAPY VS. NEUROFEEDBACK

Traditional psychotherapists have two intervention tools: talk and medication. Assessments are based upon subjective self-reports, psychiatric interviewing, testing, family history, and institutional reports. Direct brain interventions and assessments are not part of the weekly therapy agenda. Talk therapy continues to be a potent modality. It promotes the healing of psychological issues, whereas medication alters—not heals—the electrochemical activities in the brain. Talk therapy may result in real changes in the metabolic activity of the brain over an extended period of time. But not all conditions will improve with talk therapy. Direct changes in the metabolic activity of the brain can be achieved though medication. Those changes are not permanent, however, and side effects are common.

Given all that we now know about the brain and our capabilities of non-invasively viewing the brain in action, therapists are increasingly turning toward brain-based therapies in a variety of therapeutic situations. Neurofeedback training works directly with the brain. Each client trains at his or her own pace. Progress can be monitored and reviewed with trainees at every session. Some trainees report sensations of greater mental clarity and less mental fog during the first training session. Others require more sessions before they notice a significant difference. Training can open a door to emotional freedom and concomitant emotional releases. At those moments basic counseling skills are used to debrief trainees. Empathy and unconditional positive regard join to create an emotionally safe therapeutic environment.

Neurotherapy is a metabolic tracking and changing tool that is orchestrated by the therapist and played out by the client. For the first time, a client statement such as "I am feeling calmer" can be measured and quantified on the cerebral level. Actual numerical and graphic changes in the electroencephalogram (EEG) can be observed. The age of neurofeedback has been born amid the current technological revolution and the proliferation of personal computers (Robbins, 2000a). Clients can be empowered to change brain metabolism; medication reduction or elimination is a reality. The brain can heal, or at least improve itself, without the aid of medication.

Biofeedback is the process of recording and sending biological data back to a trainee (Criswell, 1995). Neurofeedback is a modality of biofeedback that can facilitate changes in brain wave patterns and regional cerebral blood flow (rCBF) activation. Neurofeedback trainees do not receive input in the form of electrical impulses or subliminal messages. This is an important point to stress: *there is no input.* Trainees receive feedback or output signals that relate to their own subconscious neuronal activities. Thus, neurofeedback is a self-regulation skill that inspires growth through self-awareness. Trainees are informed via auditory or graphic signals each time the brain is operating more efficiently. More important, the trainee learns how to access that improved state of mind for future use outside the training arena. Hence, true learning takes place—without harmful side effects. Neurofeedback is similar to a comprehensive exercise program because it strengthens neural pathways while increasing mental endurance and flexibility. It is more like coaching than psychotherapy.

The goals of psychotherapy include positive change, growth, and an improved sense of self. But changes cannot be measured and quantified easily; they are often limited to subjective judgments. How may times have you been *certain* that the talk therapy intervention you have employed really

6 Getting Started with Neurofeedback

made a lasting difference to your client? Consider the modality of couples counseling. What is the long-term success rate? Couples therapist Brent Atkinson has addressed this question and has described the role of the limbic system when working with clients (Atkinson, 1999):

> Controlled studies of marital therapy outcome show that following a stint of treatment, only 50 percent of couples significantly improve. But even among those couples who did make progress, a big chunk—30 to 40 percent—relapse within two years. A close reading of this outcome research reveals a still more dispiriting reality: many of the so-called "successful" couples reported still feeling unhappy with their marriage at a two-year follow-up. In the course of therapy they had merely progressed from "highly distressed" to just plain "distressed." (pp. 24–25)

Atkinson (1999) went on to eloquently describe the predominant role of the amygdala (a part of the brain's limbic system) during the clinical hour. He does not promote neurotherapy as the answer to a couple's problems, but he does demonstrate the frustration that many psychotherapists face when trying to help people change their behavior. Even though the therapist actively engages the rational side of the brain, the emotional component of the brain often wins out. Atkinson asserts that therapists must be aware of limbic power because it can be quiet during counseling sessions but be active during real-life situations. Knowledge of the neurobiology behind this fact is crucial: we know that the emotional portion of the brain—the limbic system—lies beneath the prefrontal context—the executive of the brain. Real changes to the emotional self are hard to come by, and there may be a neural explanation for this fact.

I am not suggesting that couples therapy is not a valuable modality. Hidden feelings and emotions need a safe place to be expressed and examined. Personal issues can be discussed and resolved. Despite the value of this treatment, however, many couples are simply unable to make long-lasting changes. The majority of couples are not therapeutic failures; they are not psychologically resistant to change. Rather, they have progressed as far as the talk therapy arena can take them.

This is but one example of psychotherapy's limitations. Recognizing this fact, many clinicians have added adjuncts to their clinical practice such as eye movement desensitization and reprocessing (EMDR) and other "power" therapy techniques (Wylie, 1996). The mind has the power to heal itself, but very often it lacks an effective tool to do so. Interventions at different and deeper levels are required to produce further change and growth. Neurofeedback is one such intervention that is just now coming into its own, and technological advances continue to improve the efficacy of neurotherapy.

NEUROFEEDBACK: TAKING THE SHAME OUT OF MENTAL ILLNESS

The brain is becoming more and more of an open book that can be read through the use of noninvasive imaging techniques. Recent developments in computer technology have opened the way for clinicians in private practice to examine brain functions safely. Brain imaging or quantitative EEG (QEEG) is no longer limited to large institutions such as hospitals. It can be added to your small private practice. Clients can be shown pictorial images that will help them understand what is happening within their own cerebral cortex. Multicolor brain maps show what parts of the cerebral cortex are operating outside of normal limits. The ability to show a client what's wrong cannot be overstated. For example, depressed clients may feel that they are to blame for their condition because of being weak-willed or lacking in personal fortitude. However, many depressed clients have an abnormal pattern of EEG slowing in the anterior left hemisphere that has been with them since birth (Davidson, 1998). Therefore, having depression is not a cause for shame or guilt. Depression often relates to brain dynamics. More important, neurofeedback training can do something about those dynamics.

Each region of the brain is associated with specific functional operations (Springer & Deutsch, 1998). For example, if a client struggles to solve math problems it may relate to an inadequate rCBF in the parietal lobe region. Neurofeedback technology gives the clinician tools to assess and modify parietal lobe functioning without the use of medication. It shows the client where the problem is and what can be done about it.

Throughout this book I will be presenting research data that support the rationale for neurofeedback training. Before moving ahead to Chapter 1, however, I want to touch on some of the key studies that have supported the value of neurofeedback training and brain imagining techniques. As you work in a neurotherapy practice, you will find that doctors, insurance companies, and prospective clients often ask for written information that supports the efficacy of neurofeedback training. I recommend keeping a collection of press releases, clinical studies, brochures, and other printed material that can be distributed as needed.

THE YONKERS PROJECT

If a therapy treatment is effective, then it should work for large numbers of people over long periods of time. It should not be limited to one or two case studies or anecdotal reports. The experiment at the Enrico Fermi School in Yonkers, New York, is well worth considering. Robbins (2000b) reported on the use of neurofeedback for ADHD, learning disorders, depression, and improved conduct at the Enrico Fermi School in Yonkers, New York:

> Linda Vergara, the school's principle, said she decided to try the approach when doctors diagnosed the disorder in her son in 1992. "They told me I needed to give him something to calm him down," she said.
>
> Ms. Vergara decided not to give her son Ritalin, the drug frequently used to treat the ailment, and instead took him to see Dr. Mary Jo Sabo, a psychologist in Suffern, N.Y., to try neurofeedback.
>
> Ms. Vergara said she saw her son become calmer, and he began doing his homework without being asked. She and Dr. Sabo brought the technique to Fermi, a public elementary school with 900 children.
>
> Now, *five years* after the program began nearly 300 *hundred children* have been treated at no charge with neurofeedback at Fermi and two other public schools in Yonkers for a variety of problems, including A.D.D., learning disabilities and depression.
>
> "There are children who see tremendous gains and some who see minimal changes," said Ms. Vergara. "Over all, the kids can focus better and have better self-esteem. There are fewer suspensions, better attendance and fewer late kids." (p. 7)

Three hundred children and 5 years later, neurofeedback was declared a success. Participants benefited without suffering harm or experiencing the side effects that often accompanies medication. Incidentally, in-house neurofeedback training in the Yonkers school system continued until the 9/11/2001 tragedy. At that time, funding for special projects was channeled into New York City, where it was desperately needed. Other schools in the United States continue to have in-house neurofeedback training.

ATTENTION DEFICIT HYPERACTIVITY DISORDER

For a therapy to be accepted by the wider scientific community, it must rely on clinically sound diagnostic procedures. The assessment process should not rest on the subjective talent or intuition of a skilled therapist.

Large numbers of those diagnosed with attention deficit hyperactivity disorder (ADHD) have been studied with QEEG. Their brain wave patterns were found to be discreetly different than those of the normal population. Dr. Joel Lubar, at the University of Tennessee, analyzed QEEG data for over 109 volunteers with ADHD and 11 controls. He concluded, "Excessive *theta* activity and lack of *beta* activity are the primary neurological landmarks of ADHD" (1995, p. 505, italics added). Furthermore, "during academic challenges, there were significant increases in slow (4–8 Hertz) theta activity along the midline and in the frontal regions and decreased beta activity, especially along the midline posteriorly" (p. 502). The pattern of too much theta and too little beta is characteristic of the inattentive type of ADHD. He also catalogued other subtypes of ADHD that have distinctive EEG patterns. Lubar's review of the literature revealed the following:

> Abnormalities in EEG were reported in children now classified as ADD and ADHD as early as 1938 (Jasper, Solomon & Bradley, 1938). There is extensive literature, much of it reviewed in the supplement to the *Journal of Child Neurology* published in 1991. Basically, EEG studies show excessive slow activity in central and frontal regions of the brain. These studies are supported by recent PET [positron emission tomography] scan and SPECT [single photon emission computerized tomography] scan studies that also indicate abnormalities in cerebral metabolism in these particular brain areas. (p. 501)

The *Diagnostic and Statistical Manual of Mental Disorders (DSM-IV)* (American Psychiatric Association, 1994) delineates criteria that must be met in order to make the diagnosis of ADHD, with or without hyperactivity. Impulsivity, inattention, distractibility, and hyperactivity are four of many behavioral components that may be found in ADHD. However, there is also a neurological basis that can be seen in the EEG pattern of individual sufferers—especially the inattentive type. Neurotherapists have the advantage of making a *DSM-IV* diagnosis and supporting it by EEG analysis. ADD is only one of many disorders with a neurological basis that can be supported by QEEG, PET, and SPECT brain scans.

CRI-HELP STUDY

The efficacy of any treatment can be determined by outcome studies that include both experimental and control groups. Both groups must have the same diagnostic disorder. The experimental group participates in the new treatment regimen, whereas the control group receives the traditional treatment or no treatment. Thereafter the study must be published or presented to a group of peers in the scientific community. One such study came from the application of neurotherapy to the problem of substance abuse.

CRI-Help is a substance abuse clinic in California that has integrated neurotherapy with traditional methods of treatment. Scott, Brod, Sidirof, Kaiser, and Sagan (2002) organized an outcome study among a group of 121 polysubstance abusers in residential care. Sixty-one volunteers were in the control group and 60 were in the experimental group. The control group received traditional care for substance abusers offered at CRI-help. The experimental group received additional neurofeedback treatment. Scott and colleagues (2002) presented the outcomes of the CRI-Help study to the American Psychiatric Association. They were as follows:

1. The control group had a much higher dropout rate than the experimental group. Only 27 out of 61 controls finished the study, compared to 47 out of the 60 in the experimental group.
2. The experimental group was more successful: "At one-year post study 36 of the 47 completing experimental subjects were abstinent compared to 12 of 27 control subjects."

Only 12 out of 61 in the control group, or 20%, remained abstinent 1 year after treatment ended. However, 36 out of 60 in the experimental group, or 60%, remained abstinent 1 year after treatment ended. Several conclusions may be drawn from the above statistics. First, neurofeedback training motivates participants to complete treatment programs. Second, the addition of neurofeedback to traditional therapies significantly improves clinical outcomes for substance abuse treatment. Third, adding neurotherapy to substance abuse programs will likely save money in the long run. The study at CRI-Help is the largest of several studies that have produced similar results on an institutional level (Kelley, 1997; Peniston & Kulkosky, 1991, 1999) . Substance abuse threatens the safety of many citizens throughout the world. Programs such as Alcoholics Anonymous have assisted many in the recovery process. Institutions have been set up to permit intensive in-house care of substance abusers. The fine efforts of many organizations have certainly benefited society. But what if those programs could be made more effective? Neurotherapy is an effective treatment for substance abuse.

THE PLACEBO EFFECT

All treatments lend themselves to the placebo effect. That's why Sterman's early research is of such great interest. His early research was with animals, not humans. Using noncomputerized neurofeedback equipment, he trained animals to increase the amplitude of a brain wave frequency bandwidth known as sensorimotor rhythm (SMR). Later, quite by chance, he was asked by NASA to study the seizure effects of the rocket fuel hydrazine. Sterman decided to test the effects of hydrazine exposure on cats. Ten of his 50 cats had been trained to increase SMR. Much to his surprise, the cats with enhanced SMR were seizure resistant. The cats with normal SMR activity died upon exposure to hydrazine. This event cannot be attributed to the placebo effect; changing the brain dynamics of cats made a real difference.

In the 1970s treatment for epilepsy was limited; few options existed. But, Sterman's finding offered hope for a new treatment modality. One of his staff workers, Margaret Fairbanks, suffered from epilepsy. As a result, she was denied a driver's license. She decided to try the experimental treatment previously reserved for animals. Although not the first neurofeedback trainee, she was the first to ameliorate the symptoms of seizure disorder by means of neurofeedback. When her training was complete, she qualified for a driver's license—she took control of her life with the aid of neurotherapy. There was no other treatment known to her or her doctors that could have effected this change. Her training experience was not an example of the placebo effect. Since then many others have found relief from the symptoms of epilepsy through neurotherapy.

THE PURPOSE OF THIS BOOK

Neurofeedback is not a silver bullet; it will not fix all ailments, and it should not be labeled as a cure for any disorder. Rather, it is a training procedure that requires cooperation on the part of the trainee.

Getting started with a neurofeedback practice can be daunting. Most health care professionals do not have a background in neurology or an understanding of brain's electrical patterns. Furthermore, there is expensive equipment to buy, software to learn, and seminars to attend. All of this requires time, money, and effort on your part. *Getting Started with Neurofeedback* has been written to help smooth out this process and to make your entry into this field, as well as your work within the field, a success. For example, many attending their first neurofeedback seminar feel overwhelmed and confused. However, if you have read this book in advance you will get the most out of that experience with the least amount of confusion.

Getting started does not have to be a headache. If you as a clinician are looking to expand your practice, if you are ready for a challenge, if you want to see proof and data to back up your clinical work, then neurotherapy is for you. If you want to know what it means to be a neurofeedback provider before taking the plunge, then read this book. It will show you how neurofeedback can enrich your existing therapeutic practice, as either an adjunct to traditional psychotherapy or a substitute for it. It is also designed to give valuable information about working in this area to therapists who already use neurofeedback.

Part I provides a detailed definition of neurofeedback basics, including a brief history of neurofeedback, a presentation of brain basics, body anatomy, and the role of each region of the cerebral cortex. The EEG and its role in cerebral metabolism are explained. Actual neurofeedback training procedures are outlined in detail. The clinical utility of brain imaging is demonstrated. The color insert makes the EEG and QEEG brain imaging come alive. The reader is given a taste of what it means to become a neurofeedback provider.

Part II provides an overview of neurofeedback in clinical practice. The entire process from evaluation to training will be covered step by step. The neurofeedback provider is intensely interested in baseline measurements. They provide both the clinician and the client with concrete evidence of the efficacy of neurotherapy. Anecdotal reports serve to support baseline changes. Treatment plans outline the mutual task that faces both client and therapist. Homework is often assigned to enhance training goals. Lifestyle changes may be necessary to ensure success. Cognitive advancement is important, but emotional growth may be more important. Training may provide insights that can be transformed into "a corrective emotional experience" (Alexander, 1946). Alert clinicians capitalize upon those moments of insight that arise during the training hour. Regardless of the treatment modality, empathy will always be needed to engage the client in the therapeutic process.

Part III escorts the reader through the entire process of finding professional training, becoming a certified neurofeedback provider, purchasing equipment, and setting up an office. Suggestions on marketing and practice development are designed to help the newcomer make a financial success of the practice of neurotherapy.

PART I

UNDERSTANDING
NEUROFEEDBACK

1

History and Evolution
of Clinical Practice

THE HISTORY OF BIOFEEDBACK (including neurofeedback) is built upon the cornerstones of technology, electronics, behaviorism, physiology, and neurology. Innovations, experiments, and research came from the minds of individuals who would challenge current scientific thinking. Even as late as the 1950s scientists balked at the idea of conscious control over the autonomic nervous system (ANS). Within a decade however, human subjects would learn to regulate electrical signals in the cerebral cortex and individual muscles. Human subjective experience combined with scientific research created a flurry of ideological discussions and differing opinions. Conferences were organized and researchers attempted to create definitions and give names to what they were observing. The evolution of biofeedback theory had begun. Its growth would be governed by personal theory, clinical discoveries, and advancing technology. The early history of biofeedback laid the groundwork for future research and current clinical theory.

FROM BRAINWAVES TO BIOFEEDBACK: KEY HISTORIC EVENTS

Many consider the scientific research of Richard Caton to be biofeedback's first key event. In 1875 he discovered that fluctuations in the brain's electrical activity follow mental activity. His experiments included putting

15

electrodes in the open or exposed brains of animals. He also recorded some electrical activity from the closed scalp of animals (Criswell, 1995, p. 70). In the 1920s Hans Berger measured the electroencephalograph (EEG) on the *human* scalp. He was the first to record raw EEG on paper (electroencephalogram); later he would identify two different filtered waves, alpha and beta. Ten hertz is known as the Berger Rhythm (Budzynski, 1999, p. 65). Berger discovered that thinking and alertness accompany bursts in the beta frequency band that ranges from 13 cycles per second (hertz) to about 30 cycles per second. His landmark paper was published in 1929. He believed that abnormalities in EEG reflect clinical disorders (Criswell, 1995, p. 70, Cantor, 1999, p. 20). Many neurofeedback providers design training protocols in harmony with Berger's assumption. They apply neurofeedback training to regions of the brain that are known to influence cognitive and behavioral performance.

Other researchers studied the body's biological signals. Carl Jung was one of several practitioners who were investigating galvanic skin response (GSR). He observed changes in electrodermal activity when patients responded to word association exercises. He attempted to correlate physiologic responses with psychological issues. Theoretically, words with emotional content corresponded to fluctuations in his GSR meter. Evidently, the body could be used to signal the mind's activity (Criswell, 1995, p.104). More important, he demonstrated the link between psychotherapy and physiology.

During the 1930s Edgar Adrian and B.H.C. Matthews successfully replicated Berger's "measurements of electrical waves" (Robbins, 2000a, p. 20). They also studied the entrainment of brain waves with a photic stimulation "flicker" device (Budzynski, 1999, p. 65). They pioneered the use of the differential amplifier (Siever, 1999, p. 6.4). Their research showed that the brainwave patterns could be modified by specific frequencies of flashing or flickering light. Brain wave entrainment changes the EEG but it does not conform to the principles of biofeedback because it does not feed back biological information to the trainee—it is a one-way process. However, brain wave entrainment is an ally of neuronal change and growth. It lacks the specificity of neurofeedback, but studies have shown the efficacy of photic stimulation under certain conditions. Consequently, a number of neurofeedback practitioners use it as an adjunct to neurofeedback training.

As late as the 1950s scientists questioned the concept of voluntary control of the ANS. Biological processes such as heart rate variability, blood pressure, and hand temperature were assumed to be under the control of the body's automatic management system. However, by 1960, Neal E. Miller's research proved that subjects could alter ANS functions via operant conditioning (Robbins, 2000, p. 37; Schwartz & Olson, 1995, p. 4). Therefore, operant conditioning via biofeedback training was scientifically possible. Biofeedback's foundation was now secure.

In 1963, John Basmajian discovered the basic principles of electromyography (EMG). Robbins (2000a) explained the essence of his experiment:

> He was studying cells in the brain's motor cortex, which send the message to muscle cells in the body to fire. An organized nerve path in the motor cortex is called a motor unit, and a single motor unit that travels down the spine might control anywhere from a few muscle cells to hundreds of them. Basmajian chose a motor unit that controlled a few cells at the base of the thumb. He inserted a tiny needle electrode into the thumb muscle. No one could see any movement of the muscle, but half of Basmajian's sixteen subjects were able to control the firing of a single motor unit in the brain that governed that muscle. (p. 61)

Basmajian learned that a single motor unit starting in the motor cortex of the brain and extending to the thumb could come under voluntary control. He utilized an oscilloscope to obtain real-time readings that reflected the electrical activity within a muscle (Criswell, 1995, p. 87). Learning to control a single motor unit was not a practical application of biofeedback but it effectively demonstrated the mind-body connection. In just a few years Basmajian's research would open the door to controlling entire muscle groups. Flat electrodes taped to the skin would replace the single needle electrode. This noninvasive form of EMG biofeedback would be called surface EMG (SEMG).

THE BIRTH AND EVOLUTION OF CLINICAL PRACTICE

The year 1963 also to gave rise to the work of Joseph Kamiya, a teacher at the University of Chicago. He wanted to find out if conscious recognition of brain waves was possible. He trained a volunteer to recognize bursts of alpha (8–12 Hz) brain wave activity. Kamiya gave his trainee verbal reinforcement each time he entered into an alpha state. The experiment was a success. Human ability to control brain wave states via instrumentation was confirmed (Criswell, 1995, pp. 70–71). Kamiya's experiment demonstrated the typical biofeedback training loop: (a) an instrument records a specific biological activity of interest; (b) a trainee is reinforced each time the desired activity occurs; then (c) voluntary control of a biological activity becomes possible. All biofeedback modalities are based on the same two-way process innovated by Kamiya.

Kamiya opened the door to alpha enhancement training. Later Green, Green, and Walters of the Menninger Foundation, as well as Budzynski, pioneered theta enhancement training. Trainees entered into "twilight" states of emotional learning and psychological growth (Budzynski, 1999, pp. 69–70). Thus, dynamic psychotherapy interventions could be mobilized by facilitating the client's entry into alpha and theta brain wave states. These biofeedback pioneers had assisted in the birth of applied psychophysiology—the joining of psychotherapy with any biofeedback modality. However, the future of biofeedback would not be limited to psychological depth work. Researchers would soon adapt this new technology to the fields of medicine, mental illness, cognitive rehabilitation, and peak performance training.

Just five years after Kamya's discovery, Barry Sterman published his landmark experiment (Wyricka & Sterman, 1968). Cats were trained to increase sensorimotor rhythm (SMR) or 12–15 Hz. This frequency bandwidth usually increases when motor activity decreases. Thus, the cats were rewarded each time that SMR increased, which likely accompanied a decrease in physical movements. Unrelated to his study, NASA requested that Sterman study the effects of human exposure to hydrazine (rocket fuel) and its relationship to seizure disorder. Sterman started his research with 50 cats. *Ten out of the 50 had been trained to elevate SMR.* All 50 were injected with hydrazine. Much to Sterman's surprise, the 10 specially trained cats were seizure resistant. The other 40 developed seizures 1 hour after being injected (Budzynski, 1999, p. 72; Robbinsa, 2000, pp. 41–42). Sterman had serendipitously discovered a medical application for this new technology.

Sterman was one of many researchers engrossed in the science of changing biological signals with feedback equipment. Consequently, in 1968, a gathering of researchers convened to compare notes on this new technology. The convention delegates included Elmer Green, Barry Sterman, Thomas Budzynski, Joe Kamiya, and many others. With Barbara Brown as its first president, the assembly adopted a descriptive name to define this new scientific field: biofeedback (Robbins, 2000a, pp. 65–66). Neurofeedback is one of many biofeedback modalities.

In that same year, 1968, Thomas Budzynski and John Stoyva collaborated to study the effects of SEMG biofeedback on muscle tension (skin sensors were used rather than needle electrodes). They successfully trained entire muscle groups by placing sensors over the belly of the muscle rather than isolating a single motor unit with a needle sensor. In their study, sensors were placed over the frontalis muscles in order to reduce muscle tension on the forehead (Criswell, 1995, pp. 87–89). Neurofeedback practitioners are interested in muscle tension in the face, scalp, and neck because it can interfere with EEG recordings.

By late 1971, Mary Fairbanks—a sufferer of epilepsy—began neurofeedback training with Sterman. It was hypothesized that her seizure disorder would improve if she trained SMR to increase along the sensorimotor cortex of the brain. The left hemispheric region of the sensorimotor cortex was chosen for the experiment. EEG training equipment was designed to flash a green light when SMR increased and a red light when it decreased. The incidence of seizure activity was greatly reduced after 3 months of neurofeedback training. Fairbanks was well enough to obtain a driver's license (Robbins, 2000a, p. 46). Others followed in her footsteps with similar results.

Some of Sterman's colleagues became pioneers in neurofeedback research and development. Joel Lubar continues to be one of the key researchers in the study of attention, learning, and the EEG. Margaret Ayers developed her own line of equipment, opened up the first commercial neurofeedback clinic, and specializes in the treatment of brain trauma. Sterman, Lubar, and Ayers have generated a fountain of research-based information. They have focused their efforts on cognitive rehabilitation and mental disorders rather than on biofeedback for psychological depth work.

QEEG assessments with normative databases became a reality in the 1970s and 1980s. The pioneers in the development of EEG brain imaging and "large normative and discriminative EEG databases" were Frank Duffy, E. Roy John, and Robert Thatcher (Budzynski, 1999, p. 73). It was now possible to compare brain wave patterns of each individual to a sample normative population. QEEG data acquisition is the process of gathering EEG data from multiple scalp sites. Typically, 19 sensors are placed in exacting scalp locations. QEEG data provides the clinician with a broad picture of the cerebral cortex in action. Brain imaging with normative databases leads to the production of topographical brain maps (examples can be seen in the color insert).

Neurologists also acquire QEEG data for the purpose of examining the waveform or morphology of the raw EEG. If they discover the presence of spikes in the wave morphology then seizure disorder may be present (see Appendix for examples).

About the same time that normative databases were being created, Lexicor Medical Technology, Inc., developed a 19-channel system for QEEG data acquisition. They also manufactured a two-channel EEG neurofeed-back training system that "became the mainstay instrument of the modern Neurofeedback area" (Budzynski, 1999, p. 74). Lexicor brought the field of neurotherapy into the computer age. No longer would published studies rely upon stand-alone (noncomputerized) units for data acquisition or training. Computer driven neurofeedback equipment is now produced by several manufacturers of commercial-grade equipment.

In the early 1980s the power of neurofeedback was relatively unknown. It needed a public relations director. Margaret Ayers introduced Siegfried and Sue Othmer to neurofeedback. Ayers had assisted the Othmers in the treatment of their son. Afterward, they formed their own neurofeedback enterprise, EEG-Spectrum. They became the center of neurofeedback publicity. The Othmers promoted the use computer graphics and effective sounds for deep-states training (Robbins, 2000a, pp. 105–129). They highlighted the link between neurotherapy and psychotherapy. During the 1990s EEG-Spectrum conducted numerous training programs that emphasized the value of following the client's emotional and physiological responses during the training process.

In 1989, Eugene Peniston and Paul Kulkosky used a specific neurofeedback protocol for the treatment of posttraumatic stress disorder (PTSD). They facilitated twilight states of learning by rewarding both alpha and theta. Their protocol has come to be called deep-states training (Robbins, 2000a). Guided visualizations and skin temperature (ST) training were also part of the protocol design. The first landmark study included a small population of Vietnam veterans. Two years later Peniston and Kulkosky studied the effect of neurofeedback training with veterans who had dual diagnoses of alcoholism and PTSD. Both studies had positive outcomes (Peniston & Kulkosky, 1999). They were not the first to explore deep-states training but they were unique in its application to specific disorders in a controlled environment. Formerly, deep states or twilight states of learning were relegated to the domain of each trainee's own subjective inner world. Now the efficacy of alpha/theta neurotherapy would be subjected to the rigors of scientific outcome studies.

CURRENT TRENDS IN NEUROTHERAPY

The major events in the history of neurofeedback have led to the development of theory in clinical practice. Sterman's discovery evolved into a treatment for epilepsy. Others would apply this concept to various clinical disorders. Meanwhile, the work of Kamiya would also bear fruit. Neurotherapy proved to be an effective method for trauma resolution, substance abuse treatment, psychological depth work, and peak performance training. Consequently, neurotherapy evolved into two branches growing and thriving side by side. One branch focused on normalizing the EEG, whereas the other branch focused on personal growth and mental flexibility. The person getting started in neurofeedback may naively assume that all neurofeedback providers follow a similar theoretical path with similar treatment interventions. However, the practice of neurotherapy is diverse.

Some neurotherapists are like *cognitive* therapists, who challenge abnormal thinking because the emphasis is on correcting abnormal EEG patterns. Single-channel site-selective training protocols guided by QEEG data are common. Other neurotherapists are like *dynamic* psychotherapists, who design interventions to make global rather than regional changes in the EEG. Multiple-channel training is used more often than single-channel training. Flexibility and personal growth are integral parts of this model. Peak performance training is included in this category. Lastly, there are many clinicians with an *eclectic* style, who incorporate a variety of interventions. Sometimes treatment begins along the sensorimotor cortex. In other cases treatment is guided by peer-reviewed studies. Various means are used to gather EEG data during the first phase of treatment.

Another factor that differentiates one neurotherapist from another is the amount of time and energy that go into the initial assessment. Initial evaluations may take as little as $1\frac{1}{2}$ h or as much as $4\frac{1}{2}$ h. Longer assessments include QEEG data acquisition, computerized testing, behavioral checklists, psychiatric interviewing, and medical and psychosocial history taking. Some clinicians will not begin neurofeedback training without QEEG data and topographical brain maps to guide protocol selection. Other clinicians assess the EEG by alternate means and limit QEEG data acquisition to clients with traumatic brain injury. Yet other clinicians acquire very little EEG data during the assessment phase; treatment protocols are shaped in accordance with the client's reaction to the treatment protocol.

2

Brain Basics and Body Anatomy
and Physiology

NEUROTHERAPISTS HAVE AN IN-DEPTH KNOWLEDGE of neuronal communications and the operations of various regions of the brain. More important, they can apply their expertise to the client's presenting problem. The rationale for treatment protocols is based on solid research and clinical practice. There is often a direct relationship between regional brain functioning and symptoms. While it is not necessary to be a neurologist, it is necessary to have a working knowledge of the brain, the nervous system, and the endocrine system's role in the fight-or-flight response. Chapter 2 explores the functions of each of the four lobes of the cerebral cortex. It has been organized for neurofeedback providers and not for a general audience. Knowledge of the brain and its functions will guide sensor placement and form a partial basis for treatment.

THE NERVOUS SYSTEM

The nervous system is the command center of the body (see Figure 2.1). It sends and receives signals every second of the day. It is one of the most intricate communication systems in the physical universe. The basic unit of the nervous system is the neuron. Billions of neuronal cells form an intricate network of connections throughout the body. The nervous system has two parts: the central nervous system (CNS) and the peripheral

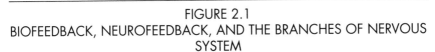

FIGURE 2.1
BIOFEEDBACK, NEUROFEEDBACK, AND THE BRANCHES OF NERVOUS
SYSTEM

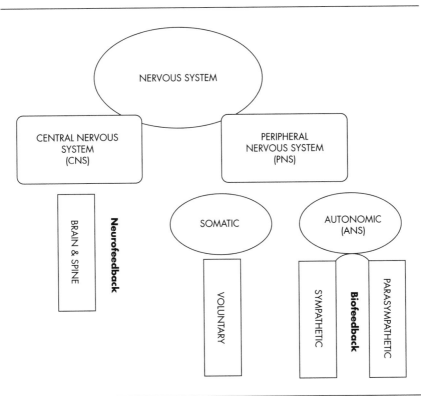

nervous system (PNS). Information travels within and among these two divisions via neural tissue. The CNS includes the brain and the spinal cord. There are 12 pairs of cranial nerves and 31 pairs of spinal nerves. The PNS picks up much of its information from the spinal cord and makes connections with the rest of the body.

The PNS has two divisions: somatic (voluntary) and the autonomic (involuntary). The autonomic nervous system (ANS) has two divisions: sympathetic (activating) and parasympathetic (deactivating). For example, the sympathetic nervous system accelerates the beating of the heart, whereas the parasympathetic nervous system slows it down. The basic unit of communication is the neuron. Neuronal transmission is an electrochemical event. It can be detected and measured from the brain and from various muscle systems throughout the body. Measurements are recorded in microvolts (amplitude) and cycles per second (frequency). The electroencephalograph (EEG) is a graphical representation of neuronal activities in the cerebrum. The electromyograph (EMG) is a graphical representation of neuronal activities in muscles located anywhere in the body or head.

The most prominent part of the brain is the cerebrum; it is divided into left and right hemispheres. Almost every brain structure comes in pairs. The outer layer of cerebrum, the cerebral cortex, is responsible for higher mental functions. It is about 1/8 inch (3 mm) thick. It is divided into four corresponding lobes in each hemisphere. Each lobe is named in conjunction with the cranial bones above it and is associated with specialized tasks. Beneath the lobes of the cerebral cortex is a complex network of connections and structures. One of these structures is the limbic system; it is a key to understanding emotions, memory, and the fight-or-flight response. Some of the parts of the limbic system include:

- amygdala (associated with deep emotions and fear);
- hippocampus (crucial for memory storage and emotions);
- anterior thalamic nuclei (necessary for sensory data processing).

The hypothalamus, just below the thalamus, is a control center for the ANS and survival functions. The cerebellum, or little brain (located in the hindbrain), is responsible for coordination of motor movements and equilibrium. The brain stem holds up the brain as a stem holds a head of broccoli; it contains the reticular activating system (RAS), which helps to regulate the cycle of sleep and wakefulness.

The endocrine system works with the nervous system. It sends messages by secreting hormones that activate glands in various locations, whereas the nervous system sends messages from one neuron to another in a chain-link fashion. The endocrine system glands located in the body are the adrenal, thyroid, parathyroid, pancreas, testes, and ovaries. The endocrine glands located in the brain are the pituitary and the pineal glands. The endocrine system and the CNS talk to each other. The pituitary receives messages from the hypothalamus. (Marieb, 1995). The pituitary then activates other members of the endocrine system. Neuroendocrine exchanges happen all the time. For our purposes, only the fight-or-flight response will be discussed because it is of great interest to the mental health professional.

The fight-or-flight response is a neuroendocrine event that happens after a real or imagined threat is recorded by the thalamus. The thalamus responds by sending out two messages: the first signal is sent for instant analysis by the limbic system. Lightning-fast messages go between the amygdala and hippocampus, climaxing at the hypothalamus. The hypothalamus-pituitary-adrenal axis prepares the body for the perceived emergency: the endocrine and the sympathetic nervous systems go into action (Sills, 2001, p. 348). An avalanche of physiological changes begins, including increased muscle tension, breathing, brain wave frequency, blood pressure, and heart rate, and decreased skin temperature. Adrenal (medulla) glands begin secreting the corticoids (adrenaline, epinephrine, and norepinephrine), which inhibit basic bodily functions such as digestion, tissue repair, and the immune system. Meanwhile, back in the cerebrum, a *second* signal from the thalamus reaches the frontal lobes (the executive part of the cerebral cortex) for rational assessment (after the fight-or-flight response has already begun).

Now, if the frontal lobes make the decision to shut down, the fight-or-flight response, it may take as long as 3 min to reverse the process. However, if the frontal lobes are in agreement, the process continues, be it fight-or-flight. If neither fight nor flight can effect a solution—for example, a serious auto accident—then the next stage begins. Once completely overwhelmed, the energy created by the stress response is abruptly halted. The result is a shock to the system. Immediately preceding this shock, emotions (fear and rage) can become so strong that dissociation from normal conscious awareness sets in, along with numbness; the victim is frozen or immobilized. The parasympathetic nervous system goes into action and releases neurohormones. Pain may no longer be experienced as adrenaline and endorphins are flooding the system (Sills, 2001, pp. 349–356).

Some clients suffering from anxiety activate the fight-or-flight response too often, as if there were a hair trigger in their limbic system. In some cases, anxiety can be reduced if prefrontal lobes are strengthened. When the executive portion of the brain works well, the second signal coming from the thalamus is received in a rational manner. Or, better yet, when the executive portion of the brain is working well, life is just not as frightening.

Biofeedback training promotes greater control over the cerebral cortex and the ANS. Biofeedback gives the trainee power to control unconscious or involuntary physiological processes. Heart rate variability, skin temperature (ST), and brain wave patterns are no longer the sole propriety of the subconscious nervous system activity for those who have mastered the principles and training afforded by biofeedback. The mind-body connection can be quantified, measured, and observed on computer or visual display. The trainee and the trainer can see the progress simultaneously.

NEURONAL COMMUNICATION

The basic unit of the nervous system is the nerve otherwise known as the neuron. The brain has billions of neurons with trillions of connections. Neurons are arranged in a complex yet well-defined circuitry that is only partially understood by modern science. Neuronal communication is throughout the nervous system. Many neurons in the CNS are multipolar in design (Figure 2.2). For the purposes of our discussion, imagine a multipolar neuron on its side, stretched out from right to left. On the far right are the dendrites, which receive information and transfer it to the cell body or soma. Next come the axon. Some axons are gray, whereas others are white. White axons are coated with myelin. Mylenated axons transfer signals faster than unmylenated (gray) axons. Mylenation increases with maturation.

Most of the cell bodies are found within the CNS. The "little gray cells" that help detective Hercule Poirot solve the case are the cell bodies (soma) covering the outer cerebral cortex; these same cell bodies have white myelinated axons extending beneath the surface. At the ends of the axons are the terminal buttons. They are filled with neurotransmitters ready to be released for the purpose of sending information. The spaces (gaps) that separate axon terminal buttons from receptor dendrites are called synapses. Communication is one-directional.

FIGURE 2.2
THE MULTIPOLAR NEURON

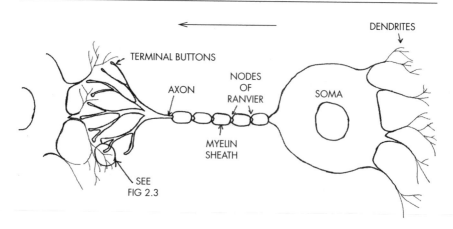

There are three types of neurons: sensory neurons, motor neurons, and association neurons. They are responsible for all of the connections in the brain:

- *Sensory neurons* carry information from the skin or other organs upward toward the CNS. The impulse is received by the sensory cortex—the anterior portion of the parietal lobes.
- *Motor neurons* send information downward and away from the CNS to various muscles. The origin of the signal comes from the motor cortex—the posterior portion of the frontal lobes. The axons of most sensory and motor neurons travel inside the body's information highway: the spinal column.
- *Association neurons*, or interneurons, help make the connection between sensory and motor neurons; they are the most numerous kind of neurons in the CNS.

Communication between neurons is an electrochemical event. A nerve impulse, also called an action potential, is an electrical charge that travels from the cell body toward the terminal buttons at the ends of the axons. A stimulated cell body sends a signal toward the terminal buttons. The impulse travels along the axon in bucket-brigade fashion; each membrane has the job of stimulating the next membrane down the line. The whole process resembles a chain reaction and is known as depolarization. At this point the terminal buttons release neurotransmitters into the synapse. Dendrites from adjacent neurons pick up the message and try to keep the ball rolling, from neuron to neuron, until the reason for the initial impulse is accomplished. Sometimes an action potential starts and then quickly stops due to a weak signal. Consequently, it never reaches a threshold of power. Action potentials happen in an all-or-none fashion.

Once an individual neuron has completed an action potential, it begins to repolarize in order to rejuvenate itself. The time period needed to do this is called a refractory period, in which no further communication can take place.

Brain waves are formed by a dual action—a push-pull process. A cycle starts when a terminal button releases the neurotransmitter in order to excite the adjacent neuron. It ends when the process reverses due to an inhibitory response. Two terms define the process of making brain waves: 1) Excitatory postsynaptic potential (EPSP); 2) Inhibitory postsynaptic potential (IPSP). Each dendrite of the adjacent neuron can be excited or depolarized by the release of an excitation neurotransmitter. The inhibitory process is invoked by the release of an inhibitory neurotransmitter.

The thalamus and other cortical localities create EEG rhythmic activity. Signals move upward toward the cerebral cortex, then back downward to the thalamus, over and over again. Now imagine the total rhythm caused by millions of communicating neurons. One sensor placed on the scalp can pick up a portion of this rhythmic activity at the cortical level. The information is then sent to an EEG unit that displays the end product: brain waves.

Brain waves are a byproduct of EPSPs and IPSPs and *not* a direct measurement of action potentials. Neurotransmitters are chemicals that are sent into the synaptic gap from the synaptic button in order to excite dendrites located in adjacent neurons.

There are many neurotransmitters, including serotonin, dopamine, gamma-aminobutyric acid (GABA), and epinephrine. They are stored in numerous individual sacs, called vesicles, within the axon terminal—ready to be released into the synapse (Figure 2.3). Once the neurotransmitter has done its job, it returns to the terminal button. Each button has channels that allow for the entry and exit of neurotransmitters. Prozac, Paxil, and Zoloft were all designed to plug some of the channels in order to keep more serotonin in the synapse. Those drugs are known as selective serotonin reuptake inhibitors (SSRIs). Glenmullen (2000) described the reuptake process:

> After a signal has been sent, the cell from which it originates cleans up unused serotonin by reabsorbing it in a process called "reuptake." Reuptake keeps signals crisp, terminating them in a timely fashion, which prevents lingering serotonin from continuing to stimulate the receiving cell. Prozac-type drugs inhibit—or block—reuptake, thereby boosting the level of serotonin, prolonging serotonin signals in the brain. (p. 17)

Glennmullen (2000) points out the dangers associated with long-term use of psychotropic drugs. But there are also side effects associated with medication withdrawal. Neurofeedback training often reduces or eliminates the need for psychotropic medications because of its power to correct abnormal EEG patterns. Therefore, trainees need to be prepared for one or more of the side effects that accompany withdrawal 50% of the time. Physical effects may include dizziness, weight gain, flulike symptoms, sleep disturbances, and sensations that resemble electrical shocks. Emotional effects may include increased anxiety, crying spells, agitation, anger, and suicidality.

If medication levels are maintained despite improvement, then the trainee may experience symptoms of overdose. Typical symptoms of

FIGURE 2.3
NEUROTRANSMITTERS

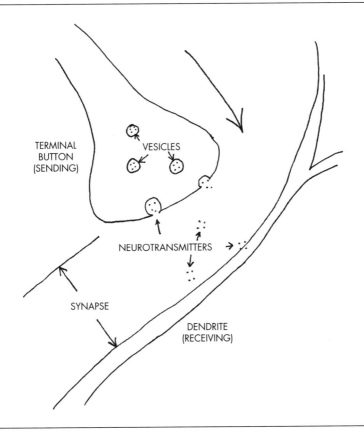

antidepressant overdose include agitation and restlessness. Get to know the psychotropic drugs being used by the trainee. Purchase one or more professional guides to prescription drugs and become aware of potential side effects. Avoid giving advice. Have clients read the information for themselves. Do not hesitate to send them back to the prescribing doctor for medication adjustment. If needed, communicate with doctors and psychiatrists during the withdrawal process. Warn clients that going "cold turkey" can be dangerous. When consulting with medical doctors, use instruments such as the Beck Depression Inventory (BDI) to demonstrate the progress of the trainee. Finally, warn clients about the dangers of mixing supplements such as St. John's Wort and (5-HTP) with SSRIs or other psychotropic medications.

OTHER CEREBRAL PROCESSES

Neurofeedback training is most often identified with the electrical activity of the brain. However, there is a growing interest in regional cerebral blood flow (rCBF) activity. Neurotherapists using Hemoencephalography (HEG) neurofeedback equipment can teach trainees to improve cerebral blood flow in key areas of the brain. In some cases, HEG neurofeedback is more effective than electroencephalography (EEG) neurofeedback. Understanding the relationship between rCBF and the EEG is essential knowledge for all neurotherapists.

Cerebral Blood Flow

No brain wave activity would occur unless the brain was supplied with enough oxygen and glucose. Cerebral blood flow (CBF) carries these needed elements to various brain structures in order to prevent brain damage:

> The adult brain requires 750 milliliters (almost a quart) of oxygenated blood every minute to maintain normal activities. Of the total amount of oxygen delivered to the body tissues by arteries, 20 percent is consumed by the brain alone. Under normal conditions cessation of blood flow to the brain for 5 to 10 seconds is sufficient to cause temporary changes in neuronal activity. Interruption of flow for 5 to 10 minutes can produce irreversible neuronal damage. Delivery of blood to the brain is accomplished by two pairs of arteries. (Diamond, Scheibel, & Elson, 1985, p. 9-1)

CBF on the cortical level has been recorded countless times via brain imaging techniques such as positron emission tomography (PET) and (SPECT) single positron emission computerized tomography. Both PET and SPECT scans have indicated that abnormal blood flow patterns are indicators of various disorders including, but not limited to, obsessive-compulsive disorder (OCD), and attention deficit/hyperactivity disorder (ADHD). Likely, underactive regions of the brain have inadequate supply of oxygenated blood. The brain at work requires more oxygenated blood in specified regions than the brain at rest. Improving the quality of blood flow in the brain translates into enhanced mental capacity. The correlation between regional cerebral blood flow (rCBF) and EEG activity is explained by the following two references:

Research by Lubar, Angelakis, Frederick, and Stathopoulou (2001) showed the relationship among EEG, hemoencephalography (HEG), and cortical slowing:

> Cerebral blood flow (CBF) measures, like PET and fMRI [functional Magnetic Resonance Imaging], support the association of slow-wave EEG with brain deactivation. Cognitive neuroimaging studies using CBF measures have shown increases in cerebral metabolism at brain areas responsible for different reading modalities.... Increases in cerebral metabolism have been correlated with increases in *fast* frequency EEG amplitude; and decreases in cerebral metabolism have been correlated with increases in *slow* frequency EEG amplitude. (p. 8)

Davidson's (1998) research showed the relationship between decreased blood flow and decreased neural activity in the left prefrontal cortex for depressives:

> Studies of regional brain function with neuroimaging of patients with psychiatric depressions have fairly consistently revealed a pattern of decreased blood flow or metabolism in left prefrontal regions at rest.... We have conducted several studies examining *regional brain electrical activity* in depression.... We view this pattern of left prefrontal hypoactivation as a neural reflection of the decreased capacity for pleasure, loss of interest, and generalised decline in goal-directed motivation and behaviour. (pp. 319–320)

Cerebral Spinal Fluid

The brain is so heavy that it could be crushed under its own weight. Cerebral spinal fluid (CSF) prevents this from happening. The brain floats within the cushion of fluid—it is surrounded and nourished by CSF. It is gives the brain a liquid cushion that minimizes the damage coming from blows to the head. CSF also moves though the ventricles and other pathways inside the head and partly into the spinal cord. It is replenished on a regular basis to provide the brain with a fresh supply of nutrients. When sensors are put on the head, signals must travel through CSF.

BRAIN STRUCTURES

There are four outer brain lobes that make up each hemisphere of the cerebral cortex. The brain is a highly complicated structure; there are countless connections beneath each lobe that influence the operations of each lobe. To make matters more complex, each lobe can be divided into smaller functional units that sometimes lie on the border separating each lobe. The list of important regions includes right-hemisphere (RH) and left-hemisphere (LH) differences, the four lobes, and three specialized areas within the four lobes. Sensor placement is often guided by our knowledge of brain lobes.

Lateralization

The LH is usually the dominant hemisphere (Figure 2.4). It is responsible for activities on the right side of the body. Most people are right-handed; it is the dominant hand. The LH keeps track of many details. If you were a forest ranger, the LH would examine individual trees and animals for defects, whereas the RH would take a much broader point of view: animal and tree health would be viewed as part of a larger system and not as

FIGURE 2.4
CEREBRAL CORTEX FUNCTIONS SIMPLIFIED

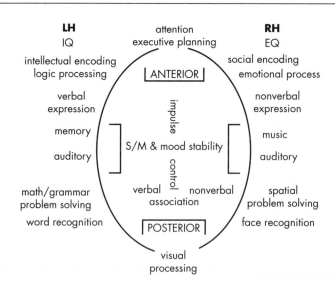

individual, unrelated parts. The RH sees the forest as a complete unit. Some people are good at details; others are better at seeing the whole picture. The healthy brain can switch from LH to RH as needed. Those who have practiced meditation for many years often become adept at right-to-left switching. They have trained themselves to output high-amplitude synchronous alpha waves.

The LH is good at logic, math, and analytical reasoning. It oversees the three R's: reading, 'riting, and 'rithmetic. Verbal expression and understanding are linked to Broca's area and Wernicke's area of the LH. The LH is crucial to finding details during the research process; it governs grammatical principles and spelling. Verbal memories are stored in the LH.

The RH is usually the nondominant hemisphere. It is responsible for activities on the left side of the body. It governs emotions and music comprehension better than the LH. The sweet tones of singing and the bitter sounds of swear words all come from the RH. The RH knows why a joke is funny. RH functions include creativity and perception, visual-spatial processing, not getting lost, and recognizing familiar places. My RH just knows where I am—without thinking about it. Logic may be on the left, but intuition and insight are on the right. Perhaps one of the most important features of the RH is its human qualities such as facial recognition, empathy, and early self concept.

Problems result when there is no clear winner in the LH-RH competition. Two disorders that may reflect this struggle are dyslexia and stuttering. For example, in 70% to 80% of normal adults and children the planum temporale (the center of Wernicke's speech area) is larger than the corresponding lateral RH location (Preis, Jancke, Schmitz-Hillebrecht & Steinmetz, 1999). But such is not the case for dyslexics. Postmortem studies have indicated a symmetrical relationship—the right planum was similar in size to the left planum in dyslexics. In the case of stuttering, a functional difference has been observed in brain imaging studies. Normal reading and speech activate the left superior temporal gyrus, whereas stuttering activates the corresponding RH location (Springer & Deutsch, 1998, pp. 274–280). How does the LH-RH competition play out in the case of left-handers? Contrary to popular opinion, research has indicated that "only about 20 percent show right-brain dominance. Concurrently, left-handers also have a higher incidence of language impairment, stuttering, and dyslexia" (Ratey, 2001, p. 275).

Women and men differ when it comes to LH-RH differences. "A women's brain has a thicker corpus callosum [a major connection between the two hemispheres] than a man's, with women having up to 30 percent more connections between left and right" (Pease & Pease, 2000, p. 51). That means they have bigger and better connections between the emotional RH and the logical LH. This difference may contribute to a woman's ability to express and understand interpersonal emotions. Carter (1998) noted other functional differences between men and women:

> When they do complex mental tasks there is a tendency for women to bring both sides of the brain to bear on the problem, while men often use only the side most obviously suited to do it. This pattern of activity suggest that in some ways women take a broader view of life, bringing more aspects of the situation into play when making decisions, for example. Men, on the other hand, are more focused. (p. 71)

When it comes to linguistic abilities, women use more of the brain on both sides of the brain when compared to men; they usually speak at an earlier age than men (Pease & Pease, 2000, p. 70). Dual-hemispheric processing helps women to manage dyslexia better than men. However, men typically rely more heavily upon the left hemisphere for language processing. That is why, a LH stroke will damage a man's language skills more than a woman's because she has the RH edge (Ratey, 2001, p. 275). When it comes to emotion, men rely mostly on the RH whereas women activate both sides of the brain (Pease & Pease, 2000, p. 134).

When it comes to spatial abilities the tables are reversed: men use more of their brain, on both sides of their brain, than women. They are better at left-right recognition, determining which way is north, reading maps, and playing three-dimensional games or puzzles. Most engineers, pilots, and air traffic controllers are men. Contrary to popular opinion, male and female occupational differences may not simply be a case of stereotyping or bias.

Male and female brains are wired differently. This ought to be taken into consideration by neurofeedback providers who are assessing for neurological deficits or recommending a change in family structure. For example, ask parents how much time is spent playing video games (boy) or on the telephone (girl). It must be noted that 10–20% of males and females may show cross-gender abilities, and individual differences abound.

How often does the LH dominate when men and women are grouped together? Ratey, (2001) presented the following statistics:

> Language resides predominantly in the left hemisphere in 90 percent of the population. About 5 percent have their main language areas in the right hemisphere, and another 5 percent split language fairly evenly between the hemispheres. (p. 274)

Electrical and metabolic differences from LH to RH are associated with disorders such as anxiety and depression. Davidson (1998) researched the relationship between cerebral cortex asymmetry and psychiatric disorders. He proposed the following conclusion:

> We have hypothesised that the decrease in left prefrontal activation may be specific to depression, whereas the increase in right-sided prefrontal activation (as well as right parietal activation) may be specific to certain components of anxiety. . . . One common region we believe to be associated with both anxiety and depression is the amygdala. (p. 321)

Davidson's research indicated that RH-LH asymmetries, especially in the prefrontal cortex, are traits that can be detected in infants and some animals. Neurofeedback protocols often target these asymmetries in an effort to stem the tide of anxiety and depression.

On the subject of traumatic brain injury and stroke, Ayers (1999) reports the following LH and RH symptoms:

> Consistent with neurological findings generally, I have found that injuries on the right side often result in mood swings, personality change, problems with visuospatial organization, temper outbursts, impulsivity, and poor organization. Injuries on the left side often involve problems with language, such as lack of spontaneous speech, difficulty retrieving words, aphasia, paraphasia, agraphia or alexia, and/or problems with logic, math and judgment. (p. 206)

Psychiatric interviewing and cognitive evaluation will likely identify if one hemisphere is over- or underactive. Thus, it may be possible to know which side of the brain is suspect even before EEG measurements are taken. Hemispheric asymmetry is only one of many possible problems; knowing the functions of each brain structure is another key to diagnostic and treatment success. The following section is designed to introduce the reader to various technical words and terminology employed by neurologists and found within anatomical textbooks.

Terminology

Specific terms are employed to locate brain structures and other anatomical features. Neurologists often describe brain regions with anatomical directional terms. However, Neurotherapists rely on the International 10–20 system that assigns letters and numbers to 19 primary sites on the scalp.

The International 10–20 System

Each region of the cerebral cortex has been assigned a letter and/or a number designation. Sensors are placed on the head according to the International 10–20 system. The international 10–20 system provides meaningful letters and numbers to brain positions. Odd numbers are on the left side of the brain; even numbers are on the right. When this book uses a forward slash (/) dividing two sites it means in between. For example, C3/ T3 refers to a midway location. When it uses a dash (-) it means along the same path or both. For example, C3–T3 means include both sites.

- *F* for Frontal lobes.
- *Fp* for Frontal poles.
- *T* for Temporal lobes.
- *O* for Occipital lobes.
- *P* for Parietal Lobes.
- *C* for Central and sensorimotor cortex.
- *Z* for the centerline that separates left and right hemispheres.

Figure 2.5 shows the location of each of the 10–20 positions. It is also useful to have a "dummy" head in the office that has each of the 10–20 positions marked on the head. Hairdressers have Styrofoam heads that can be used for this purpose.

Next consider the anatomical directional terms:

Posterior	Toward the rear of the head
Anterior	Toward the front of the head
Vertex	Central position (Cz) (also Pz and Fz)
Dorsal	Toward the top of the head
Ventral	Toward the bottom of the head
Medial	Midline of brain
Lateral	To the left or the right of the midline
Superior	Closer to the top (dorsal)
Inferior	Closer to the bottom (ventral)

Fissures are the long deep grooves in the cerebral cortex that follow the boundaries between lobes. The wall or elevated ridge on each side of a deep groove is called a gyrus. For example, the surface of the deep groove that divides the LH and RH is called the cingulate gyrus. The cingulate gyrus is considered to be the cortical portion of the limbic system

FIGURE 2.5
INTERNATIONAL 10–20 SYSTEM

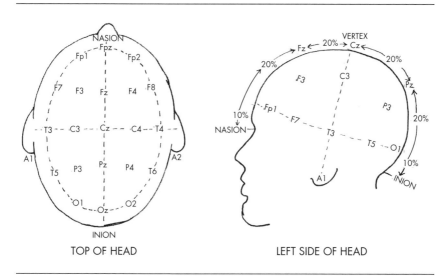

TOP OF HEAD   LEFT SIDE OF HEAD

(Pinel & Edwards, 1998, p. 118). Shorter grooves are called sulcus. The grooves in the prefrontal lobes are called the orbital gyrus; they are located just above the eye sockets. The angular gyrus makes up the boundary separating the temporal and parietal lobes. The central fissure creates a dividing line between the somatosensory cortex and motor cortex that extends from the left lateral sulcus to the right lateral sulcus. The lateral sulcus forms part of the superior boundary of the temporal lobes.

Here is a translation of the 10–20 system into brain locations along the cingulate gyrus, the division between the LH and RH (Figure 2.6):

Fpz   anterior ventral medial (prefrontal cortex)
Fz   anterior dorsal medial (prefrontal cortex)
Cz   central dorsal medial (somatosensory/motor cortex)—the
       central fissure and the cingulate gyrus intersect at the vertex.
Pz   posterior dorsal medial (parietal lobe)
Oz   posterior ventral medial (occipital lobe)

Here is the translation of the 10–20 system into brain locations of frontal lobes:

    Fp1   anterior ventral lateral left (orbital gyrus)
    Fp2   anterior ventral lateral right (orbital gyrus)
    F3   anterior dorsal lateral left
    F4   anterior dorsal lateral right
    F7   anterior lateral left
    F8   anterior lateral right

The following regions have been assigned names:

- Broca's area—(LH only: F7/T3)
- Wernicke's area—(LH only: posterior superior temporal lobe)
- Auditory cortices, each abutting the lateral sulcus
  (LH: C3/T3; RH: C4/T4)
- Parieto-occipital—(LH: P3/O1; RH: P4/O2)
- Temporo-parieto-occipito—(LH: T5/P3/O1; RH: T4/P4/O1)
- Sensorimotor cortex divides frontal and parietal lobes—(C3-Cz-C4)

    The somato*sensory* cortex is in the parietal lobe.

    The primary *motor* cortex is in the frontal lobe.

    The pre–motor cortex is anterior to the primary motor cortex.

FIGURE 2.6
NEUROANATOMY DIRECTIONAL TERMS

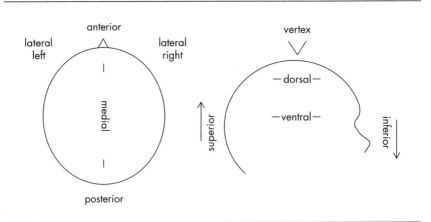

LOBE SPECIALIZATION AND FUNCTIONS

Much of our understanding of lobe functions comes from brain imaging and from observations made by neurologists when a local brain lesion occurs. Lesions may come from injuries, disease, or surgical interventions. Neurologists have observed that lesions occurring in specific regions of the brain produce specific symptoms. Conversely, specific symptoms relate to specific regions (Figure 2.7). The rationale for treatment, in part, rests on this assumption. It may be asserted that sensor placement is guided by matching specific brain functions with specific symptoms. Having the following information at hand will simplify the entire treatment process.

Frontal Lobes

Sites: frontal poles—Fp1, Fp2, Fpz; frontal—Fz, F3, F4, F7, F8
Key functions: attention, memory, social awareness, character, motivation, planning; pre-frontal lobes have connections (neuronal networks) leading to the amygdala.

Frontal lobes are responsible for immediate and sustained attention, social skills, emotions, empathy, time management, working memory, moral fiber or character, executive planning, and initiative. They identify problems and may send them to other brain regions for a solution. One of the most famous cases of prefrontal lobe damage happened at the turn of the century in Vermont. Phineas Gage, a railroad foreman, was the victim of a fluke explosion that jettisoned a metal spike through the ventral medial portion of the brain just dorsal lateral left of Fz. It did not damage Broca's area so Gage was able to communicate with others. His vision—in his undamaged eye—was perfect; his motor skills were intact. What was changed was his personality. His moral character was severely compromised. He was no longer the fine, upstanding member of the community he was before the accident. His social skills and empathy for his fellow man had literally been destroyed (Damasio, 1994, pp. 4–33). The brain is not just a cognitive processing organism; it also is the seat of our conscience. Emotions, morals, and the social self cannot be isolated to frontal lobe activities; other deeper structures are also involved. For example, Ratey clarified the relationship between the frontal lobes and the amygdala: "The frontal cortex, responsible for the brain's most complex processing, has the heaviest projections to the amygdala, and the two work together as part of the network that is the social brain" (2001, p. 312).

FIGURE 2.7
MAJOR STRUCTURES OF THE CEREBRAL CORTEX

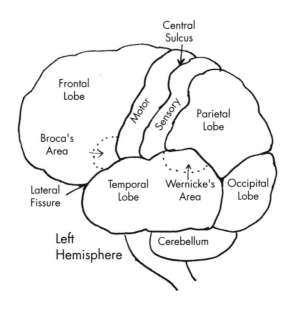

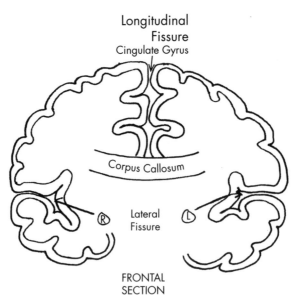

Neurofeedback training along the anterior dorsal (Fz) and ventral (Fpz) portions of the brain may have an impact on social behavior and moral fortitude. Weaknesses in this area are evident in oppositional defiant and antisocial behaviors. This behavior may parallel excessive EEG slowing and inadequate CBF throughout other prefrontal areas as well—especially Fp1 and Fp2. Clients with excessive fear as a result of trauma, anxiety, and neglect may likely have an overactive amygdala. Neurofeedback training in the right prefrontal cortex may lead to "a reduction in fear as well as a sense of calm and well-being" (Fisher, 2004, p. 89).

Checking clients for frontal lobe problems often involves testing. But even without testing, some assessments can be made. Do the clients appear to be in a fog and unable to concentrate? Do they get into trouble with school or community authorities? Are they fearful? Are they ethical and moral? Do they care about other people? Do they have good social skills? Did it take them twice as long as usual to fill out the paperwork? Do they seem unmotivated and disconnected? If negative, depressed, or anxious, suspect frontal asymmetries when the EEG is checked.

Parietal Lobes

Sites: Pz, P3, P4
Key functions: math, naming objects, complex grammar, spatial awareness.

Parietal lobes solve problems that have been conceptualized by the frontal lobes. They have been labeled the association cortex. Complex grammar, the naming of objects, sentence construction, and mathematical processing are traceable to the left parietal lobe. Acalculia or dyscalculia is a disturbance in the mental ability to calculate math problems. It should be noted that some forms of math involve spatial processing—for example, geometry—and so the right parietal lobe is also suspect. Math calculation begins with the working memory (near F7), whereas problem solving engages the parietal lobes. If times tables are not memorized and attention is poor, the parietal lobes may not be fully engaged in the problem. Map orientation, knowing the difference between right and left, and spatial recognition are all functions of the right parietal lobe.

Specialization has its limits. For example, PET scans have shown that the naming of objects involves several brain regions, including the posterior frontal cortex, the inferior parietal cortex, and the superior temporal cortex.

Sense of direction also encompasses more than one region: the inferior prefrontal cortex, the posterior parietal cortex, and the inferior temporal cortex (Pinel & Edwards, 1998, pp. 208–211).

Ratey (2001) commented on another symptom that may accompany posterior parietal lobe deficits:

> Damage to the posterior parietal cortex can cause a classic deficit called Balint's syndrome, in which patients are unable to attend to multiple objects simultaneously; they cannot see the forest for the trees. The damage limits a person's ability to shift attention from one location to another, and perhaps from one sensory modality to another. (p. 116)

Clients with parietal lobe problems may have more car accidents because they are not able to attend to both sides of the visual field. They might have trouble playing computer games like solitaire, which require scanning from left to right. If they draw pictures and the left half of the picture seems incomplete, this indicates a deficit in the right parietal lobe.

Commenting on the RH and the parietal lobe, Ratey (2001) also concluded:

> The right hemisphere, particularly the parietal lobe, is responsible for analyzing external space and the body's position in it. The parietal lobe is the "where" area of sensory perception. ... Studies in lesions in the right parietal indicate that it is involved in attention, music, body image, body scheme, face recognition, and the physical act of dressing. Further the entire right hemisphere plays a role in the attentional system and in feeling and displaying emotion. (p. 320)

If a new client has trouble following the directions to my office, or if they report a pattern of getting lost or getting turned around, then I suspect a parietal lobe problem. If the client fails to recognize a simple tune, can't remember faces, or easily gets turned around and becomes lost, then both the right posterior temporal lobe and parietal lobe may be suspect.

Ask the client to write a few sentences, draw a simple picture, or play "monkey see monkey do." Have them do a few simple math (word) problems. How well did they perform? How accurate is their picture? How difficult was it for them to follow hand and body movements? Were the math problems answered with ease or with difficulty or not at all? For anxious clients, it is important to remember Davidson's (1998) find that right parietal lobe may have increased activation.

Temporal Lobes

Sites: T3, T4, T5, T6
Key functions: LH—verbal memories, word recognition, reading, language, emotion; RH—
music, facial recognition, social cues, object recognition; proximity to the amygdala
(emotion) and hippocampus (memory).

Luria (1973) indicated that lesions to the left midtemporal zone interfere with verbal memory making. Damage to this zone prevents the storage of longer passages of information, although short phrases may be retained. Consequently, it becomes difficult to keep up with a conversation because information is being lost. Lesions to the right temporal lobe often result in the inability to recognize intricate rhythmic melodies. Music appreciation may be lost (1973, pp. 135–143).

The temporal lobe houses the auditory cortex in close proximity to the hippocampus. Consequently, it is critical to the memory-making process, especially verbal memories. Springer and Deutsch's (1998) review of the literature comparing CBF and memory, explained that memory can be placed into three different categories: short-term memory, working memory, and long-term memory. Each activity tends to activate different parts of the brain, as shown in PET scans. Short-term memory, which includes recalling a seven-digit number such as a telephone number, activates "Broca's area and the left inferior parietal cortex." If a short-term-memory task is visual or spatial in nature, then the RH is activated, including "right occipital, parietal, and prefrontal cortices." If a short-term-memory task is phonetic, then suspect damage points to the left posterior/inferior parietal lobe (1998, pp. 207–211). Phonological memory takes in the correct order and transmission of speech sounds; it contains the phonetic pattern of a language.

Long-term memory can be divided into two branches: semantic and episodic. Semantic memory includes the recall of objects and word understanding, especially in language, and is associated with left-temporal-lobe (Wernicke's area) problems. Episodic memory involves functional tasks such as remembering to pay the bills, to fill the gas tank, how to play baseball, where glasses and keys were placed, and so on. Deep lesions to the midtemporal extending into the hippocampal lobes result in a dysfunctional episodic memory. It may also be hypothesized that "left prefrontal cortical regions are more involved in retrieval of information from semantic memory and in simultaneously encoding novel aspects of the retrieved information into episodic memory. Right prefrontal cortical regions, on the other hand, are involved in episodic memory retrieval" (Springer & Deutsch, 1998, pp. 215–216).

Working memory is an example of short-term plus long-term memory joined in a problem-solving task such as math or reading. Studies show an activation of the frontal lobes in the case of verbal or mental tasks (Springer & Deutsch, 1998, p. 206) When it comes to memory problems, it is not possible to isolate the problem to the temporal lobes.

Another condition that may involve both the frontal cortex and temporal lobe is dyslexia. Wernicke's area (understanding) is located at the posterior-superior temporal lobe. Broca's area (expression) is located F7/T3. PET scans have revealed the following with reference to dyslexia:

> Some types of dyslexia may be due to what is known as a dissociation disorder—a missing or inactive connection between two brain modules. A study in which PET scans were made of dyslexics' and non-dyslexic's brains while they attempted a complex reading task, suggests that the two main language areas, Wernicke's and Broca's, do not work in concert in dyslexics. This appears to be because an important neural link in the vicinity of the insula cortex is not activated during such tasks as it is in others. (Carter, 1998, p. 152)

Broca's area is activated when discriminating between two similar sounds, but so are the midtemporal lobe and Wernicke's area. All three areas must be suspected in cases of dyslexia (Springer & Deutsch, 1998, pp. 170–171).

Whereas the LH is associated with word recognition, the right temporal lobe is associated with facial recognition:

> A deficit in the ability to recognize faces is called facial agnosia or prospag-nosia, derived from the Greek words for face (*prosopon*) and not knowing (*agnosia*). Prosogagnosia seems to be a result of an impairment in the medial occipitotemporal cortex of the brain, due to stroke or brain damage. Although bilateral damage usually causes the full-fledged syndrome, damage to the right hemisphere alone is far more debilitating than damage to the left. (Ratey, 2001, p. 316)

Lesions to the temporal lobes may also contribute to the "auras of déjà vu, jamais vu, and formed visual hallucinations" (Rowan & Tolunsky, 2003, p. 47). Those terms are translated as *already* viewed and *never* viewed respectively. The temporal lobe is also near the amygdala, and so it may be another factor in an angry or aggressive child. Amen (1998) commented on the change in his nephew Andrew's personality that came from a left temporal lobe tumor:

> But then his personality changed. He appeared depressed. He had serious ag-
> gressive outbursts and he complained to his mother of suicidal and homicidal
> thoughts (very abnormal for a nine-year-old). He drew pictures of himself
> hanging from a tree. He drew pictures of himself shooting other children.
> (p. 11)

After Andrew's operation to remove his tumor, his condition improved and
he returned to his former likable self. His story is reminiscent of Phineas
Gage's story because a personality change followed damage to a specialized
brain region.

EEG slowing in the temporal lobes is often seen following concussions
"since head injuries, regardless of the site of impact, often involve the scrap-
ing of the temporal lobes along the inner part of the sharp, bony middle
fossa" (Hughes, 1994, p. 122). Actually, problems with temporal lobe slowing "are the most common kind of EEG abnormality in the majority of EEG
laboratories . . . the major pathological changes in aging, anoxic conditions,
head injury and many other etiologies are found *in* the temporal lobe, especially within the depth of this lobe, the amygdala and hippocampus"
(p. 120).

The anterior left temporal lobe, due to its proximity to the amygdala,
may also be implicated in depression. Davidson, Abercrombie, Nitschke &
Putnam (1999) reported the following:

> Investigators found that blood flow in the left dorsolateral prefrontal cortex
> and the left anterior temporal cortex is negatively correlated with severity of
> negative symptoms, suggesting that these cortical zones play a role in gen-
> erating positive affect, motivation and goal-setting, and that their inactivity
> leads to negative symptoms. (p. 230)

Papp, Coplan, and Gorman's (1992) review of the literature also revealed a
pattern of CBF change in the temporal lobes (especially the *right* temporal
lobe) of subjects with anxiety disorder and panic disorder. "Mild anxiety increases CBF, whereas severe anxiety reduces CBF values and cerebral
metabolism" (1992, pp. 314–316).

Temporal lobe functions affect us in various ways. LH functions are associated with reading (word recognition), learning, memory, and a positive
mood. RH functions are associated with music, facial recognition, anxiety,
and sense of direction. Comprehensive tests and questions are needed to
isolate temporal lobe problems.

Occipital Lobes

Sites: Oz, O₁, O₂

Key functions: visual field: helps to locate objects in the environment, see colors and recognize drawings and correctly identify objects; reading, writing, and spelling depend upon an accurate visual field; some connections extend to the amygdala.

The occipital lobes are closely associated with the visual cortex. During the assessment phase, it is important to rule out vision problems before concluding that other lobes must be responsible for a learning disorder. For example, some children with ADHD who are challenged by reading tasks benefit from neurofeedback training to help them focus as well as vision therapy to help them process. The occipital lobe borders the parietal and temporal lobes. EEG abnormalities in posterior locations in those two lobes often extend into occipital lobe regions. Visual memories and accurate reading require accurate vision. Furthermore, traumatic memories that accompany visual flashbacks are often processed in the occipital lobes. Two visual processing problems to look for are:

- Visual agnosia (inability to perceive and draw complete objects)
- Simultaneous agnosia (inability to see multiple objects at the same time)

Luria (1973) described simultaneous agnosia:

They cannot place a dot in the centre of a circle or a cross, because they perceive only the circle (or the cross), or the pencil point at any one time; they cannot trace the outline of an object or join the strokes together during writing; if they see the pencil point they lose the line, or if they see the line they can no longer see the pencil point. (p. 121)

Luria's description suggests a simple cognitive test. Sometimes conversations with parents reveal severe problems with writing, coloring, or other visual spatial activities in their children. Posterior parietal lobes should also be suspect when considering visual spatial activities. Adults also may have problems in the occipital lobes due to traumatic brain injury or a stroke.

Clients suffering from posttraumatic stress disorder (PTSD) may benefit from training in the occipital lobes. Davidson and Irwin (1999) reported a unique connection between the visual cortex, the amygdala, and PTSD:

Moreover, the intensity of fear displayed in the faces was systematically related to increases in blood flow in the left amygdala. In a subsequent re-analysis of these data, Morris and colleagues found that increase blood flow in the amygdala predicted increased blood flow in extrastriate visual cortex during fear but not during happy presentations. These findings indicate functional connectivity between these regions is altered as a function of emotional expression condition. (p. 15)

Neurofeedback specialists who work with PTSD often place sensors on the visual cortex when doing deep-states training. Depression and anxiety have also been known to remit after deep-states training. The efficacy of this approach is in harmony with the above findings.

Sensory and Motor (Sensorimotor) Cortex

Sites: C3, C4, Cz

Note: The sensory and motor cortices run parallel to each other and are divided by the central sulcus. The two cortices combined are sometimes called the sensorimotor cortex. However, the sensory cortex alone may also be called the primary somatosensory cortex or just the somatosensory cortex. The primary motor cortex may called just the motor cortex.

Key functions of primary motor cortex: conscious control of all skeletal muscle movements.

Key functions of the primary somatosensory cortex: spatial discrimination and the ability to identify where bodily sensations originate.

The sensorimotor cortex marks the division between the parietal lobes and the frontal lobes. The primary motor cortex is anterior and within the frontal lobes. The primary somatosensory cortex is posterior and within the parietal lobes. Together the sensory and motor cortices reach downward to both the left and right temporal lobes to the lateral sulcus. Considering the careful placement of these two adjacent structures lends support to the notion that they not only divide the anterior from the posterior but they also serve as a junction that coordinates movement that is in part guided by sensation. Much of what we do and who we are translates into moving our legs, hands, torso, or neck into action.

From the Greek root soma, for body, the somatosensory system is responsible for both the external senses of touch, temperature, pain, and the internal senses of joint position, visceral state, and pain. (Damasio, 1994, p. 65)

Damage to the RH portion of the somatosensory cortex "compromises reasoning/decision making and emotion/feeling, and, in addition, disrupts the processes of basic body signaling" (p. 70).

The functions of the primary motor cortex have been associated with skillful movements and smooth repetitive operations such as typing, playing musical instruments, handwriting, the operation of complex machinery, and fluid speaking. It is the hub and switching station between voluntary muscles of the body and the brain. Wilder Pennfield's research into the sensorimotor cortex led him to map out many of its functions. He found discreet locations that correspond to actual movements such as hands, legs, mouth, jaw, and so on. Considering the far-reaching effects of this dual cortex, it is no wonder those early pioneers in the field of neurotherapy started training along the sensorimotor cortex. One of the brain waves, sensorimotor rhythm (SMR), got its name from this cortex. Barry Sterman trained Margaret Fairbanks along the sensor/motor cortex (C3) to increase SMR. She was the first sufferer of epilepsy to receive neurofeedback training. In many ways, she was the first success story.

Training along the sensorimotor cortex is implied for stroke, epilepsy, paralysis, ADHD and disorders of sensory/motor integration. Keep in mind that the RH controls the left side of the body and visa versa. However, the sensorimotor cortex has other functions. Ratey explained that the motor cortex helps the cerebral cortex to encode both physical and cognitive tasks. He asserted that "The brain circuits used to order, sequence, and time a *mental* act are the same ones used to order, sequence, and time a *physical* act" (2001, p. 149). That means that the somatosensory cortex shares in orchestrating both physical and mental processes. It governs more than just sensory and motor functions. Therefore, clients who have trouble seeing the logical sequence of cognitive tasks may benefit from neurofeedback training along the LH sensorimotor cortex (C3). Training along the RH sensorimotor cortex (C4) may invoke feelings, emotions or calmness. Training at the median or Cz may facilitate a mixed response.

Cingulate Gyrus

Sites: Fpz, Fz, Cz, Pz (also called the cingulate *or the* Z *line)*
Key functions: anterior cingulate gyrus—contributes to mental flexibility, cooperation, attention; helps the brain to shift gears and the young child to make transitions; helps the mind to let go of problems and concerns; helps the body to stop ritualistic movements and tics; contributes to the brain circuitry that oversees motivation, the social self, and our personality; is closely aligned with the amygdala. posterior cingulate gyrus— is closely aligned with parahippocampal cortices and shares in the memory-making

process; provides orientation in space, as well as eye and sensory monitoring services (Voght, Finch, & Olson, 1992, pp. 435–443). The division between anterior and posterior is generally considered to be at Cz.

The entire cingulate gyrus (anterior plus posterior) divides the LH and RH. The anterior cingulate cortex is closely associated with the anterior ventral medial site that is central to the prefrontal cortex. The anterior cingulate is in the frontal lobes and the posterior cingulate is in the parietal lobes. The cingulate gyrus intersects the central sulcus at the vertex. Hence, EEG neurofeedback training at the vertex (Cz) influences three cortices simultaneously: somatosensory, motor, and cingulate. The cingulate is called the cortical portion of the amygdala. Damasio (1994) summed up the operations of the cingulate in this way:

> I would like to propose that there is a particular region in the human brain where the systems concerned with emotion/feeling, attention, and working memory interact so intimately that they constitute the source for the energy of both external action (movement) and internal action (thought animation reasoning). This fountainhead region is the anterior cingulate cortex, another piece of the limbic puzzle. (p. 71)

A "hot" cingulate means that it is overactive and causing problems. Several problems are closely associated with the anterior cingulate cortex. Three problems in particular relate to cingulate malfunctions: OCD, ADD/ADHD, and Tourette's syndrome.

OCD may cause obsessional thoughts or compulsive rituals or both. It is accompanied by worrying, anxiety, mental tension, and physical tension. Mind and sometimes the body are stuck in ritualistic thoughts or behaviors. Telling the sufferer to lighten up will only make the condition worse. Schwartz (Schwartz & Beyette, 1996) specializes in the diagnoses and treatment of OCD using PET. Hundreds of neuro-images have revealed an abnormal pattern of CBF unique to OCD. Schwartz developed a rigid four-step cognitive-behavioral program to counteract symptoms of OCD. PET scans taken before and after treatment have proven that positive changes in brain activity can be accomplished without the use of drugs. The mind can heal the brain. Clients with OCD should be encouraged to read *Brainlock: Free Yourself from Obsessive Compulsive Behavior* (Schwartz & Beyette, 1996).

Brain structures that contribute to OCD include the anterior cingulate gyrus, orbital gyrus (just above the eyes in the prefrontal cortex), and deeper structures such as the caudate nucleus. Evidently, the brain gets locked into obsessions or rituals in a closed-loop fashion. Ratey (2001) summed it up in this way:

> The anterior cingulate tells the orbitofrontal cortex what it should pay attention to, while the orbitofrontal cortex itself identifies what seems to be an error in behavior. It says, "Error, error, this action is a mistake." When the signals about attention and error conflict, motor programs get caught up in the turmoil. A panic message results, telling the brain to activate to get out of danger or to correct the problem by taking action, such as returning to the house, for the third time to turn off the stove that is already off. The typical OCDer is a perfectionist who is interminably searching for error. He or she explodes with worry and gets caught up in a never-ending do-loop of concern and rumination. (p. 152)

Sufferers of OCD typically have abnormal metabolic activity along posterior and anterior regions of the cingulate gyrus. The goal for the neurofeedback provider is to find out what EEG abnormalities are negatively impacting key brain structures. Training may include the anterior or posterior cingulate as well as the orbital cortex (Fp1 and Fp2). Hammond (2003a) conducted an extensive review of the literature on OCD as well as an intensive EEG analysis of OCD subjects. Several OCD subtypes have been identified and differentiated according to specific EEG characteristics.

Unwanted verbal expressions and movements mark Tourette's syndrome—similar to OCD. The anterior cingulate cortex and the left dorsolateral prefrontal cortex (near F3/F7) are underactive in the brains of Tourette's syndrome sufferers. Deeper structures such as the left basal ganglia also contribute to the problem (Carter, 1998). If underactivity means EEG slowing, then neurofeedback providers have the option of increasing CBF with HEG neurofeedback or activating those sites with EEG neurofeedback. Clients with tics may also benefit from similar protocols.

Neurofeedback specialists have researched ADD/ADHD more than any other disorder. Two million grade school children are thought to have ADD/ADHD. This disorder can manifest itself with or without hyperactivity. The four basic components of this disorder are inattention (selective attention), distraction, hyperactivity, and impulsivity. Adults and children have this disorder, there is a genetic component, and it runs in families. Adults tend to lose the hyperactivity symptom but continue to struggle with inattention and impulsivity symptoms. Girls are often overlooked because they are less likely to be hyperactive—"the squeaky wheel gets the grease."

Other disorders mimic ADD/ADHD, such as reactive attachment disorder, OCD, generalized anxiety disorder, PTSD, mania, learning disorders, and others. Immature and spirited children are sometimes falsely given this label and inappropriately medicated.

It is reasonable to say that many potential clients will have ADD/ADHD as either a primary or a secondary disorder. The assessment chapter will present suggestions on diagnoses and treatment in detail. But the task for the moment is to determine which brain structures are involved. Several different brain localities may be suspect when assessing ADD/ADHD. But the cingulate gyrus and the anterior ventral medial region may be the first places to look.

The anterior cingulate cortex is known to monitor and control attention and impulse control; it keeps us motivated and on task. It is in the home of the primary and secondary motor cortices that control movement and activity. Some children with ADD/ADHD have difficulty understanding the consequences for their behavior. They may become hyperfocused, locked into a subject or activity for hours at a time. Getting mentally locked into something relates to the OCD loop; not seeing the consequences is reminiscent of Phineas Gage, who was pierced in the anterior cingulate region. Cortical slowing along the anterior cingulate is often found to be the cause of this disorder.

Joel Lubar, a leader and early pioneer, trains most ADD/ADHD children along the cingulate. Other clinicians, including Margaret Ayers, Mary J. Sabo, and the Othmers, have been known to train along the sensorimotor cortex to treat this disorder. Hershel Toomim often trains directly on the prefrontal lobes at Fp1, Fp2, and Fpz (which is part of the anterior cingulate cortex). Knowledge of this disorder and its treatment are primary to most neurofeedback practices.

NEUROPLASTICITY AND THE CEREBRAL CORTEX

While still in the womb the brain is organized into structures and neural circuitry that have formed into basic circuitry. At birth the sensorimotor cortex begins to assign discreet locations and space that will be allotted to each limb, finger, and moving part of the body. The development of the rest of the cerebral cortex follows. The prefrontal cortex is not complete until late adolescence. At birth there are too many neural circuits. The brain "prunes" off what it deems as unnecessary and retains and strengthens essential circuits. Many young children, for example, have the capacity for eidetic imagery (photographic memory), but this skill is usually pruned off to make room for more important skills. Synaptic connections that are not actively used are lost. Billions are pruned off during the early part of life.

Brain imaging techniques have supported the concept of neuroplasticity. During formative years, if the brain receives physical trauma to one location, then other locations take over the job. It is possible for the RH to assume responsibility for a LH function, but there may be a price to pay. One adolescent boy suffered damage to

> his *right* [italics added] parietal lobe, a structure that supports visual and spatial skills, suffered a lesion. Yet despite the injury, the boy developed normal visual and spatial skills. Oddly, however he had great difficulty with math, which is normally a function of the *left* [italics added] parietal lobe. Through brain imaging, researchers learned that functions ordinarily controlled by the (injured) right side of the brain had moved over to the left hemisphere. Spatial skills typically develop before math skills do. As a result, when it came time for the child to learn math, the region of his brain that would ordinarily be responsible for that function had already been taken and there was little neural real estate left to support mathematical reasoning. (Schwartz & Begley, 2002, p. 100)

Adults who have had strokes and other brain injuries can also enlist adjacent portions of the brain into action. Though not as successful as children are, adults continue to have a measure of plasticity. However, it requires effort and cognitive retraining to make the needed changes. Neuroplasticity is good news for neurofeedback providers. It supports our basic assumption that the brain can be strengthened (or even changed) if it is challenged.

DEEPER BRAIN STRUCTURES

Beneath the layers of the cerebral cortex lay key supporting structures. A brief description of a few of the key structures follows.

Limbic System

The limbic system is thought to be the seat of emotion, even though the right cerebral hemisphere also is involved in processing emotions and feelings. Within the limbic system we find the hippocampus, amygdala, olfactory button, septum, a portion of the thalamus, and the fornix. The hypothalamus is included as part of the limbic system by some but not all texts.

The hippocampus stores conscious memories; it orchestrates the process of making a memory permanent. Information that is combined with emotion may be stored faster because the hippocampus is contained within the limbic system. It is in proximity to the temporal lobes. The left temporal lobe seems to work closely with the hippocampus in the memory-making process. Egregious verbal memories are likely stored via hippocampus processes. Victims of trauma with lifelong PTSD may have underdeveloped or smaller hippocampus structures.

The amygdala stores unconscious memories. Egregious non-verbal memories are likely stored via amygdala processes. Early childhood trauma may still govern adult behavior. Sharp negative reactions may follow a simple trigger in the environment, such as a particular smell, facial expression, hair color, or style of clothing. The reaction does not necessarily follow a clear memory of details; rather, it is an inward knowing. It is a memory that has been driven in by fear (van der Kolk, McFarlane, & Weisaeth, 1996, p. 230). The aggression of temporal lobe epilepsy may be in part driven by its proximity to the amygdala in the brain. There are many cerebral cortex connections to the amygdala, including the anterior ventral medial cortex, the visual cortex, and the temporal lobes. The emotion of the amygdala is not always dark; it also is involved in positive feelings and emotions.

The thalamus is an editor for sorting and directing sensory information and emotions. It moderates between sensory information and the cerebral cortex. Its influence over the cerebral cortex and the EEG were reported by Marieb (1995):

> In addition to sensory inputs, virtually *all* inputs ascending to the cerebral cortex are funneled through the thalamic nuclei.... Thus the thalamus plays a key role in meditating sensation, motor activities, cortical arousal, and memory. It is truly the gateway to the cerebral cortex. (pp. 393–395)

The hypothalamus is just below the thalamus. It is a key player in the control of the endocrine system and the ANS. It influences eating, body temperature, sleep, and emotional responses. It has the job of activating the fight-or-flight response. It arouses the sympathetic nervous system and the endocrine system, preparing the body to take action. It also is part of the chain of command that calms things down by activating the parasympathetic nervous system.

TABLE 2.1
Brain Lobe Functions and Symptom Chart

	SITES	FUNCTIONS	PROBLEMS AND CONSIDERATIONS
Parietal Lobes	P3, Pz, P4	LH: Problem solving, math, complex grammar, attention, association RH: Spatial awareness, geometry	Dyscalculia sense of direction learning disorders
Cingulate Gyrus	Fpz, Fz, Cz, Pz, Oz	Mental flexibility, cooperation, attention, motivation, morals	Obsessions, compulsions, tics, perfectionism, worry, ADHD symptoms, OCD & OCD spectrum
Sensorimotor Cortex	C3, Cz, C4	LH: attention, mental processing RH: calmness, emotion, empathy Combined: fine motor skills, manual dexterity, sensory and motor integration and processing	Paralysis (stroke), seizure disorder, poor handwriting, ADHD symptoms
Frontal Lobes including the frontal poles	Fp1, Fp2, Fpz, Fz, F3, F7, F4, F8	LH: Working memory, concentration, executive planning, positive emotions. RH: Episodic memory, social awareness Frontal poles: attention, judgment	LH: depression RH: anxiety, fear poor executive functioning
Temporal Lobes	T3, T5 T4, T6	LH: word recognition, reading, language, memory RH: object recognition, music, social cues Facial recognition	Anger, rage, dyslexia, long-term memory, closed head injury

(Cont.)

TABLE 2.1 *(continued)*			
Occipital Lobes	O1, O2, Oz	Visual learning, reading, occipito-parieto-temporal functions	Learning disorders
Broca's Area	F7-T3	Verbal expression	Dyslexia, poor spelling, poor reading or verbal comprehension
Wernicke's Area	Parieto-temporal junction	Verbal-understanding	
Left Hemisphere	All odd numbered sites	Logical sequencing, detail oriented, language abilities, word retrieval, fluency, reading, math, science, problem solving, verbal memory	Depression (underactivation)
Right Hemisphere	All even numbered sites	Episodic memory encoding, social awareness, eye contact, music, humor, empathy, spatial awareness, art, insight, intuition, non-verbal memory, seeing the whole picture.	Anxiety (overactivation)

Reticular Formation

The reticular formation sends a continuous flow of impulses toward the cerebral cortex. It keeps the brain alert, awake, and ready to receive more information. "The outstanding feature of the reticular neurons is their far-flung axonal connections . . . such wide spread connections make reticular neurons ideal for governing the arousal of the brain as a whole." The reticular activating system (RAS) is an "arm of the reticular formation." It filters out sensory data. For example, it can shut out sensory data in noisy and crowded environments to prevent sensory overload. The hypothalamus and other neuronal circuitry shut down the reticular activating system when it's time for sleep (Marieb, 1995, p. 402).

Cerebellum

The word *cerebellum* literally means "little brain." It is beneath the occipital lobes and it protrudes beyond them. It keeps us erect and governs posture. The lobes of the cerebellum work in conjunction with the cerebral cortex to carry out voluntary muscle movements. It processes information coming from proprioceptors throughout the body. It then becomes possible to direct and coordinate muscle movements smoothly and efficiently. For example, as a youngster my ability to catch, throw, and do gymnastics was average to above average. However, as an adult I find that I have a poor sense of direction and often lose when playing checkers. Therefore, I have concluded that my cerebellum functions well, whereas my RH temporoparieto-occipital region functions poorly.

CONCLUSION

A working knowledge of brain anatomy helps the neurotherapist in discussions with clients who want to know why there is a problem and what can be done about it. It is important to convey the rationale for treatment interventions without becoming dogmatic. Accurate use of terminology is essential when conversing with doctors and neurologists.

A family evaluation often precedes an EEG evaluation. Psychological factors must be taken into account. If neurotherapy is indicated, then the next step is to compare presenting symptoms with likely neurological counterparts. If irregular or abnormal EEG patterns are found in clinically significant regions, then correcting those abnormalities will likely result in symptom reduction and positive changes.

3

Biofeedback Modalities and the Body

THE PURPOSE OF THIS CHAPTER is to create a bridge of understanding between mind and body feedback therapies. Some may feel that biofeedback for the body has little to do with biofeedback for the brain. That feeling is not supported by the facts; research has demonstrated the "science behind mind-body medicine" (Pert, 1997). The mind and body are uniquely connected—clients bring to treatment a head plus the body beneath it. Neurofeedback providers are aware of biofeedback's power to augment neurofeedback training. The body is a valuable ally in the quest for wellness.

The most important nonequipment modality for self-regulation is controlled breathing. Neurofeedback programs often begin by showing the client how to breathe properly. It is an essential skill for all clients with anxiety disorders, regardless of the treatment that follows. I have repeatedly helped anxious clients to significantly reduce anxiety levels within 1 week when they perform daily diaphragmatic breathing exercises.

BREATHING THERAPIES

The brain needs oxygen and glucose to survive. Knowledge of this system may help to impress upon potential clients the need to do effective breath work—a key to successful biofeedback treatment. Diaphragmatic breathing is taught in conjunction with most other biofeedback modalities. In most cases it can be mastered without equipment. However, some biofeedback therapists use *strain gauges*, which are wrapped around the chest or abdomen to train proper breathing patterns. Other therapists place surface electromyography (SEMG) sensors in the upper chest region or the abdomen for the same purpose.

Normal ventilation depends upon the movement of the diaphragm and intercostal muscles; the lungs have no muscle system. The diaphragm is like two double sheets of muscles that extend upward toward the chest beneath the lungs. It contracts during inspiration and rests during expiration. Normal breath rates are 12–15 breaths per minute (Schwartz, 1995). However, training lower breath rates (4–8 breaths per minute) will likely lower levels of tension and anxiety.

Clients with anxiety often have higher breath rates and forced inspiration that result in an exaggerated expansion of the upper chest (thoracic cavity). Rapid breathing (tachypnea) can lead to hyperventilation, which causes carbon dioxide to be exhaled faster than it can be produced. Alveolar hyperventilation causes an excessive loss of carbon dioxide from the blood, which contributes to respiratory alkalosis—increased blood pH (Marieb, 1995).

Blood alkalosis causes arteries to constrict and inhibits the flow of blood to the brain. Consequently, the brain receives a reduced supply of oxygen. Dizziness and symptoms of anxiety emerge: the heart begins to pound, panic takes over—it feels like suffocation—and in a desperate attempt to survive, inhalation becomes deeper, which causes a further carbon dioxide imbalance and more anxiety. Breathing into a paper bag increases carbon dioxide. In some cases it can limit the symptoms of panic attack.

I demonstrate proper breathing to almost all of my new clients—including children. Train yourself to do diaphragmatic breathing before you train someone else. Here's how: Remove tight-fitting clothing and put on a top that shows your profile. Get a watch with a second hand. Count the number of complete breaths you take (that is, both inhale and exhale) in 1 min. The optimum rate is 4–8 breaths per minute while relaxed. Breath rates of 15–25 are too fast. Next, observe the way your lungs fill with air: Stand sideways in front of a mirror and take a deep breath. What moved? Your chest, your abdomen, or, a combination of the two? If your chest moved the most, then you are a *reverse breather*—sometimes known as a shallow breather. There are two factors in correct breathing: rate of breath and method of breathing. Learning to slow down your breath rate goes hand in hand with abdominal or diaphragmatic breathing. Fill the abdomen first and foremost rather than the chest cavity. If you have no medical restrictions, do the following:

- Exhale while pushing in your stomach with both hands.
- Try to talk. If you can still talk, then air remains in your lungs.
- Evacuate the air until you can no longer talk.
- Inhale. You should observe that only your stomach is moving.
- Your chest should not be moving.
- Repeat.

If you are having trouble mastering this skill, get a partner. Ask your partner to apply light pressure to your back and stomach simultaneously (like playing the accordion) when you are exhaling. Release the hand pressure when inhaling. Repeat out loud: "Belly in, belly out." Have your partner work with you until you have mastered the technique. Sometimes it's helpful to lie on your back and put a large book on your stomach. Watch the book go up and down while your chest remains still. Once this skill has been mastered, work on adjusting your breath rate to 4–8 breaths per minute. Learning and teaching this technique is an excellent way to begin a treatment program. Some anxious clients resist the idea of taking time for themselves during the day—they want to practice at bedtime, when they are already feeling more relaxed. Practicing diaphragmatic breathing for 15 min each day during the daylight hours, however, works best.

BIOFEEDBACK FOR THE BODY

Biofeedback is the process of learning to control physiological functions by the use of instrumentation. Biofeedback training requires attaching sensors to the body for the purpose of acquiring biological signals such as those produced by muscles, sweat glands, body temperature, and heart rhythm. Biological signals are fed to trainees with the goal of gaining mental control over subconscious biological processes. The trainee receives moment-by-moment information about changes beneath the sensors. Information may come in the form of auditory tones, digital or analog displays, or computer graphics. Biofeedback is a self-regulation skill: Trainees learn to regulate aspects of ANS functions. Neurofeedback is a form of biofeedback. It is always used with reference to the cerebral functions. It relates either to the brain's electrical activity or to regional cerebral blood flow (rCBF). The term *biofeedback* may be used to encompass all feedback therapies, including neurofeedback. Many, but not all, clinicians use the term *biofeedback* as a way of describing feedback therapies for the body.

Biofeedback promotes a stronger sense of self. Responsibility for wellness rests with the client. Trainees hear feedback signals coming from their own biology. They are not subject to the interventions, questions, clarifications, or confrontations coming from a psychotherapist. Resistance to the therapist is hardly a factor in treatment. Resisting the feedback will result in less feedback, not more therapist interventions. The client comes face-to-face with the self. Blame for treatment failure cannot be projected upon the therapist, family members, or the world at large. Biofeedback frees the client to explore the internal workings of the self.

Biofeedback always rewards the trainee—it never punishes. The most important reward comes during the training process. Trainees hear auditory signals or see graphic movements that indicate that they are on track. In addition to the feedback signals, some neurotherapists make well-placed positive remarks during training, as if they were coaching the trainee. At the close of each session trainees are given further encouragement. They may be shown a progress report or receive a commendation. When trainees say they are tired after training, I immediately reply, "Of course you are tired. You've been working hard!"

Biofeedback training is theoretically intertwined with behaviorism. It brings to mind the principles developed by Ivan Pavlov (classical conditioning) and B. F. Skinner (operant conditioning). In classical conditioning the trainee learns a new way to elicit a natural response—the bell causes the dog to salivate as if the meat were present. In operant conditioning the trainee learns to elicit a new response following reinforcement—the monkey is reinforced by food each time it pulls the designated lever. Biofeedback is a form of operant conditioning; reinforcement comes only when the trainee emits the correct response. The reinforcement comes in the form of a tone and/or computer graphics. Unlike the monkey, the biofeedback trainee sees a grander purpose in learning a new skill—for example, better grades in school. Biofeedback trainees learn best when the challenge matches their ability to learn. Training that is too easy or too difficult usually fails to produce change.

Biofeedback modalities fall under one of two headings:

1. Peripheral biofeedback—or, biofeedback for the body—relates to the PNS and more specifically to its sympathetic and parasympathetic branches. The following *partial* list includes three peripheral biofeedback modalities:

- ○ Galvanic skin response (GSR) biofeedback
- ○ Skin temperature (ST) training (thermal) biofeedback
- ○ SEMG biofeedback

2. Neurofeedback relates to activity within the brain:

- ○ Electroencephalography (EEG) neurofeedback (electrical activity)
- ○ Hemoencephalography (HEG) neurofeedback (Cerebral blood flow [CBF])

INTEGRATING NEUROFEEDBACK WITH BIOFEEDBACK MODALITIES

Neurofeedback training influences peripheral biofeedback recordings. There is a mind-to-body connection. The body is a system; it can be compared to the mobile hanging over a child's crib. The movement of one member changes the position of the others. Neurofeedback specialists study the body and not just the brain. They integrate biofeedback and breathwork training with neurotherapy as needed. For example, anxious clients often have an overactive sympathetic nervous system. Biofeedback training improves the balance between sympathetic and parasympathetic nervous system activity. It improves the quality of neurofeedback training. Biofeedback training is used for homework assignments. For example, daily skin temperature (ST) training teaches the client relaxation through mental control. ST training prepares one for neurofeedback training—both are self-regulation skills.

It is not unusual for some neurofeedback providers to monitor bodily activity while clients engage in neurofeedback training. Peripheral biofeedback equipment provides hard data that can support the client's subjective response. For example, training may change hand temperature. An increase in hand temperature suggests relaxation, whereas a decrease suggests tension. Another way to track response to training is to monitor sweat gland production. Cold sweaty hands signal anxiety; dry warm hands signal relaxation. Muscle electrical activity is of great interest because it can happen at the same time and at almost the same place as EEG activity. The muscles of a tense client may compromise clean EEG recordings. It is prudent to be aware of physiological changes during neurofeedback training.

Consider the place that each peripheral biofeedback modality may have during neurofeedback training.

Galvanic Skin Response

Galvanic skin response (GSR) is a method of measuring the conductivity and electrical resistance of the skin. It is also called electrodermal activity feedback (EDA). The RH of the brain controls the skin conductivity on the left side of the body and visa versa. There are as many as "2000 sweat glands per square centimeter" in the hand. When aroused, the sympathetic nervous system activates the eccrine glands in the hands and the feet. A saline solution is secreted via eccrine sweat glands. Increasing sweat gland production results in a corresponding reduction in electrical resistance (Peek, 1995, pp. 77–78). (Saline or salt water is a good conductor of electricity). A simple test will demonstrate this principle:

1. Purchase an inexpensive ohmmeter/voltmeter.
2. Fill one glass with pure water.
3. Fill the other glass with water mixed with 1 tablespoon of salt.
4. Switch the meter selector to read ohms.
5. Put the two probes together—the meter should read zero.
6. Separate probes by 1 inch (25.4 mm) and submerge in pure water.
7. Keeping the probes separated, submerge in the salt water.

The ohmmeter readings are very low in the salt water because it is a good conductor of electricity; consequently there is little or zero resistance to record. On the other hand, pure water is a poor conductor of electricity— much resistance is recorded. GSR equipment measures electrical resistance: the sweatier the hand, the lower the electrical resistance; the dryer the hand, the higher the electrical resistance. Sweaty hands often indicate sympathetic nervous activity that accompanies stress and tension. Decreasing sweat production often corresponds to decreasing levels of stress and tension (Criswell, 1995, pp. 100–111). GSR can be used as a general relaxation trainer or to augment systematic desensitization. Inexpensive home trainers are available.

GSR measurements are taken from two different fingers of the same hand. Sensors are either taped or strapped to each finger. Biofeedback instrumentation signals changes in eccrine gland secretions. The trainee is reinforced whenever there is a reduction in secretions. GSR equipment can also be used as a monitoring device. Changes in GSR activity during neurofeedback training indicate changes in sympathetic nervous system activity. Usually, the hands become dryer as the trainee becomes more relaxed. However, if sweat glands dry up too quickly it suggests a negative response to training. This kind of backlash condition is known as relaxation induced anxiety (Kerson, 2002).

GSR activity is useful when evaluating the efficacy of a training protocol. *Clinical-grade equipment* is required for monitoring trainees, and some neurofeedback providers make the investment. In states with low humidity, such as Arizona, GSR equipment may have limited value, and physiological changes can be tracked in other ways. For example, increases in either breath rate or pulse rate signal a rise in sympathetic nervous system activity.

Skin Temperature Training (Thermal Biofeedback)

Skin temperature (ST) training, or hand warming, improves circulation in the extremities, which often reflects a decrease in stress—essential for anxious clients. It is also used as a treatment for hypertension, migraines, and Raynaud's disease. The temperature of our skin relates to the alternating activities of the sympathetic and parasympathetic nervous systems. It is an indirect measurement of peripheral vasoconstriction (the constriction of blood vessels). ST changes when the body undergoes a stress response. This causes blood to flow toward key areas of the body, such as the brain, spinal cord, and muscles, and away from the extremities such as the hands and the feet. The sympathetic nervous system sends out signals in order to contract smooth muscles of blood vessels, resulting in a decrease of ST. The stress response is reversed when the peripheral nervous system (PNS) sends out signals to cause vascular dilation. All this happens unconsciously in the autonomic nervous system (ANS). ST training promotes conscious control of the ANS (Criswell, 1995, pp.112–123).

Many neurofeedback providers employ ST training because it is the fastest and least expensive way to introduce a new client to neuroregulation skills. I instruct clients as follows:

1. Go to an electronics equipment retailers and purchase a digital indoor/outdoor thermometer with a straight (not disc) probe.
2. Remove any wire bracket from of the probe.
3. Tape the probe to the midsection of the middle finger from either hand (palms up).

4. Switch the temperature gauge to outdoors.
5. Raise your finger temperature to 93–95°F and hold it for 15–20 min.
6. Practice ST training at home for 5–8 days in a row before EEG training begins.

Learning to do ST training involves the process of *letting go*. What does *letting go* mean? It means replacing worry thoughts or ruminations with self-supporting thoughts or relaxing thoughts. Sometimes the temperature decreases because trainees are trying too hard. I tell them that this is a time for feeling, not thinking. I also say: "Imagine you are getting a massage. What would you be thinking about? Your bills? The argument you had with your spouse? Problems with the family? No, it would be time-out from your problems." Although not everyone is a good candidate for this treatment—some have very warm hands to begin with and others suffer from performance anxiety—fortunately, the majority of adults and children respond well to this technique. It may be necessary to refer the highly anxious client to an alternative health care provider for bodywork. Successful trainees choose from a variety of relaxation techniques:

- Diaphragmatic breathing (primary nonfeedback modality)
- Guided imagery
- Autogenics
- Relaxation tapes
- Positive self talk
- Repetitive word reciting (in silence) (reciting the names of 5–7 five to seven objects in the room repeatedly)

During EEG neurofeedback, one of the goals is for the trainee to remain alert without becoming tense. It's important to be engaged with the process without developing performance anxiety or zoning out. A state of passive awareness is needed. ST training teaches passive awareness; it is especially useful for clients who suffer from anxiety. It prepares the client for neurotherapy. It is used in the first stage of deep-states (neurofeedback) training.

Hand temperature can be checked quickly without equipment. Even an anxious person usually has a warm cheek. Put your fingers on your cheek to find out if they are cold or warm. In this way, changes in hand temperature can be readily detected. Before assigning someone to do ST training, master the skill yourself. With practice, you will be able to raise your hand temperature in the presence of clients.

Surface Electromyography

Surface electromyography (SEMG) biofeedback records the electrical activity of muscles coming from the surface of the skin. Those who engage in this form of training learn to regulate voluntary muscle activity. It is often used to promote deep relaxation and relieve muscle tension. For example, trainees can learn to relax the muscles of the neck and reduce the incidence of tension headaches. Skeletal muscles are controlled by the voluntary motor cortex. There are two ways to train muscles with biofeedback: one way is to train directly over a muscle with SEMG biofeedback; the other way is to train the part of the brain that controls the muscle namely the motor cortex via EEG-biofeedback (neurofeedback).

Neurofeedback providers have a vested interest in cranial muscle tension because of its effect upon the electrical measurements coming from the cerebral cortex. Therefore it is essential to understand the connection between the electrical energy coming form the muscles and the electrical energy coming from the cerebral cortex. First, before the electrical nature of muscles is examined, it is important to explain muscle dynamics.

Muscles have the power to contract or extend in one direction. If a muscle does pulling, it can do no pushing; if a muscle pushes, it cannot pull back to the original position. Opposing muscles or antagonists are needed to reverse direction. For example, the biceps can pull something toward the body but they can't push it away. It takes the action of the triceps to push something away from your body. While the triceps are pushing away from the body, the biceps are in a relaxed state (Keeffe, 1999). A tense muscle continues to contract (or extend) without cause—it fails to relax. The tense neurofeedback trainee is often reminded to drop his or her shoulders. Positive signals coming from the brain help the whole person to relax. Instructing your client to relax a muscle group can have far-reaching effects.

The electrical signals from muscles emanate from motor units beneath the skin. A motor unit consists of the neuron and muscle fibers. Muscle movements are produced by a series of electrical signals that are passed on from one neuron to another. It can be compared to a relay race in which each runner passes the baton to another until the anchor neuron takes it across the finish line. In this illustration, each runner is *electrical* and the baton is *chemical*. The chemical neurotransmitter acetylcholine is secreted across each gap or synapse. Further movement or contraction is accomplished by adjacent neurons (Keeffe, 1999; Krebs, 1995). SEMG equipment can record the electrical activity of motor units.

SEMG training requires the placement of electrodes on the surface of the skin and over the belly of a muscle. One channel of SEMG has three electrodes that are connected to three wires or leads. The wires are braided together. On one end, all three wires join to make a standardized plug that fits into the biofeedback unit. On the other end, each wire has a small flat round disk called an electrode. All three electrodes are taped to the skin. Two serve as actives while the third serves as the ground. The two active electrodes bridge the belly of the muscle and the ground is placed nearby.

One channel records the muscle activity over one location. Two channels record the muscle activity over two locations. Two channels of SEMG have more clinical utility than just one. Each channel has its own set of electrodes. With two channels it's possible to evaluate muscle symmetry. For example, one set of sensors can be placed on the right facial muscles and the other set can be placed over the left facial muscles. If one channel has significantly higher electrical readings than the other, then there is a problem. If both channels are *roughly equal and within normal limits*, then it can be assumed that the muscles are functioning properly. Normative values are published for each muscle group.

SEMG feedback may come in the form of tones that reflect muscle activity. For example, when successful a trainee will hear a steady but low pitch or tone that often reflects muscle relaxation. The pitch increases when muscle tension increases. In this way, many trainees learn within a few minutes how to reduce muscle tension. However, SEMG training can also be used to strengthen or rehabilitate muscles. Typically, 6–12 training sessions make up a complete SEMG program.

SEMG signals from muscles are electrical. EEG signals from the brain are electrical. Both are measured in microvolts and cycles per second (Hertz). The general range of SEMG is 20–200 Hz (Krebs, 1995). The most commonly analyzed range of EEG signals is 0–40 Hz. Therefore, SEMG and EEG signals overlap because both share the same range of electrical activity. Both produce electrical signals between 20 Hz and 40 Hz. Furthermore, SEMG electrical activity can be more powerful than EEG electrical activity. High-amplitude SEMG signals tend to drown out EEG signals. Every time a trainee coughs, clears the throat, blinks, or swallows, EEG recordings are distorted by SEMG artifact. Consequently, trainees should be educated about muscle artifact. Make them aware of facial movements. Remind them to sit still and avoid gum chewing. Some trainees have so many twitches and forehead movements that it is better to train with eyes-closed or to place sensors away from prefrontal lobes.

Clients with bruxism (teeth grinding) and TMJ (temporomandibular joint tension and pain) disorders have a great deal of muscle tension that extends to the scalp. The electrical force of SEMG becomes more apparent when EEG sensors are placed in frontal and temporal lobe positions. One way to overcome this problem is to do SEMG training. I routinely help clients with bruxism or TMJ to relax facial muscles with SEMG biofeedback. If you lack the right equipment, have the clients stretch their jaws before doing EEG neurofeedback training. Clients with general muscle tension may benefit from Jacobson's method of progressive relaxation (Criswell, 1995). Make all clients aware of muscle tension.

4

Neurofeedback Modalities
and the Brain

PSYCHOTHERAPY IS A TOOL TO ENRICH THE MIND, whereas neurotherapy is a tool to enrich the brain. The mind depends upon healthy brain metabolism when attempting to draw conclusions and make changes. Two intervention methods are better than one. The psychotherapist receives *psychological data* from the client in the form of transference, emotional expressions, and rational or irrational beliefs. The client's narrative is examined for both content and process. The psychotherapist feeds back to the client: confrontations, clarifications, empathy, or insight. The client— if he or she is ready—has the option of using that information for his or her own edification. In a similar way, the neurotherapist records the trainee's *biological data* in the form of electroencephalograph (EEG) activity or regional cerebral blood flow (rCBF). Auditory or visual signals are fed back to the trainee. Feedback informs the trainee each time progress is being made—in the very moment that it happens. Motivated trainees are empowered to make incremental changes. When cerebral efficiency is enhanced, psychological growth is potentiated.

Neurofeedback is a comprehensive treatment system that works directly with the brain. Each of us has a countless number of neurons in our cerebrum. Brain waves are associated with the electrical activation and deactivation of neurons. They cycle up and down, over and over again. The trainee is given feedback precisely at the time when the cycle of brain waves moves into a desirable pattern. For example, if someone is training to become more alert, then the feedback would be set in the following manner: Each time the cycle of brain waves moves into an *alert* state, tones are heard and computer graphics are activated. Each time the cycle of brain waves moves into a *distracted* state, tones and graphics cease. Amazingly, the brain cooperates; simple reinforcement teaches the brain how to *prolong* healthy brain wave patterns. Within a few sessions trainees often gain a heightened awareness of mental drifting. Gradually, most trainees learn to pay attention for longer periods of time—even during boring tasks in the classroom or at work.

ELECTROENCEPHALOGRAPH NEUROFEEDBACK

The electroencephalograph (EEG) is a paper or digital recording of raw unfiltered brain wave signals (Figure 4.1). Examples of the raw EEG can be seen in Appendix 1. Minute electrical signals coming from the scalp can be amplified and transformed into brain waves and data. Hospitals have departments that are equipped to examine the electrical activity of

FIGURE 4.1
ELECTROENCEPHALOGRAPHY RECORDING SYSTEM

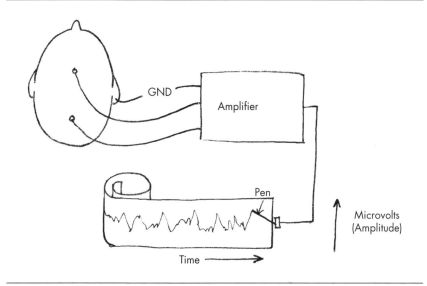

the brain. Neurologists working in hospitals analyze raw EEG data. They examine the morphology or waveform of the raw EEG for spikes when seizure disorder is suspected. Hospital equipment is for testing, not for training. EEG neurofeedback training equipment is for both training and testing. The emphasis is on frequency and amplitude rather than wave morphology. The raw signal is important and some neurofeedback providers can spot seizure spikes in the raw EEG (see Appendix 5). A good clean raw signal is also part of the evidence that there is a good hookup. But raw signals are not used for training. The raw EEG is further refined and dissected into smaller parts by means of electronic filters.

The EEG signal is amplified and then filtered by active band-pass filters. Just as a glass prism can break down white light into many colors, electronic filters can separate the raw EEG into smaller parts, called frequencies. Electronic filters can isolate a single frequency. Each brain wave frequency can be measured in terms of hertz and microvolts. One hertz means 1 cycle per second; it is the rhythm of the wave. Slow frequencies are less than 10 Hz; fast frequencies are greater than 13 Hz. Microvolts measure the amplitude or the height of the wave. Microvolt (μV) readings are variable and may range anywhere from near zero to 100 μV. Slower frequencies tend to have higher amplitudes than faster frequencies—but not always. When slow frequencies dominate, the brain is moving slowly, idling, reflecting, or getting ready to do something. When fast frequencies dominate, the brain is moving along from one task to another and sometimes it goes into high gear. Figure 4.2 shows the difference between a high amplitude slow wave and a low amplitude fast wave.

Single frequencies have been organized into discreet groups. For example, the frequency range from 1 Hz to 4 Hz forms the frequency bandwidth known as delta (1–4 Hz). Frequency bandwidths have amplitude or microvolt readings that reflect all of the activity within the bandwidth. In general, as the size of a bandwidth increases, so does the amplitude. For example, 6.9 μV was the measurement obtained at Cz from 8 to 12 Hz in one clinical sample. Notice what happens to the total amplitude measurement when the bandwidth range is changed:

8–9 Hz	1.6μV
8–10 Hz	3.3μV
8–11 Hz	5.2μV
8–12 Hz	6.9μV
8–13 Hz	8.4μV

FIGURE 4.2
HIGH AMPLITUDE SLOW WAVE ACTIVITY COMPARED TO LOW
AMPLITUDE FAST WAVE ACTIVITY

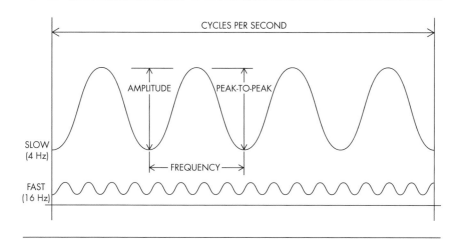

TABLE 4.1
Common Frequency Bandwidths

COMMON BANDWIDTH NAME	FREQUENCY RANGE (Hz)	GENERAL DESCRIPTION OR CHARACTERISTICS
Delta	1–4	Sleep, repair, complex problem solving
Theta	4–8	Creativity, insight, deep states
Alpha	8–12	Alertness and peacefulness, readiness, meditation
Beta	13–21	Thinking, focusing, sustained attention
SMR	12–15	Mental alertness, physical relaxation
High beta	20–32	Intensity, hyperalertness, anxiety
Gamma	38–42	Cognitive processing, learning

Other bandwidth names include theta, alpha, beta, SMR, high beta, and gamma. Each named frequency bandwidth is associated with specific characteristics. Training is often aimed at changing the amplitude of a selected frequency bandwidth. Remember: amplitudes can change within a selected frequency range. *Frequencies do not change; amplitudes change.* Table 4.1

is a list of all of the common frequency bandwidths and their general characteristics:

ONE-CHANNEL EEG TRAINING SYSTEMS

A *single-channel* EEG unit records one raw signal and separates it into parts with electronic filters. Data is acquired by placing electrodes on the scalp according to the International 10–20 system. There are two basic montages or ways to mount electrodes on the scalp. (When speaking with clients, I use the term *sensor* because it sounds less intimidating than the word *electrode*.) Learning the correct way to place sensors or electrodes on the scalp is critical to success. Recordings with a single-channel EEG require the placement of three separate leads on the head. Each wire or lead has a small cup on one end and electrical connectors on the other. The cups go on the scalp or the ears and the connectors are plugged into the EEG training system. Each of the three electrodes has a different function or designation. One electrode is the ground and can be mounted on the earlobe or any convenient place on the scalp. The other two electrodes acquire the data and are called the actives. Both actives are essentially the same, even though one of the actives is called the *reference*. Sometimes, the reference designation is useful. For example, the question, "How many miles is it to Vermont?" cannot be answered unless a starting point has been designated. However, if I asked, "How many miles is it from London to Vermont?" then the number of miles can be calculated. Vermont is the active, the point of interest. London is the reference or the starting point. Changing the starting point or the reference changes the output. There are two ways to set a reference. One way is to use the earlobe as a reference; the other way is to use a scalp location as a reference. Consider the differences between these two basic montages (Figure 4.3):

1. A *referential* (monopolar) montage is accomplished by mounting only one active electrode cup to the scalp. The reference cup is often clipped to an earlobe. The ground cup is often clipped to the remaining earlobe. Theoretically, a referential montage renders an *absolute* value because the reference earlobe placement is considered to be neutral or zero in value. Many clinicians place the reference earlobe electrode in the same hemisphere as the scalp placement. For example, if the active scalp electrode is on the left side of the

FIGURE 4.3
REFERENTIAL COMPARED TO BIPOLAR (SEQUENTIAL) MONTAGE

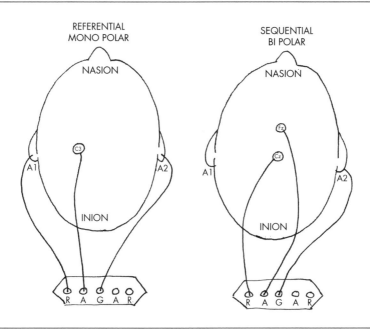

brain, then the reference is clipped to the left earlobe. If the active electrode is on the Z-line (Cz, Pz, Fz, etc.), then either ear may be chosen as the reference. (Sometimes the earlobe on the opposing side of the head is chosen to obtain a maximum differential and to control ear contamination.) A referential (monopolar) montage has one major drawback: It is the most sensitive to large amplitudes of electromyography (EMG) muscle artifact and earlobe contamination. Each facial movement of the client may cause a significant distortion of the EEG recording.

2. A bipolar (*sequential*) montage means that both the reference and the active electrode cups are mounted to the scalp, and the ground cup is clipped to either earlobe. An impedance meter should be used to ensure that both of the sensors mounted on the scalp have similar resistance measurements. Bipolar (sequential) montages will not yield absolute values. For example, if the active is at Cz and the

reference is at Pz, then the resultant measurement will be *incremental* rather than absolute because Pz has a value—it is *not* neutral. The output is rendered as the complex mathematical difference between the two chosen sites. Therefore, the absolute value at Cz cannot be obtained with this method. Bipolar (sequential) montages are chosen for several reasons. One factor relates to muscle artifact. Bipolar (sequential) montages are more resistant to muscle artifact than referential (monopolar) montages. Large amplitudes of EMG activity may stem from a singular or common muscular movement originating in the head. The process of rejecting similar electrical activity is called common mode rejection (Lubar & Lubar, 1999, p. 122). Another factor relates to communication: bipolar montages engage two regions of the brain simultaneously. Hence, two separate regions are conscripted into the same neuronal task. They are being persuaded to have a heightened awareness of each other's presence in the cerebral universe.

Mechanics of Sensor Placement

Electrode cups are usually made from silver, gold, or tin. Cups may be filled with special gels that conduct electricity; some manufacturers have designed electrodes that make use of the electrical conductivity of saline solutions. Many neurofeedback providers fill each electrode cup with Ten20 conductive paste. They add extra paste to the cup(s) located on the scalp. The scalp and earlobe positions are cleaned with alcohol or an abrasive conductive gel such as NuPrep™ ECG & EEG Abrasive Skin Prepping Gel before mounting sensors. The following sequence works well for paste-filled electrodes:

- Apply NuPrep to a nonsterile gauze pad, separate the hair until a bare spot is exposed, and clean (lightly abrade) the selected site. Scalp sensor(s) are pushed down on a clean scalp position with a small piece of a paper towel (or small cotton ball) on top. If the towel piece falls off, the connection may be inadequate. Make sure minimal hair is under the sensor. Securely attach remaining sensor(s) to earlobe(s). If an anterior or a posterior *ventral* scalp location is chosen, a headband may be required to keep the sensors from moving.

An impedance meter should be used to determine if there is good contact between the sensor and the skin. There is always some electrical resistance between the sensor cup and the skin. Electrical resistance is measure in ohms. The standard for assessments is 5,000 Ω or less (Hughes, 1994, p. 41). Reclean the scalp if necessary. Looking at the raw EEG signal on the computer screen is another indication of the quality of the connection. Never train if the raw EEG signal looks wrong. If the raw EEG is distorted, suspect one of the following:

- Excessive surface electromyography (SEMG) or muscle artifact.
- Damaged lead wires (check with an ohmmeter).
- There is a salt bridge or conductivity between two head sensors due to sweat (remove excessive sweat).
- The battery-operated equipment is not fully charged (recharge).
- The sensors are not plugged into equipment correctly (correct problem).
- The wiring in building is improperly grounded (call an electrician).
- Fluorescent lighting is causing a 60-Hz artifact.
- There is a computer communications port problem (fix computer).
- RS232 cable is incorrect or broken (find correct cable).
- There is a radio frequency interference (RFI) or electromagnetic interference (EMI) artifact (see Chapter 17 on choosing an office).
- There is an electrocardiogram (EKG) artifact.

Setting Thresholds Within One Channel of EEG

The goal of neurofeedback training is to transform an unhealthy EEG pattern into a healthy one. The client's symptoms directly relate to an abnormal distribution of bandwidths within the raw EEG. For example, the client may have too much theta while having too little beta amplitude in one region of the brain. If so, the goal of neurofeedback training would be to *decrease* theta and/or *increase* beta amplitudes. One way of monitoring the client as he or she trains is by observing the flow of EEG data. Another way is to observe the training graph on a computer screen. Figure 4.4 represents an EEG of a client who was downtraining alpha (8–12 Hz) at T5-T6 (See Figure 6.8c.) The client was trained with a BrainMaster Technologies, Inc. two-channel EEG training system.

Figure 4.4 demonstrates a good learning curve. However, the decrease in the alpha bandwidth does not reflect a permanent change: The alpha amplitude will likely return close to its original average reading in due time. More training sessions are needed to produce a long-lasting change within a frequency bandwidth at a single scalp location. There is no way to predict the

FIGURE 4.4
TRAINING GRAPH OF A GOOD LEARNER

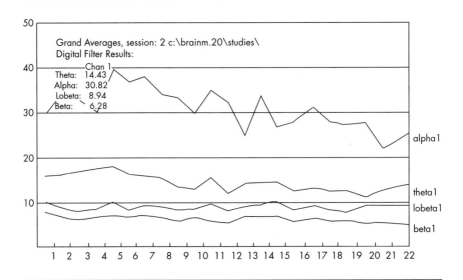

Grand Averages, session: 2 c:\brainm.20\studies\
Digital Filter Results:
Chan 1
Theta: 14.43
Alpha: 30.82
Lobeta: 8.94
Beta: 6.28

alpha1

theta1
lobeta1
beta1

exact number of sessions needed to produce satisfactory change. Regardless of the rate of progress, the goal is to *see* movement in the right direction. In Figure 4.4, the goal was to lower the amplitude of alpha (8–12 Hz). Progress needs to be monitored as the session advances; the training graph is one of the monitoring tools available to the neurotherapist.

Learning can be manifested in different ways on the session graph; it may even seem inconsistent at times. *Sometimes, amplitudes go up before they go down, or they may zigzag up and down.* For example, increases in theta during training sessions may occur if the trainee is assigned a task such as reading. Consequently, theta may go up for a *few* sessions until the trainee learns to lower theta while under task. Generally speaking, if the amplitude keeps going in the wrong direction as the session proceeds, then training should be paused or stopped. Find out what's wrong! The problem could rest either with the trainee or with the trainer. For example, the trainee could be tired, sleep deprived, daydreaming, upset, ill, thirsty, anxious, bored, or uncomfortable. On the other hand, the neurotherapist (trainer) may have made a poor decision about (a) sensor location, (b) selected frequency bandwidth(s), or the (c) duration of training. Successful training provides reasonable challenges or tasks that match the trainee's ability to perform.

Neurofeedback training can be compared to progressive weight lifting. In order to improve, the trainee must be given a task that challenges the brain. The task may be designed to enhance the strength, endurance, or flexibility of the brain. Or it may improve the communication between two or more regions of the brain. Regardless of the task, neurofeedback training usually involves the setting of thresholds. Electronic thresholds determine how easy or difficult a training task is to master. No learning can take place unless the trainee is rewarded at the appropriate time. Decreasing the amplitude of a frequency bandwidth is accomplished by an *inhibit* threshold; increasing the amplitude of a frequency bandwidth is accomplished by a *reward* threshold. An inhibit threshold is like a limbo bar because trainees are reinforced when the amplitude of a wave is lower than the set threshold. A reward threshold is like a hurdle because trainees are reinforced when the amplitude of a wave is above the set threshold. Consider the following example: If a trainee had an average of 7 μV of alpha at Cz, thresholds could be set to either decrease or increase the amplitude. To decrease the amplitude, an inhibit threshold would be used; it would be set to reinforce the trainee each time the amplitude was *less* than 7 μV. On the other hand, to increase the amplitude a reward threshold would be used; it would be set to reinforce the trainee each time the amplitude was *greater* than 7 μV.

In Figure 4.5, the wave will cycle inside and then outside of the two threshold bars. If this was an illustration of an inhibit threshold setting, feedback would be given as long as the wave was inside the bars. Moving the bars closer together would result in less feedback. Moving the bars further apart would result in more feedback. Obviously, a reward threshold setting works in precisely the opposite manner.

It is possible to set one, two, or more thresholds at the same time, that is, one for each different bandwidth. In general, increasing (rewarding) the

FIGURE 4.5
FEEDBACK BETWEEN THE THRESHOLD BARS

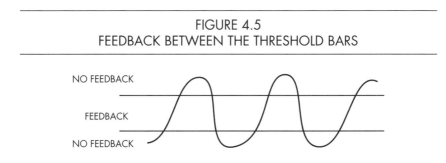

NO FEEDBACK

FEEDBACK

NO FEEDBACK

amplitude of a wave is called uptraining while decreasing (inhibiting) the amplitude is called downtraining. One style of training is called beta/SMR training. This style includes only one reward filter combined with two inhibit filters. The following exemplifies beta/SMR training because beta is rewarded while two other bandwidths are inhibited. Beta is sandwiched by one higher bandwidth and one lower bandwidth. Typically, beta is rewarded when training is in the LH, while SMR is rewarded when training is in the RH. In either case beta or SMR is in between two inhibits. A possible three-threshold setting could look like the following:

- Inhibit (theta) 4–8 Hz with a 15-μV threshold
- Reward (beta) 16–20 Hz with a 3-μV threshold
- Inhibit (high beta) 20–30 Hz with a 6-μV threshold

As shown in Figure 4.6, all three threshold conditions must be met before the trainee receives an auditory and a graphic reinforcement. In order for trainee to be reinforced, (a) theta amplitude activity must be less than 15 μV, (b) beta amplitude activity must be more than 3 μV, and (c) high-beta amplitude activity must be less than 6 μV—*all at the same time*. When the brain works at the task of keeping within threshold limits, it often results in change. Brains that are challenged by a specific task become stronger and more flexible.

FIGURE 4.6
SETTING THRESHOLDS FOR REINFORCEMENT

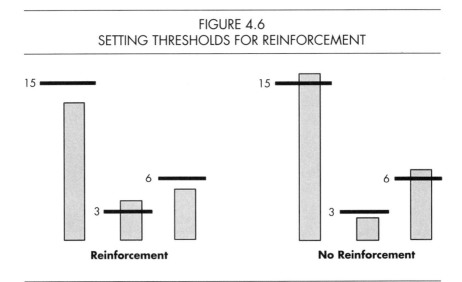

Reinforcement   No Reinforcement

During a training session, brain wave amplitudes (microvolts) may change in one or more bandpass filters. If so, then the training may become too easy or too hard. When the training becomes too hard, the rate of auditory feedback gets slower; when the training becomes too easy, the rate of auditory feedback gets faster. Therefore, listening to the feedback is one indication of trainee success or failure. Watching the training graph is another indication. A third way is by determining the percentage of success. Thresholds are set in order to achieve a certain percentage of success. Neurotherapists have learned that certain percentages promote learning. All clinical-grade equipment give an indication of the percentage of success.

What does it mean to set a threshold for 50% success? It means that the threshold bar has been set so that reinforcement is received about half of the time. Or it might be said that the amplitude of the frequency bandwidth cycles within threshold limits at least half of the time. Some (but not all) software automatically adjusts thresholds so that a predetermined percentage of success is maintained. Hence, the electronic limbo bar or hurdle automatically moves up or down as necessary. If the equipment does not allow for automatic thresholding, then the neurotherapist makes the adjustment manually.

Thresholds are set in such a way that the trainee feels successful. The trainee must always feel successful—I cannot overstate this principle. Often thresholds are set so that the trainee is reinforced 50–80% of the time—when a *single* bandpass filter is being trained. However, if *multiple* bandpass filters are used, some therapists use this general set of percentage goals when three separate bandpass filters are used:

- 70% success for one reward filter (e.g., beta)
- 20% success for the primary inhibit (e.g., theta)
- 10% success for the secondary inhibit (e.g., high beta)

Note: *Inhibit* thresholds use a reverse format, that is, an 80% reinforcement is output as 20% and a 90% reinforcement is output as 10%—opposite to the way reward thresholds are designated. This reverse format is found in most equipment.

It is not necessary to use the three bandpass filters. There is no set number of filters with corresponding thresholds that must be set. Sometimes, I train with only one frequency bandwidth. Or, I might train with two or three. I seldom train with more than three frequency bandwidths for each channel. Deciding how many bandwidths to train requires an understanding of the normal distribution of banded frequencies. Secondary bandwidths may help the trainee learn or succeed with the primary bandwidth. Typically, when three bandwidths are being trained, one bandwidth is the reward and the other two are inhibits (e.g., inhibit theta and high beta but reward beta). However, this condition may be inverted during deep-states training (e.g., reward alpha and theta while inhibiting either 15–30 Hz or 2–5 Hz [Scott, 2002]).

Sounds are *very* important. Sounds generally fall into three categories: sustained, tapping, or pitch variable. A sustained sound continues as long as threshold conditions are met. A tapping sound is one that repeats as long as threshold conditions are met. A pitch-variable sound goes higher if the client is more successful and goes lower if there is less success, or visa versa, according to the client's taste in sounds. The key is to find the sound that works best. I give clients a choice. For example, one client felt anxiety with a tapping sound; when I switched to a pitch-variable sound, she described it as music and felt better. Sounds can be even more important when doing deep-states training—they should be soothing or calming.

Graphics are important. Most graphics tend to be boring and repetitive. Most computer graphic games are not games at all—objects on the screen simply move every time the trainee is successful. EEG computer games lack the excitement so often found in the world of video games. Very few computer graphics can honestly hold the attention of trainees unless they are highly motivated. Clients with anxiety sometimes enjoy the rhythmic movement of graphics, but each person is different. When training for attention, my biggest concern is that the trainee stay alert. Preventing boredom during training can be a challenge. Therefore, I usually have them engage in one of a number of site-specific learning activities while they are training. Specific regions of the brain are responsible for specific cognitive, emotional, spatial, and visual activities. For example, if I am training someone on the left side of the brain, I may choose cognitive learning activities like reading. But if I am training in the visual cortex (occipital lobes), I may choose visual activities like solitaire, looking at picture books, using Microsoft's Paint program, or simply watching the action on the screen. Of course, graphics are of no value if the trainee has his or her eyes-closed.

TWO-CHANNEL EEG TRAINING SYSTEMS

Two-channel EEG systems acquire two independent raw EEG signals for the purpose of training or assessments. Each channel has its own set of filters that break down the EEG into frequency bandwidths. Two-channel training systems are more versatile than single-channel systems. They can compare and train two scalp locations simultaneously. Regions of the brain do not operate independently—the brain is a system. At least two EEG channels are needed to gain the systemic edge.

Each channel of a two-channel EEG training system has its own set of sensors or electrodes. Each channel has two active electrodes, whereas both channels share one ground. Both types of montages may be used when training with two channels. For example, referential montages are typically used for coherence and synchrony training, whereas bipolar (sequential) montages may be used for asymmetry training. Sensors are often placed at contralateral positions on the scalp. However, both sets of sensors may be placed within the same hemisphere. Figure 4.7 depicts a two-channel referential montage.

Dynamic Interventions with Two Channels

Some neurofeedback providers limit themselves to single-channel training. However, two-channel training is likely superior to single-channel training when the goal is to improve whole brain dynamics. Two-channel training has been effective at improving cognitive flexibility and performance as well as maladaptive lateral asymmetries and global frequency output. Protocols include: (a) coherence training because it concerns itself with communication between neurological regions, specifically two scalp sites; (b) asymmetry training, which promotes simultaneous bilateral change; (c) alpha synchrony training, used for peak performance and psychological depth issues; (d) two-channel training along the sensorimotor strip. Some consider dynamic interventions to be advanced skills. Others seldom utilize multiple-channel interventions; they focus on single-channel interventions within specific neurological regions of the brain. In either case, all neurotherapists should be aware of two-channel training options. The following is an inventory of dynamic two-channel training protocols.

Coherence Training. Coherence is a measurement of the similarity of frequency between two sites on the scalp; it is a comparison of waveform or pattern rather than amplitude. For example, a test of coherence could include two sites such as F7 and T5 in the alpha range of 8–12 Hz. Coherence is a quality measurement of communication. It "can directly reflect neural network connectivity and neural network dynamics" (Thatcher,

FIGURE 4.7
TWO CHANNEL HOOKUP

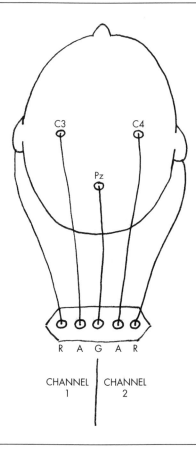

R = reference; A = active; G = ground

1999, p. 49). If someone used coherent speech, he or she would be easy to understand. If two people had a flowing relationship with many thoughts in common, it might be said that they were on each other's "wavelength." A correlation of 1.0 is the highest level of coherence, whereas a correlation of 0.0 means that there is no coherence. Hypercoherence means that two regions share too much; hypocoherence means just the opposite. Excessive hypercoherence may be observed after a closed head injury or in mental retardation. Excessive hypocoherence may be observed in some learning disorders. Genuine coherence training requires a two-channel EEG training system.

Coherence training means that only *one* frequency or frequency bandwidth is compared at any two sites on the scalp. To increase coherence, the trainee is reinforced when the correlation between both sites goes up—hence a reward threshold is set. Increasing coherence may result in increasing the amplitude within the chosen frequency bandwidth at either or both scalp locations. The exact opposite may be said about decreasing coherence.

Two-channel coherence training is a *direct* method of improving the balance or sharing between two scalp locations. Increasing coherence usually results in increasing amplitudes at both locations. Therefore, if the amplitudes within a given frequency bandwidth at two scalp locations are already too high, then increasing coherence is contraindicated. Decreasing coherence is just the opposite. However, there may be an alternative training solution. Some neurofeedback providers believe that single-channel training with bipolar (sequential) montages may be an *indirect* method of improving coherence (Walker, Norman, & Weber, 2002, pp. 31–43). If that is true, then it may be possible to decrease amplitudes while increasing coherence.

Coherence training is not always needed. All forms of neurofeedback training have the potential of changing EEG coherence. Before and after QEEG samples indicate that single-channel *referential training* can facilitate positive changes in coherence (Soutar, 2004). Furthermore, 2-channel coherence training should be limited to just a few sessions. Over training quickly leads to imbalances (Horvat, 2004). On the other hand, training with a bipolar montage is probably safer. The brain can tolerate more sessions; it is a gentler approach. Bipolar (sequential) montages also allow for inhibit and reward filters to be used simultaneously. Choose sites that relate to symptoms and have Z scores of 2.0 or greater. (See Figure 6.7c.)

Phase. EEG phase measurements compare two frequency signals on the basis of timing and phase angles. Phase computations between two sites are very useful in diagnosing traumatic brain injury (Thatcher, 1999, p. 52). Phase-training with a two-channel EEG training system must be guided by normative database computations (Mason & Brownback, 2001).

Alpha Synchrony. If two or more regions of the brain have increased activity at the same time, they are in sync. Hence, amplitudes rise and fall in unison. Synchrony is a comparison of simultaneous action at two different scalp locations. Alpha synchrony training requires a minimum of a two-EEG-channel connection. Sensors are mounted in pairs in both RH and LH such as O1 and O2. It is commonly used for peak performance and deep-states training (Norris & Currieri, 1999, pp. 223–240). However, advanced practitioners utilize several channels at multiple sites. Chapter 13 reviews alpha enhancement protocols with posterior sensor placement for beginners.

Asymmetry. Some contralateral scalp locations are normatively asymmetrical, whereas others are normatively symmetrical. Clinical disturbances may be accompanied by gross asymmetries in the EEG. Symmetry should be measured at contralateral sites such as F3 and F4. It is important to remember the following three normative patterns involving beta/alpha/theta, or the BAT triad:

1. LH beta $\geq$ RH beta
2. RH alpha $\geq$ LH alpha
3. RH theta $\cong$ LH theta (roughly equal)

Disturbances in the BAT triad often accompany mood disorders and/or anxiety disorders. If LH alpha exceeds RH alpha, suspect depression. If RH beta exceeds LH beta, suspect anxiety or anxiety mixed with depression. Significant contralateral differences in theta are also a cause for concern.

Peter Rosenfeld developed an alpha asymmetry protocol. It is designed to rectify abnormal anterior (frontal) lobe alpha asymmetries. In order to execute this protocol two separate EEG channels are set up with a bipolar (sequential) montage: Channel 1 and channel 2 both use Cz for the location of the reference electrode. The channel 1 active electrode is at F3, whereas the channel 2 active electrode is at F4. The ground is placed at any convenient place on the scalp or ears. The client receives reinforcement whenever RH alpha exceeds LH alpha: hence, whenever F4 > F3. Clinical trials have shown the efficacy of this approach. Using this protocol requires a two-channel training system plus a special software package (Baehr, Rosenfeld, Baehr & Earnest, 1999, pp. 11–18). However, it is also possible to rectify asymmetries with a single channel of EEG. For example, sensors can be placed at F3 with a referential (monopolar) montage. Filters can be set so that alpha (8–12 Hz) is inhibited while beta (15–18 Hz) is rewarded. Left hemispheric training alone may work.

Whether the clinician decides to use a two-channel or a one-channel approach, the goal is the same: Facilitate a normative EEG pattern.

Two-channel Training on the Sensorimotor Cortex. Brown and Brown (2000) recommended a two-channel protocol with a referential montage for each channel. The following is a summary of their model as I have applied it to my own practice:

> Scalp sensors are placed at LH and RH sites. C3/beta and C4/SMR protocols are executed simultaneously for 10–15 minutes. Next, for 3 minutes 20.5–21.5 Hz is rewarded at the same two sites. Finally, for 5 minutes 38.0–42.0 Hz is rewarded at the same two sites. Hence, 21 Hz and 40 Hz are reinforced in alternate patterns but not at the same time. Automatic thresholding is used for C3/beta and C4 SMR. However, manual thresholding is used for 21 Hz and 40 Hz. I make sure that manual LH and RH thresholds are equal so that both hemispheres have the same challenge.

Brown and Brown asserted that the above protocol improves alpha blocking and increases general cognitive performance: 40 Hz may well be one of the keys to improving the electrical organization of the brain. Engaging both hemispheres in this three-step cycle may also help to raise an abnormally low dominant brain wave frequency. Two-channel training protocols along the sensorimotor cortex are superior to single-channel training protocols that engage the RH and LH separately. They permit you to observe the BAT triad in action. In some cases, filter adjustments may be needed to maintain normative balances. In other cases, training simultaneously in both hemispheres is contraindicated due to gross asymmetries.

HEMOENCEPHALOGRAPHY NEUROFEEDBACK

The neurotherapist using EEG neurofeedback makes many decisions including:

- What frequency bandwidth(s) will be rewarded or inhibited?
- Should more than one frequency bandwidth be included?
- Should there be one-channel or two-channel training protocols?
- Should there be automatic or manual thresholds?
- What 10–20 position(s) will be chosen?
- Should referential or bipolar (sequential) montage be used?
- How long should a training session be?

- Should the client train with eyes-open or closed?
- Should the client train with a task or rely upon computer graphics?

The hemoencephalography (HEG) neurofeedback specialist only makes two decisions:

- What International 10–20 positions will be selected?
- What task is best performed at each chosen site?

Training is typically 10 min long for each scalp location chosen. It is possible that under certain circumstances HEG neurofeedback training may work faster than EEG neurofeedback. However, not all scalp sites are amenable to HEG neurofeedback montages. It has limitations. HEG neurofeedback application will not eliminate the need for EEG neurofeedback. Assessments are made *in part* with EEG neurofeedback equipment. Regardless, HEG neurofeedback is easier to use and learn than EEG neurofeedback.

HEG neurofeedback gives the trainee greater control over the flow of blood and the density of oxygenation at the chosen scalp location. Blood flow provides the brain with oxygen and glucose. The flow of blood also acts as a cooling system for the brain, similar to the work done by the radiator and cooling system in an automobile. On the one hand, diaphragmatic breathing and practicing inverted yoga likely improve *overall* blood circulation in the brain, which may give one the sensation of being "clearheaded" (Francina, 1997, p. 21). On the other hand, during task performance cerebral blood flow (CBF) increases to *specific* areas of the brain. If a specific region of the brain does not receive adequate blood flow at the right time, then the functions associated with that region will be compromised (Springer & Deutsch, 1998, p. 72).

Only two sensors are used to measure the quality of the circulating blood: one projects the infrared light inward while the other catches the returning rays. In this way it is possible to determine the color of the blood in the tissue. Red tissue is oxygen rich whereas blue tissue is oxygen depleted or hypoperfused. Sensors are mounted on an elastic band that wraps around the head and fastens together with Velcro. No special paste or preparation is needed. I clean the forehead of trainees with alcohol to prevent an oily buildup on my sensors. Most of the training will take place along the forehead, especially at the orbital gyrus, ventral medial cortex, or ventral lateral prefrontal lobes (Fp1, Fp1, Fpz, F7, or F8). The hookup is less than 1 min for each site along the forehead. Minor muscle movements of the forehead, eye blinks, and other facial movements have minimal effects on infrared lights (Toomim & Carmen, 1999, pp.10–14). Instruct younger trainees to limit facial movements.

Training graphs are important to monitor progress during the session. HEG cannot be measured in microvolts or amplitudes. The key is to monitor the percentage rise and fall of rCBF. The trend on the graph will rise whenever the quality of oxygenated blood improves. It is also common for the trend to fall periodically and then rise again. Sometimes the goal is to learn how to increase the overall flow of oxygenated blood to a given cerebral region. Consequently, the trend on the graph depicts a steady, even rise upward. Other times the goal is to speed up the metabolic delivery of the oxygenated blood. If so, there may be a sharp rise in the trend graph followed by a modest decline that is repeated two or three times during the 10-min session. Each person's progress looks a little different. In any case the goal is to get a percentage increase in rCBF. Most trainees become enthused when the trend graph records a significant rise in rCBF.

Trainees are instructed to concentrate and perform a task that directly relates to the region of the brain being trained. Trainees may read, do math problems or homework, study, or play a computer game such as solitaire, Freecell, Tetris, or chess. Training in the left hemisphere (LH) is enhanced by cognitive challenges. Successful trainees notice that they become better at winning games, reading, or doing math problems. *If trainees starts to zone out then they must change to other tasks to prevent boredom.* Training in the visual cortex (occipital lobes) is a form of relaxation training. It is enhanced by visual challenges, such as looking at pictures or a colorful computer screen display. Training in the RH points to use of activities that are spatial or of human interest.

Poor functioning at frontal pole sites is associated with many disorders such as schizophrenia, autism, learning disorders, attention deficit disorder (ADD), and anxiety disorders. Training often includes both right hemisphere (RH) and LH, for example, training 20 min in the LH could be followed by 10 min in the RH. One session is typically 30–40 min long. It is important to remember that HEG hypoperfusion relates to EEG hypoactivation (EEG slowing). It happens when specific areas of the brain are lacking in oxygen-rich blood. In EEG slowing, slow waves have amplitudes that are much greater than fast waves. For example, slow-wave dominance is indicated when theta (4–8 Hz) amplitudes are at least 2.5 times greater than beta

(13–21 Hz) amplitudes at Fpz. Training clients with fast-wave dominance is usually contraindicated; it may cause them to feel wired or on edge.

HEG NEUROFEEDBACK VS. EEG NEUROFEEDBACK

HEG feedback and EEG neurofeedback both place sensors in the same general International 10–20 location. HEG has the advantage of having minimum artifact when sensors are placed over prefrontal lobes and at the frontal poles (Fp1, Fp2, and Fpz). Lubar and Lubar considered eyes-open EEG neurofeedback training at frontal pole sites to be "virtually impossible" due to muscle artifacts on the forehead (1999, p. 110). Consequently, a whole new arena of training is open to the neurotherapist who employs the HEG modality. HEG neurofeedback is ideal for the child with facial tics and anterior EEG slowing. Such a child can train at the frontal poles with his/her *eyes-open* and under task.

There are drawbacks to HEG training because it is difficult to place in-frared sensors over the hairy regions of the scalp. Trainees with thick dark hair or tight springy hair present a special challenge. EEG sensors, on the other hand, are easily set in place regardless of the texture of the hair. Early reports indicate that HEG neurofeedback requires fewer training sessions than EEG neurofeedback to improve executive functioning (Toomim, 2002). Among the symptoms of poor executive functioning in the prefrontal lobes are inattention, poor planning or judgment, slow reaction time, lack of social awareness and poor impulse control.

HEG training is not designed for general relaxation training, but there is at least one exception: If sensors span the visual cortex (e.g., Oz), then the trainee should *relax* while engaging in visual tasks. For clients with trau-matic brain injury and EEG slowing or hypoperfusion in the visual cortex, training starts with 8–12 min at Fpz and ends with 10–12 min at Oz . Just one cautionary note: If any client is at risk for cerebral aneurysm or hem-orrhaging, take care—consult their neurologist before commencing HEG neurotherapy. Also keep in mind:Training in the visual cortex is greatly enhanced if the area of sensor contact is shaved.

HEG neurofeedback training works well to improve attention and build focusing and it is possible to train exclusively with HEG neurofeedback equipment. There are also occasions to combine EEG and HEG protocols within a single session. For example, some trainees benefit from 15 minutes of EEG neurofeedback for posterior beta suppression. Others have a low dominant brain wave frequency and may benefit from Brown and Brown's (2000) 3 step protocol that concludes with 40 Hz enhancement training. Typically, I train with HEG first and EEG neurofeedback second. Within one minute, the trainee can be seated, the HEG neurofeedback headband can be put in place and feedback begins.

HEG neurofeedback training is likely the best way to manage pre-frontal slowing. It is minimally effected by muscle artifact and it has already proved itself to be an effective form of neurofeedback. However, when it comes to scalp sites located within the hairy regions of the scalp, problems with specific frequencies, fast wave dominance, coherence, and asymmetry problems, as well as the need for deep relaxation EEG neurofeedback is required.

5

Compressed Spectral Array and Normal Electroencephalograph Distribution

THE COMPRESSED SPECTRAL ARRAY (CSA) is a graphic method of assessing the electroencephalograph (EEG). Each CSA provides a three-dimensional overview of frequency band distribution acquired from a single channel of EEG. It allows the clinician to determine if the proportions between frequency bands are normal or abnormal. CSA comparisons are made when data are taken from two scalp locations. *Gross* abnormalities, asymmetries, and uneven bandwidth distributions can be found in this way. Some disorders have simple but distinct EEG signatures that can be seen via CSA graphics. Indeed, some clients have been properly assessed and trained on the basis of CSA graphics. The CSA is a clinical yardstick that can provide the clinician with a broad perspective of the EEG.

Figure 5.1c is an *eyes-closed* two-dimensional display of frequency bandwidth distribution at Cz. It is a single-site snapshot, a moment in time, a fraction of a second. Bandwidths are in 4-Hz color-coded increments. Figure 5.1c is normative because bandwidth amplitudes are in correct proportions at the vertex (Cz). For example, the alpha exceeds all bandwidths, theta is in second place, and beta decreases as the frequency increases. Two-dimensional displays are often observed while the client trains. They are not static—bandwidths are in constant change, rising and falling.

However, too much variation in a two-dimensional graph is usually a reflection of artifact coming from eye movements, scalp, or facial muscles, and other body movements. In general, two-dimensional graphics give a good visual presentation of one channel of EEG.

Figures 5.2c is an *eyes-open* three-dimensional display of frequency bandwidth distribution at Cz known as a CSA. It presents the EEG in one second epochs for a total of 40 seconds. Four-hertz frequency bandwidths are laid out in a cascading fashion with color-coded graphics. Figure 5.2c is normative because bandwidth amplitudes are in correct proportions at the vertex (Cz). For example, alpha amplitudes are only marginally higher than theta, and beta decreases as the frequency increases. Clinical CSA recordings are usually taken from only a few scalp locations. They have limited diagnostic utility. Contralateral sites or anterior-to-posterior sites may be compared. Two recordings may be taken at the vertex (Cz): one with eyes-open and the other with eyes-closed. If alpha blocking is normal, then eyes-closed alpha amplitudes will be much higher than eyes-open alpha amplitudes. Only a minority of clients will have easy-to-interpret CSA recordings.

Figures 5.3c to 5.8c are clinical examples of abnormal CSA diagrams. Each one shows a different EEG pattern often found in the clinical population. Clinical disorders such as attention deficit/hyperactivity disorder (ADHD), anxiety, depression, and posttraumatic stress disorder (PTSD) have *many* different raw EEG patterns. Written explanations are included with each diagram.

NORMAL (EEG)

Montgomery, Robb, Dwyer, and Gontkovsky (1998) studied the normal EEG with a small population of "bright young college students." Each one was examined with a single EEG channel and at just one scalp location: Cz. A referential (monopolar) montage was used with the active sensor at the Cz (vertex) site on the scalp and the other two sensors clipped to the ears. They acquired two recordings at Cz, one with eyes-open and the other with eyes-closed. Four bandwidths were selected for the study. The goal of the study was to provide other clinicians with a normative standard. Knowing the *normative distribution* of bandwidths at Cz is a boon to the assessment process. Table 5.1 is a summary of their study:

TABLE 5.1
Normative Distribution of Bandwidths at Cz, Eyes-Open, and Eyes-Closed

BANDWIDTH	EYES CLOSED	EYES-OPEN
Alpha (8–12 Hz)	16.6 μV	9.3 μV
Theta (4–8 Hz)	12.4 μV	10.7 μV
Beta (13–21 Hz)	8.1 μV	6.4 μV
SMR (12–15 Hz)	5.1 μV	4.4 μV
Theta-to-beta ratio	1.6:1	1.8:1

Adapted from Montgomery et al., 1998. Adapted with the permission of the *Journal of Neurotherapy*

Several conclusions can be drawn from Table 5.1:

• Bright young adult theta-to-beta ratios are less than 2:1 at Cz.
• Alpha amplitudes exceed theta amplitudes with eyes-closed.
• Slow waves have greater amplitudes than fast waves.
• Beta (13–21 Hz) amplitudes exceed SMR (12–15 Hz).
• Alpha amplitudes sharply decrease when eyes-open (alpha blocking).

Table 5.1 is useful in comparing proportional differences between bandwidths using peak-to-peak microvolt readings—common to most EEG training systems. The table clearly shows the difference between eyes-open and eyes-closed recordings. Those same normal proportions are illustrated by Figures 5.1c and 5.2c. Clinical disturbances are often reflected by variations from the norm. For example, Figures 5.3c and 5.4c represent two types of abnormal proportions at the vertex or Cz.

Neither high beta (20–30 Hz) nor delta (1–4 Hz) was part of the study. Over the years I have come to the following experiential conclusions.

1. The normal amplitude of beta tends to be greater than or equal to high beta: 13–21 ≥ 20–30 Hz. When high beta amplitudes begin to rival or exceed beta amplitudes, then consider adding a high beta inhibit to the protocol.
2. The normal amplitude of theta (4–8 Hz) tends to be greater than delta (1–4 Hz). When delta amplitudes begin to rival or exceed theta amplitudes, then consider expanding the 4–7 Hz inhibit to include 2–7 Hz.

FIGURE 5.9
DATABASE BY AGE GROUPS

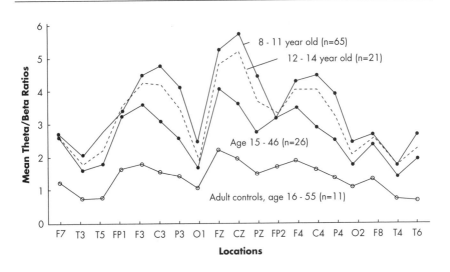

Lubar, Swartwood, Swartwood, & Timmermann. Quantitative EEG and auditory event-related potentials in the evaluation of attention-deficit/hyperactivity disorder. Effects of methyphenidrate and implications for neurofeedback training. Copyright 1995 by Journal of Psychoeducational Assessment. Reprinted by permission of journal of Psychoeducational Assessment via Copyright Clearance Center.

RATIO

Lubar, Swartwood, Swartwood, and Timmermann (1995) studied theta-to-beta ratios using 19 EEG channels at 19 scalp locations, common to quantitative EEG (QEEG) analysis. Linked-ears and referential montages were employed. Figure 5.9 depicts their results. Four small population groups were studied. The adult controls were symptom free. The other three groups were diagnosed with ADHD. In the 8- to 11-year-old category the highest theta-to-beta ratio is at Cz, almost 6:1. Figure 5.9 explains why many clinicians train to inhibit theta at Cz, Fz, C3, or C4 for children with ADHD: The highest ratios are found at those sites. Ratios exceeding 3:1

are commonly seen in children with attention deficit disorder (ADD; see Figure 5.3c).

A number of conclusions can be drawn from Figure 5.9:

- Theta-to-beta ratios decrease with age.
- Largest theta-to-beta ratios are found at Cz or Fz.
- Smallest theta-to-beta ratios are found at the temporal lobes.
- Adult controls have lower ratios than those of the ADHD population.
- Adult controls have the highest theta-to-beta ratio at Fz (2:1).

A theta-to-beta ratio greater than 3:1 constitutes a slow-wave disorder. That ratio applies most to *dorsal* sites such as Cz, C3, C4, and Fz. When I assess for ratios at *ventral* sites, I reduce the cut-off point to 2.5:1 or less. High theta-to-beta ratios at the prefrontal lobes or the frontal poles signal a problem with attention and other executive functions. Sometimes higher ratios are best observed when the subject is under task rather than at rest. In any case, high theta-to-beta ratios at any ventral site, including the temporal lobes and the occipital lobes are a cause for concern.

Measurements for Figure 5.9, were calculated using power ratios rather than amplitude ratios. The difference between the two formats is as follows:

- Power = microvolts squared/ hertz
- Amplitude = microvolts/ hertz

Amplitude ratios can be converted to power by mathematically squaring the microvolt ratio. This conversion method is adequate for making ratio determinations. Table 5.2 illustrates a recording taken at Cz.

Table 5.2 readings indicate that the client has an abnormally high theta/beta ratio, 5.2:1. In fact, the client was successfully trained at Cz

TABLE 5.2
Converting Amplitude to Power

FREQUENCY BANDWIDTH	RESULT
Theta (4–8 Hz)	29.5 μV
Beta (13–21 Hz)	12.9 μV
Ratio (theta/beta)	2.3 amplitude ratio
Ratio squared	5.2 power ratio

by inhibiting theta. Figure 5.9 can be useful if the conversion is made from microvolts to power. It must be stated that Montgomery (Table 5.1) and Lubar (Figure 5.9) did *not* use the same brand of equipment when recording data. For example, convert the μV numbers in Table 5.1 to power and then compare them to Figure 5.9. The difference between them demonstrates the fact that EEG data output varies from manufacturer to manufacturer. Even though the differences are minor, it is essential to be aware of this reality. Chapter 16 reviews this and others concerns that face clinicians when purchasing equipment.

Almost half of the children with ADHD have a slow-wave disorder with either alpha or theta being many times greater than beta. However, another group of almost equal proportion are children and adults with fast waves (13–32 Hz) greater than slow waves (1–10 Hz). Hence beta may be equal to or even exceed theta. Figure 5.4c of the color insert gives an example of an abnormal ratio wherein beta exceeds theta.

ASYMMETRY

Ratios compare the distribution of frequency bandwidths at a given site. However, sometimes the abnormality can only be seen by examining the scalp from side to side or from front to back. Such conditions are known as asymmetries.

An asymmetry is a comparison between opposing parts of the brain: usually right to left and sometimes front to back. Consider the following

TABLE 5.3
Left-to-Right Asymmetries in a Normative EEG Pattern

NORMAL EEG	SAMPLE SITES
Beta amplitudes: LH $\geq$ RH	F7 $\geq$ F8
Alpha amplitudes: LH $\leq$ RH	F3 $\leq$ F4
Theta amplitudes: LH $\cong$ RH	T3 $\cong$ T4

Note #1: Compare alpha amplitudes in figures 5.5c and 5.6c of the color insert. They show an *abnormal* eyes-closed alpha asymmetry in a depressed client: C3 alpha > C4 Alpha.
Note #2: Utilizing the above chart correctly requires clinical judgment. Consider the normative pattern of beta: Let's say that F7 (7.5 μV) > F8 (6.5 μV)—such an asymmetry may well be normative. But F7 (10 μV) > F8 (5.5 μV) may not be normative. Likely there is too much beta in the LH.

TABLE 5.4
Front-to-Back Comparisons in a Normative EEG Pattern
with an Eyes-Closed Recording

NORMAL EEG	SAMPLE SITE
Anterior beta > posterior beta	Fz > Cz > Pz
Posterior alpha > anterior alpha	Pz > Cz > Fz (eyes-closed)
Anterior theta > posterior theta	Fz > Pz

Note #1: Compare alpha/theta & beta amplitudes in figures 5.7c and 5.8c of the color insert. The slow waves are higher at Cz while the fast waves are higher at Pz—abnormal pattern. Client has PTSD with symptoms of depression, anxiety, and dissociation.

right to left asymmetries in a normative EEG pattern. They represent what I have called the *BAT triad* (beta/alpha/theta). For example the third item in Table 5.3 indicates that a normal EEG should have relatively the same theta amplitude in both hemispheres at contralateral scalp sites. For example, T3 theta amplitudes should be roughly equal to T4 theta.

Anterior (frontal) to Posterior (rear) differences have also been observed. Consider the following front to back comparisons in a normative EEG pattern with and the *eyes-closed* recording in Table 5.4:

Table 5.4 suggests that there will be a gradual downward slope in alpha μVs in *normal* recordings. Lets say that eyes-closed alpha was as follows:

$$Pz\ (18\mu V) > Cz\ (13\mu V) > Fz\ (10\mu V)$$

Now consider an *abnormal* downward slope:

$$Pz\ (34\mu V) > Cz\ (12\mu V) > Fz\ (10\mu V).$$

So, quite a bit of clinical judgment is involved when trying to make anterior-to- posterior assessments.

In general, look for the *maximum amplitude at vertex* (Cz). For example, amplitude measurements taken at Cz ought to be greater than those acquired at the temporal lobe sites. Thus, it can be said that Cz amplitudes "extend" to other dorsal sites such as "Fz, Pz; F3, F4; C3, C4; P3, P4" (Blume & Kaibara, 1995, p. 41). Thus, it may also be concluded that normative Fz theta > Fpz theta. Or, **dorsal** total amplitudes > **ventral** amplitudes but more so with eyes-opened recordings.

6

Brain Maps, Quantitative Electroencephalograph, and Normative Databases

IN GENERAL, MAPS, when they are interpreted correctly, are directional guides that keep the traveler on course. Getting lost in the clinical arena leads to ineffective training or even treatment failure. Efficient traveling requires *advance* knowledge of the main route and possible alternatives. In the same way, a brain map can be used to guide neurotherapy protocol decisions. Of course, a map in itself is rarely enough to ensure clinical success. It must be supported by cognitive testing, questionnaires, and psychiatric interviewing. Indeed, symptoms are guideposts that can direct the neurotherapist to specific regions of the brain. Of course, more than one region of the brain may be responsible for a given cognitive, spatial, or emotional disturbance. Brain maps do more than locate problems; they also translate them in the language of the electroencephalograph (EEG).

Quantitative EEG (QEEG) refers to a comprehensive analysis of individual frequencies or frequency bandwidths that make up the raw EEG. Figures 6.1c, 6.3c, and 6.5c depict raw QEEG data taken from nineteen scalp locations as defined by the International 10–20 system (Cantor, 1999). However, even one scalp location can make up a QEEG analysis (Montgomery, Robb, Dwyer, & Contkovsky, 1998). The data acquired from QEEG can be used to create topographic brain maps or color-coded simulations of the electrical activity of the cerebral cortex. If the data has been processed via normative database software, then the color-coding represents normative values. In most cases, topographical brain maps make the job of being a neurotherapist easier.

QEEG data acquisition and brain mapping have become the standard for the industry for clients with a history of traumatic brain injury (TBI). Why? Because cortical damage may create complex problems and multiple abnormal EEG patterns. Non-QEEG assessments may be inadequate and sometimes misleading. To make matters worse, it's not always clear who has TBI because the impact to the brain may have happened in childhood or the distant past. Hyperactive children are prone to accidents and head injuries, domestic violence is prevalent, car accidents happen every day; life puts all of us in harm's way. Of course, some skilled practitioners may be able to ferret out some problems without a map; they have a broad understanding of the EEG, brain anatomy, and clinical experience. For the cognitive style of neurotherapy, however, obtaining a brain map is usually the first order of clinical business (see Figure 6.16c).

QEEG COMPARED TO SINGLE PHOTON EMISSION COMPUTED TOMOGRAPHY

QEEG measures brain wave activity, whereas, single photon emission computed tomography (SPECT) "looks directly at cerebral blood flow and indirectly at brain activity (or metabolism)" (Amen, 2001, p.46). QEEG is like a brief motion picture of the brain's electrical activity, whereas SPECT is like a time-averaged snapshot of brain's metabolic activity. SPECT requires the intake or injection of radioactive chemicals. QEEG is noninvasive— 19 sensors placed on the head to track brain wave activity. QEEG relates to EEG neurofeedback. SPECT relates to hemoencephalography (HEG) neurofeedback, the study of rCBF.

Daniel Amen specializes in the use of SPECT in the diagnoses and treatment of attention deficit disorder (ADD) and other clinical disorders. After viewing over 10,000 neuroimages, he has identified six distinctive patterns of cerebral blood flow (CBF) associated with ADD. Sometimes, Amen prescribed medication for symptom relief. However, a natural treatment program also works; it includes dietary changes, supplements, exercise, lifestyle changes, and EEG biofeedback. Before-and-after SPECT scans demonstrate that abnormal patterns of brain activity can be changed *without* the use of medication (Amen, 2001, pp.155, 265–274).

UCLA has developed a normative database for SPECT. Normative databases require the gathering and comparing of data from hundreds of volunteers. Color-coding is used to identify which regions of the brain are operating outside of normal limits. Obtaining a brain map from UCLA is a costly process at this point in time. Hershel Toomin has, on occasion, used the data provided by UCLA to guide HEG neurofeedback treatment protocols. However, he has found that rCBF activity also relates to cognitive performance: *MicroCog: Assessment of Cognitive Functioning* software and continuous performance tests are used to assess rCBF. When under task the brain demands an increase of blood flow to the region responsible for accomplishing the task. Improving the regional demand for blood often accompanies improved cognitive performance (www.biocompresearch.org).

QEEG AND NORMATIVE DATABASES

Typically, QEEG data comes from the 19 scalp locations designated by the International 10–20 system. After data are acquired, a QEEG technician removes artifacts from the data that come from muscle movements, eye blinks, electrocardiogram (EKG), and other corrupting factors. Finally, the refined data are processed by normative database software. Color-coded maps and data in digital format are often printed. In the color insert, a number of brain maps have been displayed. Each circle represents the head. Each period or dot on the head represents one of the International 10–20 scalp locations. The nose is at the top of each circle so that the left hemisphere (LH) is to the left and the right hemisphere (RH) is to the right.

Two different types of normative database software samples comprise the color insert of this book: (a) NxLink, designed by E. Roy John, L. S. Prischep, and P. Easton and (b) Lifespan Normative EEG database, or NeuroGuide, designed by Robert Thatcher. Each one is color-coded differently. For example, NxLink uses black for the norm, whereas NeuroGuide uses green for the norm. (Both use statistical analysis and z-values.) Other software programs are available and well worth considering. The reader is encouraged to review the *Journal of Neurotherapy* (volume 7, numbers 3/4, 2003). The entire issue is dedicated to current trends in QEEG, and normative database software.

Normative database software compares your client's data with the data of other members within a sample population: NxLink "database includes measures from some 782 normal individuals. Of this total 356 cases were between the ages of 6 to 16 and 426 cases were between the ages of 16 to 90," whereas NeuroGuide "database now contains information from 625 individuals, covering the age range two months to 82.6 years" (Johnstone & Gunkelman, 2003, pp. 42–43). Normative databases tend to be culture free.

> Normative QEEG descriptors were found to be independent from cultural and ethnic factors. High reliability was found in studies from Barbados, China, Cuba, Germany, Holland, Japan, Korea, Mexico, Netherlands, Sweden, the United States and Venezuela. . . . The independence of the EEG spectrum from cultural and ethnic factors is a remarkable characteristic of the EEG. It has been suggested that it reflects the common genetic heritage of mankind.(Congedo & Lubar, 2003, p. 4).

Normative database software has been used in the diagnostic process. Specific "QEEG signatures have been found" that relate to a number of disorders including "attention deficit disorder with and without hyperactivity, learning disabilities, dementia, schizophrenia, unipolar and bipolar depression, anxiety disorders, obsessive compulsive disorder, alcohol and substance abuse, head injury, lesions, tumors, epilepsy and cerebrovascular diseases (Congedo & Lubar, 2003, p. 5).

What is an *QEEG signature*? It often refers to a specific QEEG pattern that has been found within a specific clinical population. Figures 5.3c–5.8c provide one- and two-channel QEEG signatures that may accompany attention deficit / hyperactivity disorder (ADHD), depression, anxiety, and other clinical disturbances. Most disorders have *several* QEEG signatures. ADHD varies greatly from client to client. For example, Figure 6.10c depicts central EEG slowing whereas figure 6.11c depicts excessive posterior fast waves (10–17 Hz)—and yet both clients have ADHD. Other examples of common ADHD signatures may be seen at 6.17c and 6.19c. In the case of anxiety disorders, 6.18c depicts several different manifestations of clinical anxiety that can be seen in the EEG. Therefore, the practitioner must be aware of the possibilities.

Normative database software interprets data via statistical analysis. A normal distribution curve or Gaussian distribution is defined by various mathematical properties including standard deviation. Clients often vary one or more standard deviations from the norm with regard to power, coherence, and asymmetry in one or more regions of the cerebral cortex. Both NxLink and NeuroGuide indicate variance by standard deviations or Z-scores. Color-coding corresponds with the degree of variance. It is *not* necessary to have a working knowledge of statistics in order to be able to read and understand a brain map. But it *is* necessary to understand the terminology that is built into the map.

MAP TERMINOLOGY

In many ways, color-coded brain maps are self-explanatory. They identify areas of the brain that are outside of normal limits and would likely benefit from training. However, an accurate interpretation of maps requires an understanding of map terminology and potential pitfalls. It's also important to understand why the numbers output by maps differ from the numbers output by typical EEG training systems. The following is a list of common terms utilized by normative database software:

Power vs. Amplitude

The terms amplitude and power can be simplified as follows: *amplitude* means microvolts/hertz, whereas *power* means microvolts squared/hertz (Thatcher, 1999, p.46). Raw QEEG data are measured in amplitudes. Normative database software often converts the data into power. For example, NxLink uses *power*, not amplitude, when displaying and processing data. Table 6.1 includes 2 of the 19 standard International 10–20 sites, O1 and O2. Note the alpha numbers.

The 106.88 number at O2 reflects *power*, not amplitude. A typical EEG training system check would render amplitudes of only $31\mu V$ at O2 and $26\ \mu V$ at O1. Amplitude readings are not printed in the NxLink report.

TABLE 6.1
Monopolar Power (μV^2): Sites O1 and O2

SITE	O1 (μV^2)	O2 (μV^2)
Total	123.57	191.82
Delta	28.77	44.65
Theta	23.38	30.50
Alpha	62.02	106.88
Beta	9.40	10.25

Note. Adapted from NxLink, Monopolar Power (μV^2).

Power values will always be different than the amplitude readings obtained from your EEG training system. Do not confuse power readings with amplitude readings. Do not use power readings as baselines for standard EEG training systems.

Amplitude measurements are rendered in microvolts. Many EEG training systems provide *peak-to-peak* microvolt measurements, also called magnitude recordings: The full height of the wave is being measured, from the top peak of the wave all the way to the bottom peak of the wave (see Figure 4.2). Appendices 1 and 2 include the peak-to-peak microvolt recordings for two of the topographical maps in the color insert.

Absolute vs. Relative

Both the NxLink (Figure 6.2c) and NeuroGuide (Figure 6.4c) designate some topographical heads as *absolute* and others as *relative*. The first row of color-coded heads in the NxLink reviews the absolute z-scores, whereas the second row reviews the relative z-scores. Comparing both formats in either the NxLink or the NeuroGuide reveals that absolute and relative may look quite different from each other. (Compare the theta bandwidth in the absolute and relative bandwidths of Figure 6.8c.) Absolute measurements reflect what is directly beneath the sensor, without taking into account the physical characteristics of the skull.

> A typical method to control for differences in scalp resistance and skull thickness, etc., is to calculate *relative power* and/or *relative amplitude*. Relative amplitude is a percentage measure and is defined as amplitude in a frequency band divided by total amplitude (i.e., total amplitude is the sum of amplitude in all frequencies). In other words, relative amplitude is a measure of the proportion of total amplitude within a given frequency band and is thus independent of skull thickness, skin resistance, and other, but not all, non-brain sources of electrical activity (e.g., eye movement artifact, EKG artifact, are not controlled for). (Thatcher, 1999, p. 46)

Consequently, if the client's skull is very thick, then absolute measurements will tend to have low Z-values, whereas if the skull is very thin the absolute measurements will tend to have high Z-values. Of course, if the skull thickness is average, then absolute Z-values are less likely to be distorted.

When examining brain maps, I seldom make clinical judgments based on absolute readings. (See Figure 6.9c—compare absolute and relative power rows.) Relative maps are more accurate most of the time, *but not all of the time*. Relative power maps are a percentage measure of the total amplitude. For example, if the total amplitude of a QEEG recording is raised by the presence of electromyography (EMG) mixed with beta, then other frequency bands will be devalued. To illustrate, if you contributed $10 toward a $100 present, then you might conclude that your share was 10%. What if you had forgotten there was a 40% tax? Consequently, the real cost of the present would become $140 ($100 + $40), which would decrease your share to about 7%. The EMG is like the tax because it can increase the total amplitude of the QEEG recording. Increasing the total amplitude will likely decrease the relative value of other bandwidths. However, the absolute power map will not be distorted because it does not take into account the total amplitude. Your $10 share will not be compared to the other contributors; it will maintain a $10 value. Therefore, when the relative map sharply disagrees with the absolute map, it behooves the clinician to determine the reason for the difference. It's important to keep in mind that EMG mixed with beta may create a fast-wave bias in the relative topographical map. The anxious client who has tense scalp and jaw muscles as well as a thicker or thinner skull may be difficult to assess with topographical brain maps derived from normative database software. (See Figures 6.21c and 6.22c.)

Two-Channel Recordings and Skull Thickness

A typical EEG training system does not make adjustments for the physical characteristics of the skull. It amplifies the signal coming from the scalp and then transforms the raw EEG by using electronic filters. Data amplitude is absolute; it is rendered in microvolts. Recordings from thick skulls will probably be lower than from thin skulls. Consequently, do not be thrown by variable μV numbers. If client A has higher theta amplitudes than client B, it does not necessarily mean that client A has a slow-wave disorder. It could mean that client A has a thin skull, whereas client B has a thick one. That having been said, ratios and bandwidth distributions have the same clinical utility regardless of skull thickness. There are two simple ways to detect EEG slowing: (a) theta-to-beta ratios exceeding 3:1, and (b) eyes-closed theta amplitudes exceeding alpha amplitudes. Skull thickness does not have to be taken into account when determining ratios or general bandwidth distribution proportions.

Absolute readings with two-channel EEG training systems have the most value when large or gross abnormalities are present. Two-channel recordings are excellent at detecting asymmetries at contralateral sites, RH and LH comparisons. Remember that absolute readings with one- and two-channel training systems reflect the raw EEG. They are rendered in peak-to-peak microvolt measurements (magnitude) unless otherwise stated by the manufacturer.

Link vs. Laplacian Montages

NxLink is limited to linked-ear montages. Referential (monopolar) montages are similar to linked-ear montages. The ear is theoretically neutral; however, linked-ear montages may be subject to temporal lobe contamination. Other montages have been used when processing EEG data. For example, NeuroGuide processes data with both linked-ear and Laplacian montages. The Laplacian montage takes into account the electrical activity of surrounding electrodes (Johnston & Gunkelman, 2003). Laplacian math equations allow for the curve of the skull and the approximate distribution of data between each electrode. It is a complex form of extrapolation that can make use of computer digital analysis. Laplacian montages provide an additional way to look at EEG data. NeuroGuide's relative power Laplacian montages may be more specific than its relative power linears montages: compare Figures 6.13c and 6.14c—it is the same client with eyes-closed.

Eyes-Open vs. Eyes-Closed Renderings

The NeuroGuide can process both eyes-open or eyes-closed data, whereas, the NxLink is limited to eyes-closed recordings. Eyes-closed recordings are usually more accurate than eyes-open recordings because they minimize the artifacts coming from eye movements (Congedo & Lubar, 2003). Fortunately, eyes-closed training is possible and at times desirable. But when training in the eyes-open condition, NeuroGuide may have greater clinical significance. For example, Figures 6.13c and 6.15c compare the same client. Note: 6.13c is an eyes-closed recording, whereas Figure 6.15c is an eyes-open recording. Even though this is the same person, the Z-scores are quite different. Although I am not suggesting that NxLink should not be consulted when determining eyes-open training protocols, in general NeuroGuide has an advantage over NxLink when eyes-open training is needed.

Single-Hertz Bins vs. Frequency Bandwidths

Both NxLink and NeuroGuide create maps with banded EEG such as delta, theta, alpha, and beta. NeuroGuide also renders maps using single-hertz bins. Single-hertz bins provide more exacting data than frequency bandwidths. Data may be "obscured with the use of relatively wide bands as normed in the Neurometric database" or NxLink (Johnstone & Gunkelman, 2003, p. 43). Remember the case of the man who drowned in a lake that averaged only 4ft deep; he drowned because part of the lake was 20ft deep even though most of the lake was less than 4ft deep. The posted average depth *obscured* the danger. In the same way, NeuroGuide's single-hertz bins prevent obscurity because they look at each individual frequency from 1 to 30 Hz. Single hertz bins promote greater precision in frequency bandwidth selection. Figures 6.12c and 6.13c are for the same person. NxLink identifies P3 and T5 as problem sites. NxLink indicates that both alpha and theta have raised Z-values, whereas NeuroGuide limits the target range to just 6–9 Hz. Consequently, single-hertz bins are usually superior to wideband frequency renderings. Downtraining 6–9 Hz is more precise than downtraining the both alpha the theta (4–12 Hz).

NxLink provides the following frequency bandwidths:

- Delta 1–4 Hz
- Theta 4–8 Hz
- Alpha 8–12 Hz
- Beta 12.5–25 Hz.

Contralateral vs. Ipsilateral Hemispheric Coherence

Coherence is a measurement of the similarity of frequency between two sites on the scalp; it is a comparison of waveform or pattern rather than amplitude. NxLink provides eyes-closed linked-ear interhemispheric (both hemispheres) coherence measurements that have proved to have great clinical utility. Figure 6.8c shows hypocoherence in the alpha range between T5 and T6. Coherence measurements are rendered as shades of colors that correspond to standard deviations from the norm. NeuroGuide's coherence measurements are for both *inter*hemispheric (contralateral—both hemispheres) and *intra*hemispheric (ipsilateral—each hemisphere), as well as eyes-open and eyes-closed. Coherence is rendered as data and color-coded lines and Z-scores. Frequency bandwidths are used rather than single-hertz bins. There is a growing interest in correcting coherence problems with single-channel bipolar (sequential) montages as well as two-channel coherence training. Interestingly Figures 6.7c and 6.8c are for the same person in the eyes-closed state. Notice the difference between NeuroGuide and NxLink (review Figure 4.4).

Asymmetry

When two contralateral scalp locations are asymmetrical, it means that they are significantly different. NxLink renders asymmetry as shades of colors that correspond to standard deviations from the norm. Anterior asymmetries are markers for depression and anxiety, but any gross asymmetry is cause for concern. Figures 5.5c and 5.6c show a central alpha asymmetry; Figure 6.12c shows posterior alpha asymmetry is related to depression. However, anterior alpha asymmetries are also likely in cases of depression. A NeuroGuide sample of asymmetry is not included.

Dominant Frequency

The frequency with the highest microvolt reading in the raw EEG is the dominant oscillating rhythm. The raw EEG may range from 0 to 32 Hz, depending upon the equipment being used. The goal is to find the highest amplitude reading by examining all 19 scalp locations. The adult dominant brain frequency of 10 Hz is reached by 13 years of age. The younger the child, the lower the dominant brain frequency (Lubar, Angelakis, Frederick, & Stathopoulos, 2001, p. 21). Knowing your client's dominant brain frequency may guide treatment (see Figure 6.18c rows 5 and 6, and 6.23c). If it is too low, then a slow-wave disorder is likely; if it is too high, then anxiety or insomnia may be present.

In addition to knowing the dominant frequency from 0 to 32 Hz, there is also clinical utility in knowing the dominant frequency within a selected bandwidth. For example, in order to find the dominant alpha frequency, it would be necessary to check each single-hertz bin within the alpha range of 8–12 Hz. Each individual frequency would be compared in order to calculate which one has the highest amplitude. Consider the following:

- 8 Hz 1.0 μV
- 9 Hz 1.5 μV
- 10 Hz 2.3 μV

- 11 Hz 2.0 μV
- 12 Hz 2.1 μV

Clearly, 10 Hz is the dominant alpha frequency. In practice, dominant frequency measurements are calculated in decimal form such as 10.01, 10.12, 10.55 Hz. Dominant frequency is very similar to but not exactly the same as mean frequency. Most normative database software produces mean frequency data rather than dominant frequency data.

Knowledge of the dominant frequency can be useful when looking for abnormalities. For example, normal alpha rhythm should have the "same dominant frequency in each hemisphere" (Blume & Kaibara, 1995, p. 39). Comparing lateral dominant scores may reveal a problem. Alpha dominant frequencies are also considered to be indicators of intelligence. Suldo, Olson, and Evans (2001) reviewed the literature and revealed the following mean alpha frequencies in various populations:

- Healthy middle-aged adults (M = 9.5 Hz)
- Adults with multi-infarct dementia (M = 8.5–9.0 Hz)
- College students with superior memory, under task (M = 11.39 Hz)
- College students with poorer memory, under task (M = 10.23 Hz)

Table 6.2 includes the monopolar mean frequencies at T5 and T6. In this case, the low-alpha dominant scores do not reflect dementia; rather, this client has TBI as well as major depression. The client with low mean alpha will likely have a slow-wave disorder. Figure 6.12c is the topographical map behind the following numbers:

TABLE 6.2
Monopolar Mean Frequency (Hz) for Bandwidths T5 and T6

SITE	T5 (Hz)	T6 (Hz)
Total	8.48	8.5
Delta	2.39	2.35
Theta	5.98	5.98
Alpha ⟵	8.78 ⟵	8.91 ⟵
Beta	16.96	17.44

Adapted from NxLink, Monopolar Mean Frequency (Hz).

Diagnostic Options

Both NeuroGuide and NxLink have diagnostic features that may place your client in a specific clinical-disorder population. For example, Figure 6.16c is a sample of NeuroGuide's "traumatic brain injury discriminant analysis." This color-coded page is a valuable tool to help clients with TBI to gain an understanding of their brain injury. NxLink, too, has a discriminant analysis package, which provides brief written diagnostic reports. NxLink may state that the data indicate unipolar or bipolar depression. Not all depressed clients have an EEG signature that fits within the NxLink or any other discriminant—there are just too many variables. The discriminant analysis is not flawless. Therefore, inform clients of their discriminant analysis report without making dogmatic statements. The following is an example of the way NxLink frames a diagnostic statement for a client with a complex EEG pattern:

- This patient's discriminant scores suggest the presence of a Major Affective Disorder ($p <= 0.025$) of the Unipolar subtype ($p <= 0.05$)
- The features making the largest contribution to the Major Affective Disorder statement are:

  - Normed Bipolar Coherence Combined for Anterior,
  - Normed Bipolar Relative Power Total for T3-F7

- The features making the largest contribution to the Unipolar Statement are:

  - Normed Monopolar Relative Power Beta for Cz,
  - Normed Monopolar Asymmetry Delta for O1-O2,
  - Normed Monopolar Relative Power alpha for Left Lateral

This classification is a multivariate statistical summary of a neurometric evaluation and serves only as an adjunct to other clinical evaluations

Artifacting

Raw EEG data must be artifacted before it can be processed by any normative database software. Both NxLink and NeuroGuide have features that make artifacting the raw EEG data more convenient. Additional training is usually required before one can master the art of artifacting. Appendix 1 (Figure A1.1) has an example of artifact in a 19-channel recording.

Food and Drug Administration

NxLink "has received a 510(k) clearance by the United States Food and Drug Administration (FDA, July, 1998, #K974748), indicating that construction of the database has been scrutinized for good manufacturing practices (GMPs). The 510(k) also signifies the legitimacy of marketing claims made concerning the database" (Johnstone & Gunkelman, 2003, p.43). However, "NeuroGuide was considered to not require FDA 510(k) clearance, based on both the non-medical nature of the intended use and the fact that databases are considered tables of numbers involving library functions. Overall, the construction and composition of this database are relatively well documented" (Johnstone & Gunkelman, 2003, p.44). Most normative databases have a non-medical nature. But, that does not diminish their clinical utility.

ACQUIRING QEEG DATA

Many neurotherapists use the QEEG data acquisition hardware Neurosearch-24, manufactured by Lexicor Medical Technology, Inc. which has the FDA 510(k) clearence. Data acquisition software is written in DOS rather than a Windows operating system. A board must be inserted into the host computer. Lexicor's data-acquisition software is easy to learn. However, once the data has been acquired most neurofeedback providers use one of the normative database software programs to artifact the data or they send the non-artifacted data to an independent contractor for processing. Independent contractors often provide treatment recommendations and a written summary. Such a report serves as a second opinion—a valuable commodity for the new practitioner. Lexicor no longer manufactures QEEG data aquisition systems. When you are ready to purchase a 19-channel system make sure it has FDA clearance and that it is compatible with most current normative database software. In the future, the best QEEG acquisition systems will be Windows and not DOS driven. No doubt, they will be able to provide data on the fly. Clinicians will be able to perform simple cognitive tests on clients throughout the data acquisition procedure. Features such as dominant brain wave frequency will be immediately available. Peak-to-peak amplitude data and not just power data would be available to the clinician. Neurofeedback training, data artifacting, and multiple channel assessments will take on a seamless appearance.

Lexicor provides a list of instructions that can be handed out to clients the week before QEEG data is acquired.

- Alcohol should be avoided for 1–2 days before the test.
- A good night's sleep is needed.
- Do not come in hungry—avoid sugary snacks.
- Bring in some water to drink.
- Hair must be washed the day of the test.
- Hair must be dry for the test to prevent a salt bridge.
- Do not use hair conditioners, sprays, gels, etc.
- Earrings may have to be removed.
- Avoid over-the-counter (OTC) medications.
- Report prescription medication use.

Data are gathered simultaneously from 19 scalp locations. Rather than using 19 separate leads, most clinicians use an elastic cap made by Electro-Cap International, Inc., of Eaton, Ohio. Each color-coded cap size has 19 holes plus 2 earlobe clips that correspond to the International 10–20 system. Each of the 21 sensors has lead wires joined together into a wiring harness. The harness is first connected to an impedance meter. The client sits still while the technician begins the process of ensuring a good connection. A special conductive gel is injected into each hole. The QEEG technician takes great pains to make sure the electrical resistance at each of the 21 positions is less than 5,000 Ω. Once the hookup is within acceptable limits, the wiring harness is removed from the impedance meter and the client is instructed to recline in a suitable chair. The wiring harness is then plugged into the QEEG data acquisition system.

The client is encouraged to look at 19 wavy lines of raw EEG data displayed on a computer monitor. Next, the technician instructs the client to perform a series of facial or bodily movements in an attempt to educate the client about muscle artifact. For example, when the client rolls the eyes there is a big distortion at most of the frontal lobe locations. If the client bites down, then temporal lobe locations will most likely be distorted. Other sources of muscle artifact include gulping, blinking, frowning, gum chewing, fidgeting and tongue movements. If there is too much artifact, then the recording will not be usable.

Muscle movements (surface electromyography [SEMG] recordings) generally range from 15 to 300 Hz. EEG recordings range from 1 to 32 Hz in most data acquisition systems. The two frequency ranges overlap each other. For example, a 25-Hz recording may be muscle or brain wave activity; sometimes its difficult to know which one is which. That's why many neurofeedback providers send their QEEG data to an expert to be processed—skilled technicians have learned how to artifact QEEG recordings. In any case, training the client to relax is your first line of defense against the dreaded foe: artifact.

The QEEG technician often gathers as much as 10 min of data for each segment. That is, one recording of 10 min with eyes-closed, another recording of 10 min with eyes-open, and, when necessary, 10 min while the client is performing a cognitive task. Some learning disorders are best seen when the client tries to do a math problem, or read, or remember. Generally, during an eyes-open QEEG recording clients are asked to look forward at one object in the room in order to minimize eye movements. Short breaks are taken (as needed) to help the client endure the 10 min of sitting still. Sometimes the client requests a break—by raising a hand. Sometimes the QEEG technician halts the data acquisition process because of artifact. During an eyes-closed QEEG recording, some clients will become tense, others sleepy. It is important to ask clients if they are becoming sleepy or feeling uneasy. Once complete, the raw EEG data are ready to be cleaned up and processed by QEEG normative database software. Each 10-min recording should yield approximately 2 min of reasonably good data.

Artifacting QEEG data is an advanced skill that can be learned at seminars. Technicians who gather data must have some knowledge of artifacting. An excellent book to read is *The Art of Artifacting* (Hammond & Gunkelman, 2001); it can be obtained from the International Society for Neuronal Regulation (ISNR).

The raw QEEG data obtained by neurotherapists are exactly the same as the data acquired by neurologists at hospitals. Consequently, when seizure disorder is suspected, it may be wise to have a neurologist examine the data and wave morphology for seizure spikes.

7

Review of Common Banded Frequencies

STUDENTS OF THE ELECTROENCEPHALOGRAPH (EEG) are often bombarded with generalizations such as alpha meditation, beta alert, theta fog, or sensorimotor rhythm (SMR) calm. Those descriptions are both helpful and misleading. They suggest that each frequency bandwidth is one-dimensional or independent. Frequency bandwidths are definitive parts of the whole raw EEG. The electrical nature of the cerebral cortex operates best when it is flexible. For example, during periods of study and reflection the brain needs to shift from beta for focusing to alpha for reflection, and theta stands in the wings ready to burst into action to provide a creative solution. Such activities are commonplace in the normative EEG. However, things can get out of balance: one or more bandwidths can dominate in a way that limits flexibility. Consequently, each bandwidth is associated with both positive and negative characteristics. Each one falls into a specific frequency range. Discreet waveform patterns or morphology are found in the *raw* EEG (Figures 6.1c, 6.3c, and 6.5c). Some banded frequencies have both rhythmic and arrhythmic patterns.

DELTA (1–4 OR 1–3.5 HZ)

Delta is associated with sleep and thus predominant in infants. Robert Thatcher (1999), an expert on normative databases, commented on the prevalence of delta:

> at birth approximately 40% of the amplitude is in the delta frequency band
> and only approximately 10% of the EEG amplitude in the alpha frequency
> band. In a normal adult, the percent of amplitude in the delta frequency band
> is typically less than 5%, whereas the percent amplitude in the alpha band is
> approximately 70% in occipital areas ... Thus, EEG amplitude in the delta
> frequency range is not necessarily a sign of pathology or abnormal thalamic
> hyperpolarization, rather it may be a normal part of the EEG. (p. 47)

High-amplitude *rhythmic* delta in adults is an indication of traumatic brain injury and other disorders, whereas *arrhythmic* delta has been observed in college students during problem-solving tasks (Lubar, Angelakis, Frederick &
Stathopoulou, 2001). Referential montages may show high amplitude delta
because of earlobe and eye-movement artifacts. It may be advisable to
reassess using a bipolar (sequential) montage. Some children with attention deficit/hyperactivity disorder (ADHD) or learning disorders may have
widespread delta as well as theta. Inhibiting part of the delta band with the
theta band may be indicated (e.g., 2–7 Hz instead of just 4–7 Hz). Delta
frequency bands may be *inhibited but never rewarded*.

THETA (4–7, 4–7.5, OR 4–8 HZ)

Theta may have a sinusoidal rhythm or it may have a square top (Figure
6.1c). Waves may be rhythmic or arrhythmic. Theta is associated with
creativity and spontaneity, but also with distractibility and inattention,
daydreaming, depression, and anxiety. Theta that is excessive or laterally
asymmetrical may reflect depression, anxiety, and other emotional disorders. (Contralateral theta amplitudes are normally similar.) Children have
higher theta amplitudes than older adults (Blume & Kaibara, 1995, p. 40).
Normative theta-to-beta ratios are about 2:1 in adults and 2.5:1 in children.
Higher ratios are common in children diagnosed with ADHD. Theta-to-
beta ratios exceeding 3:1 suggest a slow-wave disorder (Figure 5.3c). It is
common to find ratios of up to 6:1 in children. Slow-wave disorders usually
refer to excessive theta; however, delta (1–4 Hz) and slow alpha (8–10 Hz)
are also included in the slow-wave category. EEG slowing is associated with
foggy thinking, slow reaction time, poor calculation, poor judgment, and
impulse control.

    Neurofeedback providers often downtrain theta activity when atten-
tion deficit disorder (ADD)/ADHD is present. Training to inhibit slow

waves works well with many children. However, adult theta may have a different role than childhood theta. Brain wave activity alters across the life span. Downtraining theta may benefit adults and children in different ways. Lubar, Angelakis, Frederick, and Stathopoulou (2001) proposed that neurofeedback training could accelerate brain maturation:

> Slow activity (4–7 Hz) in children may be equivalent to higher rhythms, be-tween 7 and 9 Hz in adults. It has been shown, for example, that the posterior dominant frequency follows such a developmental pattern of frequency in-crease, starting from 6–9 Hz at preschool ages and reaching the adult level of 8–12 Hz around the age of 13. In this case, children with attention deficit dis-order may be developmentally delayed, and what Neurofeedback suppresses is the dominant oscillating rhythm. (p. 21)

When downtraining theta in children is appropriate, it is often com-bined with a beta or SMR reward. However, expect to see larger changes in theta amplitudes and much smaller changes in beta amplitudes. Therefore, downtraining theta alone may be just as effective in some cases. Another approach to remediating abnormally high theta-to-beta ratios is ratio train-ing. The trainee is reinforced each time the ratio between slow waves and fast waves decreases (Rossiter, 2002, pp. 9–35). Software for doing ratio training is not common to every neurofeedback training system.

Downtraining theta may be appropriate for any scalp location with a high theta-to-beta ratio. Striefel (1999) cautioned neurotherapists to avoid *up-training* theta if the client has a history of seizure disorder. Furthermore, if the client suffers from posttraumatic stress disorder (PTSD), uptraining or rewarding theta may trigger unwanted flashbacks. As a licensed psychother-apist I employ deep-states training, which includes uptraining both *posterior* theta and alpha if the client has chosen to work through past trauma. See the compressed spectral array (CSA) in Figures 5.7c and 5.8c. Chapter 13 will review alpha/theta or deep-states training. Theta is not uptrained in frontal lobes because frontal slowing is not desirable.

ALPHA (8–12 OR 8–13 HZ)

Classic alpha looks like a rhythmic sinusoidal wave. (See Figure 6.5c.) It normally ranges from 9 to 13 Hz during wakefulness and drops to 7–8 Hz during drowsiness. Sometimes activity between 9 and 11 Hz is not true alpha activity; when it resembles a series of interconnected arches it is called mu rhythm. Alpha blocking refers to the sharp decrease in alpha when the eyes-open. On the other hand, mu waves do not change when eyes-open. Alpha is prominent in the occipital, parietal, and posterior temporal lobes. Mu rhythms may be found only in the sensorimotor cortex or occasionally in the parietal lobes (Blume & Kaibara, 1995, p. 39). Avoid uptraining mu rhythms (Lubar & Lubar, 2002). Of course, the best way to know if it is a mu rhythm is by observing morphology or waveform of the raw EEG.

Alpha is associated with meditation and a sense of inner calm or peacefulness. High anterior amplitudes are common in children known to be daydreamers as well as in cases of depression. Abnormally high amplitude anterior (frontal) alpha may be present in ADD/ADHD, depression, and other disorders. (See Figure 6.9c.) Alpha amplitudes are normally higher in posterior regions and lower in anterior regions of the brain (Blume & Kaibara, 1995, p. 39). Normative "alpha is often equal in amplitude on the two sides (bilateral symmetry), but a slight decrease(<25%) of amplitude on the left is common" (Hughes, 1994, p. 55). However, when a client has depression, it is common to find an *increase* of amplitude on left. Neurotherapists are ever alert for the following abnormal asymmetry: LH alpha > RH alpha. (See CSA in Figures 5.5c and 5.6c compare with Figure 6.12c.) Alpha may be divided into slow and fast alpha.

> 8–10 Hz   Alpha 1 (slow alpha)
> 10–12 Hz   Alpha 2 (relaxed and alert)

Anterior (frontal) alpha may be downtrained for depression, anxiety, ADD/ADHD, traumatic brain injuries (TBI), and other problems. Downtraining alpha in the left hemisphere (LH) is a common protocol for depression. *Posterior* alpha may be uptrained to remediate anxiety disorders such as general anxiety disorder, but it is contraindicated when high amplitudes of alpha are present. See the example of high mean-frequency alpha in Figure 6.18c. Above-average dominant alpha frequencies may reflect superior intelligence or possibly anxiety and insomnia.

For adults, "alpha is sometimes referred to as the posterior dominant rhythm (PDR)" (Rowan & Tolunsky, 2003, p. 25). When it comes to the elderly, some "maintain a steady 10 Hz frequency throughout life. . . . The usual progression, however is a gradual decline in the frequency of the posterior dominant rhythm. A specific disease may not be evident, but the slower PDR probably reflects a degree of cerebral dysfunction" (p. 32). Alpha PDR should be relatively equal in both hemispheres, if not, suspect possible cognitive deficits.

Those with depression may have a PDR well below 10 Hz. Neuro-feedback training in posterior sites such as P3, P4, O1 or O2 may help mitigate depression and raise the trainee's general level of energy. Studies have indicated the neurofeedback training that targets "the patient's existing dominant brainwave" may be yet another effective way to remit the symptoms of depression (Hammond, 1999, p. 63). Depressed trainees and those with age related cognitive decline with low alpha dominant rhythm might well benefit from this protocol. This protocol is likely contraindicated for anxious clients.

Alpha is associated with idleness of the visual system. It increases with eyes-closed and usually decreases with eyes-open. This phenomenon is called alpha blocking: compare the eyes-closed recording of Figure 5.1c with the eyes-open recording of 5.2c. If the alpha amplitude does just the opposite, i.e., decreases with eyes-closed, it usually means "drowsiness" (Stampi, Stone, & Michirnori, 1995, pp. 368–376). In "5 percent" of the population decreases in eyes-open alpha "has no clinical significance" (Rowan & Tolunsky, 2003, p. 26).

Changes in alpha amplitudes also occur when eyes are open. For example, when the brain is challenged by complex tasks such as reading comprehension, anterior alpha amplitudes are suppressed. Some adults or children with ADD/ADHD, however, experience mental fog when trying to focus because they are unable to suppress slower waves. "This increase in alpha during a cognitive task is known as *inversion*, in that higher alpha or theta levels occur during task" (Siever, 2004, p. 24). Therefore, in addition to inhibiting 4–8 Hz theta activity, it may be helpful to include 8–10 Hz alpha. Lubar and Lubar "often train adults to inhibit 4–10 Hz activity or 6–10 Hz activity, and to increase beta activity between 16 and 22 Hz" (1999, p.138).

Uptraining (posterior) alpha with theta is used for deep-states training—a single-channel protocol in which one scalp position is chosen, such as O1, O2, Oz, Pz, and P4. Clinical trials have successfully used deep-states training to remediate PTSD and addictions (Peniston & Kulkosky, 1991). In some cases alpha needs to be suppressed when doing deep-states therapy (Scott, Brod, Siderof, Kaiser, & Sagan, 2002). See Chapter 13 for more information on alpha/theta (A T) training.

Alpha synchrony training is a two-channel protocol in which contralateral sites on the scalp are encouraged to increase alpha amplitudes simultaneously. Often posterior sites such as O1 and O2 are chosen because they are on the visual cortex. Alpha synchrony training may be used for deep-states training or for peak performance training. It is possible to do synchrony training with more than four channels, but this practice is not for newcomers to the field (McKnight & Fehmi, 2001, pp. 45–61).

SENSORIMOTOR RHYTHM (12–15 OR 12–16 HZ)

Sensorimotor rhythm (SMR) may reflect a state of being internally oriented. Some call it low beta. True SMR predominates only in the sensorimotor cortex (sensorimotor strip): C3, Cz, or C4. SMR increases when the brain's motor circuitry is idle. Consequently, SMR amplitude increases with stillness and decreases with movement (Othmer, Othmer, & Kaiser, 1999, p. 267). Barry Sterman and colleagues pioneered SMR training, first with cats and then with humans suffering with epilepsy. He rewarded 12–15 Hz at C3 or at T3 with stand-alone (noncomputerized) equipment (Robbins, 2000a, p. 44). Eventually, his protocol was combined with theta inhibition for both epilepsy and hyperactivity (Budzynski, 1999. p. 72).

During stage II sleep, "the EEG pattern becomes more irregular; *sleep spindles*—sudden, short high-voltage wave bursts occurring at 12–14 Hz—appear, and arousal is more difficult" (Marieb, 1995, p. 492).

Downtraining within the 12–15-Hz frequency range may be called for when abnormally high amplitudes are present (see Figure 6.11c). One paper indicated that as many as 56% of ADHD clients have excessive SMR (Gurnee, 2003). On the other hand, hyperactive clients with below-normal levels of SMR will likely benefit from uptraining at Cz or C4.

BETA/SMR PROTOCOLS

Rewarding SMR in the RH is a common practice, whereas rewarding 15–18 or 16–20 Hz beta in the LH is a common practice. Beta/SMR protocols are often applied along the sensorimotor strip: C3, C4, or Cz. Hence, the expression "C3/beta training" implies that 15–18 Hz beta is uptrained while theta (EEG slowing) is downtrained. The expression "C4/SMR" implies that 12–15 Hz (SMR) is uptrained while theta (EEG slowing) is downtrained (Othmer, Othmer, & Kaiser, 1999, p. 285). However, either beta or SMR uptraining may be used at Cz. Usually, beta is uptrained at Cz for more alertness, whereas SMR is uptrained at Cz to remit impulsivity or hyperactivity: in both cases slow-wave and high-beta (20–30 Hz) inhibition is added to the protocol. Similar training concepts have been applied with bipolar (sequential) montages at C3-to-T3 and C3-to-Cz or C4-to-T4 and C4-to-Cz sets. Beta/SMR protocols are not limited to single channel protocols. C3/beta and C4/SMR may be trained simultaneously with a two-channel protocol using a referential montage as suggested by Brown and Brown (2000). Regardless of the method chosen, all protocols should be based on concrete EEG or quantitative EEG data.

BETA (13–21 HZ)

Beta comprises fast wave activity, or, "any rhythmic activity > 13 Hz" (Blume & Kaibara, 1995, p. 39). (See Figure 6.3c.) It has been associated with being focused, analytic, externally oriented, or in a state of relaxed thinking. Dominant beta frequencies are higher in adults than children (Lubar & Lubar, 1999). "Maximal beta amplitude is usually in the frontocentral regions, but it may be widespread. It does not respond to eye opening, as does the alpha. During drowsiness, beta may seem to increase in amplitude" (Rowan & Tolunsky, 2003, p. 27). Beta bandwidths are defined in several different ranges. For example, E. Roy John's (NxLink) normative database defines beta as 12.5–25 Hz. Others define beta as 13–21, 15–20, or 13–32 Hz. When communicating with other clinicians about beta, define the term in the form of frequency range.

In 1999, Davidson proposed that *hypo*activation of the left frontal cortex is a marker for depression, whereas *hyper*activation of the right frontal cortex is a marker for anxiety. Their research suggested that uptraining LH anterior beta may help clients with depression, whereas downtraining right hemisphere (RH) anterior beta may help clients with anxiety. The key is to match symptoms with EEG measurements. For example, if a client is agitated and anxious and the EEG shows that RH beta is significantly greater than LH beta, then downtraining beta is indicated. Or, if a client has depression and the EEG shows excessive slow-wave activity in the LH, then uptraining the appropriate beta bandwidth while inhibiting slow-wave activity is indicated. But one key to successful beta training, be it reward or inhibit, is to determine which part of the beta frequency bandwidth is outside normal limits.

Excessive beta is commonly found in many disorders, such as: ADD, obsessive compulsive disorder (OCD), sleep disorders, bruxism, learning disorders, anxiety disorders, depression, and many other psychiatric problems. It is common to find that anterior RH beta exceeds LH beta in this population. Beta amplitudes may be equal to or greater than theta amplitudes: beta ≥ theta. (See Figure 5.4c.) Clients with excessive beta may be anxious, on edge, or uneasy. They are usually reverse breathers who will benefit from breath-work training. Neurofeedback training alone may not be enough. Help clients to become active participants in the process outside of the office. Homework assignments include 15–20 min each day of skin temperature (ST) training, breathwork, or some other form of relaxation training—alone or in a group.

Caution must be observed when *uptraining* beta because the beta range overlaps with the electromyography (EMG) range of electrical activity. "Never train an artifact!" warns Adam Crane, a biofeedback trainer. Therefore, if the incoming signal is actually EMG rather than EEG, then the trainee will be learning to increase cranial muscle tension (sometimes neck tension). This potential problem can be minimized if trainees are encouraged to drop their shoulders, do a body scan, and avoid poor posture. If legs must be crossed, then use a half yoga position or cross the legs at ankle level only. Make sure that fast waves are truly beta waves and not surface electromyography (SEMG) waves in disguise. Watch clients' body language, their forehead, shoulders, and posture. Ask them to relax or stretch. Looking at the raw EEG signal may also help: beta has a rhythmic signal whereas EMG has a choppy sharp signal (Figure 7.1).

FIGURE 7.1
RHYTHMIC BETA COMPARED TO EMG ACTIVITY

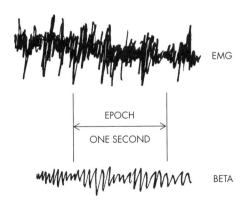

HIGH BETA (20–32 HZ)

High beta is associated with peak performance, cognitive processing, worry, anxiety, overthinking, ruminating, and OCD. (See Figure 6.18c row 5, titled "High Mean Frequency Beta: Anxiety, Alcoholism, Insomnia.") High beta is often inhibited during training but rarely rewarded. Excessive 20–32 Hz beta could be a marker for any one of a number of disorders, or it could imply that the brain is compensating for excessive theta. Downtraining theta may be equally as important as downtraining high beta. It is a common practice when doing beta/SMR protocols to add a high-beta inhibit along with the customary slow-wave inhibit and fast-wave reward.

Widespread and excessive beta ranging 13–32 Hz is difficult to downtrain. Thresholds may be set to inhibit 13–32 Hz with no reward— sometimes it works (see Figure A7.2). Training in increments of 5–7 minutes may promote learning—pause for a few minutes in-between training segments. Other clients are limited in their ability to master this form of training. They are uptight and their sympathetic nervous system seems to be on high alert. I have had the best success when the trainee breathes from the diaphragm. Sometimes adding a reward makes all the difference. For example, it may be reasonable to add an alpha reward to the beta inhibit. If so, limit training to central, posterior and RH sites. Uptraining alpha in the LH, especially at anterior sites, is seldom used due to its association with depression. Another option is to remove the beta inhibit and to uptrain alpha alone at posterior sites: for example, two-channel synchrony training at O1 and O2 or one-channel alpha enhancement at a posterior site may teach the trainee to relax. Protocols should be chosen based upon EEG data, if LH alpha> RH alpha then alpha enhancement should be limited to the RH.

GAMMA (40 OR 38–42 HZ)

Forty hertz is part of the gamma bandwidth. Synchronous bursts of 40-Hz activity have been found during problem-solving tasks for adults and children. It is often lacking when learning disorders or mental deficits are present. Forty-hertz rhythm is found throughout the scalp rather than at one discreet location. It seems to help organize the brain, promote learning, and allow for mental sharpness. It is activated when the brain needs to be active and idle when no specialized task is at hand (Hammond, 2000, pp. 95–100). If a trainee is presented with a series of cognitive challenges, gamma is at work. Two-channel synchrony training at C3 and C4 in the 38–42 Hz range can be alternated with 20.5–21.5 Hz training (Brown & Brown, 2000). This protocol may be useful for clients who have trouble organizing and executing information or those with learning disorders.

Johnstone and Gunkelman (2003) reported on the "development of the first standardized International Brain Database." One of the features of this yet-to-be-finished database is as follows:

> Another of the most interesting new analysis methods is of 40 Hz activity (Gamma synchrony). Gamma synchrony related to cognitive processing has been observed even up to the whole brain level, and with widely separated EEG electrodes (e.g., between hemispheres). It seems, therefore, that synchrony may be an important coding mechanism across multiple scales of brain organization. (p. 46)

The future of normative database software and neurofeedback technology will be built upon the basic understanding of the EEG and neurology.

PART II

NEUROFEEDBACK IN CLINICAL PRACTICE

8

Consultation Phase

NEUROFEEDBACK PROVIDERS ARE EDUCATORS. They have the challenge of teaching others about a relatively unknown technology for change and growth. Potential clients have the greatest need to understand the process and sequence of neurofeedback training. They may have little or no idea how neurofeedback works. For example, one person called and requested a single session treatment because he heard that it might help him. He incorrectly believed that treatment commenced with the first visit. However, once he heard that an in-depth assessment proceeds training, his interest quickly faded. Other prospective clients know more about neurofeedback. They may have heard about it from friends, journal articles, Jim Robbin's book, or from the Internet. Even well-informed individuals, however, need a consultation; it is the first step. It is the time to build structure without overwhelming the client with too much information. The cognitive therapist might say: "The client must be *socialized* to the neurofeedback model." Preparing a client's mind to train his or her own brain involves answering questions. Most new clients have similar questions. Some may be answered on the phone; others require a formal setting. The newly interested client needs to know the following:

- How does neurofeedback work?
- Is it dangerous?
- Will it work for me?
- Is it covered by health insurance?
- What is the first step?

An effective consultation will separate the curiosity seeker from the serious client. It translates the client's concerns into the language of neurotherapy. Change is understood to be the byproduct of training—it is a process, not an event. Neurofeedback is not a drug; the client is an active participant. The consultation phase motivates potential clients to invest in themselves by giving them a vision of improved cognitive performance and personal growth.

HOW DOES NEUROFEEDBACK WORK?

Brain waves rise and fall in rhythmic and arrhythmic patterns. Neurofeedback thresholds are set to reinforce the wave at just the right time in the natural cycle. For example, if a beep is sounded every time your pattern of brain waves moves into an alert state, then focusing is enhanced. This concept can be demonstrated as follows: I hold my left arm out as if it were a limbo bar while I move my right hand in a waveform pattern. I say out loud "Beep, beep, beep" as long as my right hand remains below the limbo bar. I stop saying beep when it rises above the bar. As soon as my hand goes below the bar again, the beeping resumes. I repeat this action a few times. The brain is a marvelous organ; it pairs the beeping with the change in brain wave patterns. The brain knows you want to hear the beep, so the brain cooperates and works with the training—it's as simple as that! This explanation may work for some, whereas for others it's simpler to say, "Healthy brain wave patterns are reinforced by neurofeedback training— frequent training will likely increase your ability to stay focused without equipment."

Neurofeedback training can be compared to other training modalities. For example, physical fitness experts recommend that you exercise at least two or three times per week. It's also important to eat the right foods and to keep reasonably active, even on nontraining days. Training may also be compared to learning to play a musical instrument. The student practices several times per week to prepare for the next lesson. Discipline is an integral part of most training programs. In the same way, neurotherapy training is often done two to three times per week. Trainees keep their brain active on nontraining days with activities such as reading or studying or relaxation exercises. Adequate sleep and good nutrition also boost training results. Children with ADD may need more structure in the home. Neurofeedback training can become an adjunct to supervision in the home, but never a replacement.

Neurofeedback training is all about learning. Each person's rate of learning is unique; some respond more quickly than others do. The total number of sessions may vary—anywhere from 15 to 60 sessions, or more, depending on the severity of the disorder.

WILL NEUROTHERAPY WORK FOR ME?

When clients ponder the efficacy of neurotherapy I reply as follows: "Most people can learn to change brain wave patterns with neurofeedback equipment. Conditions such as depression, anxiety, and attention deficit disorder (ADD) usually respond well to treatment. Neurofeedback is the process of normalizing brain wave patterns in specific regions of the brain that influence our emotional state and cognitive performance. It can also be used to balance out the electrical distribution in the brain. It has been successfully applied to a number of conditions." After making that statement, I give the client a general tour of neurological functions. If you have marked a Styrofoam head according to the International 10–20 system, it may be used as a prop. Focus on the part(s) of the cerebral cortex that most likely contribute to the presenting problem:

- Left hemisphere (LH) is for logic, planning, and details.
- Right hemisphere (RH) is for emotions and social awareness.
- Parietal lobes influence the ability to do complex grammar and problem solving.
- Temporal lobes are for (RH) facial recognition or (LH) word recognition.
- Cingulate gyrus is for smooth transitions, cooperation, and attention.
- Sensorimotor cortex is for fine motor skills—a calm motor system.
- Occipital lobes are for visual learning, pattern recognition, and spatial orientation.
- Frontal lobes are for executive functions, working memory, and attention.

By this time in the discussion, clients can begin to grasp their problem in neurological terms. They have a better understanding of how neurofeedback can enhance cerebral cortex activity. (Keep the discussion simple without being dogmatic—the brain is a system with interdependent parts.) The color insert of this book can also be used as a teaching aid. For example, the electroencephalograph (EEG) signature cards (Figures 6.17c, 6.18c, &

6.19c) will introduce the client to brain maps and individual differences. High theta-to-beta ratios are clearly depicted in Figure 5.3c: Most clients can readily see that the theta is disproportionately high.

Finally, the client may be given handouts, such as articles published in well-known newspapers and journals, along with brochures. Handouts serve to reinforce the purpose of the consultation. The introduction of this book may be also be used to present information in support of the efficacy of neurotherapy. I encourage some new clients to read Jim Robbins's book, *A Symphony in the Brain*. I also direct potential clients to my Web site, www.eegvermont.com, because it has links to key Internet sites. Each client is different. Some consultations are less than an hour, whereas others are more than an hour. Consultation fees are adjusted accordingly.

COSTS AND HEALTH INSURANCE

My time and energy are precious commodities in limited supply. When I first started out in neurotherapy, I would spend hours on the phone answering questions. However, that practice was unfruitful. There are many curious people out there looking for a new and better therapy. If someone wants further information, they are welcome to come to my office for a *paid* consultation. Extended telephone conversations are limited to *serious* potential long-distance clients—who are considering a major investment before commencing long-distance training. One or two conversations at most should provide enough information. My first goal is to help sincere candidates to make their way into my office. I review all of my fees during the consultation. My evaluation fee includes a brief psychiatric interview, psychosocial history, cognitive and psychological testing, along with a QEEG processed by normative database software. One session may be spent to review results. It's a package fee. I never give neurofeedback demonstrations. Neurofeedback is a costly investment for the educated consumer. If a potential client cannot afford the package fee, likely he or she cannot afford training. I will not set up a health insurance account until the client has made a verbal commitment. In some cases the consultation genuinely falls within the framework of family therapy, individual therapy, or perhaps psychiatric interviewing.

I have spent a great deal of time, energy, and money trying to persuade insurance companies to cover biofeedback/neurofeedback. I have given up. At the time of this writing, major health management organizations

(HMOs) and preferred provider organizations (PPOs) do *not* cover biofeed-back/neurofeedback in the northeastern part of the United States of America. There are a few exceptions, and it is possible to be reimbursed, but proceed with caution. Rely upon insurance companies, when they have agreed in advance to cover biofeedback/neurofeedback. Otherwise, it is unwise to rely upon insurance company benefits. However, as a licensed provider, I am entitled to charge for covered benefits. I charge for the time that I spend counseling the client or the family. Some clients who have been injured will say that their liability insurance will cover treatment and testing. If that is so, then have the client put the money up front and have the insurance company reimburse them directly.

Many neurofeedback providers throughout the United States refuse to take any health insurance payments, and I certainly understand their position. It is my hope that all health insurance companies will cover neurotherapy in the future. I believe that neurotherapy will save them money in the long run. However, until then, guard your financial future. The following review of the current procedural terminology (CPT) may be helpful for areas of the United States that have more flexible insurance coverage (American Medical Association, 1998). The CPT codes do not differentiate between peripheral biofeedback and neurofeedback. Typical peripheral biofeedback treatment for many common disorders is 6 to 12 treatments. Do not be surprised when a health insurance organization questions the *medical necessity* for treatment beyond the 12-session barrier. The following CPT codes may be used for reimbursement:

- 90876 (biofeedback with counseling)
- 90901 (biofeedback without counseling)
- 90801 (psychiatric interviewing and evaluation)
- 90847 (family therapy)
- 90804 (25 min of psychotherapy)
- 99090 (analysis of computerized data) (normative database analysis)
- 96115 (computer-assisted cognitive testing) (MicroCog, Test of Variables of Attention [TOVA], and Intermediate Visual and Auditory [IVA])
- 95957 (QEEG)

Typically, I use 90804 to cover the counseling part of the session. However, if the client is doing deep-states training then 90806 often qualifies for reimbursement. The client pays the usual copay plus an additional charge for neurofeedback, the noncovered service. The code 95957 is for a

19-channel quantitative EEG (QEEG), not for a 2-channel assessment. The code 99090 sometimes works for a one-time analysis of QEEG data. The code 96115 may be covered if your state license authorizes you to do testing. Many neurofeedback providers give discounts for noninsurance clients who pay in advance—10 sessions at a time. Rates for neurotherapy treatments vary widely throughout the country. Your equipment purchases and training fees were expensive; new equipment will most likely be purchased in the future. Office rentals are often higher for neurotherapists than for psychotherapists—more square footage is probably needed. Adjust your rates accordingly.

My practice of neurofeedback is growing slowly, whereas in other areas where the economy is much better and folks do not rely upon insurance reimbursement for mental health services neurotherapy is doing better. If a professional counselor knows that the folks in his or her area cannot afford out-of-pocket mental health services then the *full-time* practice of neurotherapy may be contraindicated at this time. (See Chapter 17 for suggestions.)

INDICATIONS AND CONTRAINDICATIONS FOR NEUROTHERAPY

Clients have to decide whether or not neurofeedback training is for them. Neurotherapists for their part have to decide whether or not neurofeedback training should be applied to the particular problem or case at hand. Some seeking help should be referred to other health practitioners before they are ready to commence neurotherapy. Others may require a more experienced neurofeedback provider. There are some cases that should never be treated with neurotherapy. The consultation phase has already given you some clues about the client's emotional and financial ability to undergo the neurotherapy process. The goal is to make sure that neurotherapy is the treatment of choice. There are a number of factors to consider in making this decision:

Indications and Suggestions

Begin with clients who have discreet problems that relate to specific regions of the cerebral cortex. It may be wise to avoid potential clients who present with a series of vague or unusual complaints. An ideal candidate for training is the child (8–12 years of age) with simple attention deficit/hyperactivity disorder (ADHD). Learning disorders and dyslexia may be secondary issues—attention is the primary issue. This hypothetical client comes from a loving family and a relatively structured environment. The parents are willing to do whatever is reasonable, and they have the finances to cover treatment. You make several suggestions about diet, exercise, limiting video game playing, and so on, and they are willing to comply (see my handout, "For Children Who Are in Training," in Appendix 3). They do not expect you to "fix" their child, but they are hoping for a definite improvement. They can make arrangements for at least 1–2 months to bring in their child to train two or three times per week. Other ideal candidates are ones who present with depression (and perhaps mild to moderate anxiety) who are not currently being medicated. They are willing to do basic cognitive assignments and reasonable physical exercise on nontherapy days. They have appropriate finances and are willing to come in for treatment more than once per week. They have stable family structures, steady employment or household duties; support base of encouraging friends are at hand.

Ideal candidates for training have structure in their life; they are not running from one crisis to another. They do not have a pattern of interpersonal problems. They do not make it a habit of speaking harshly about the school system, employers, and others in authority, although they may point out a few genuine problems they have observed.

Clients on medication may also be good candidates, but symptoms of withdrawal must be taken into account (Glenmullen, 2000, pp. 64–105). The goal of treatment is to improve performance or mood. If this includes medication reduction or elimination, so be it. Be careful about making statements that suggest the goal of treatment is to eliminate medication. It may cause clients to end drug-management therapy before they are ready to do so. It may cause them to equate success with medication elimination rather than feeling and functioning better. Do not assume the role of a psychiatrist.

Some children will not sit still for training unless they are on a stimulant medication. Training may eventually lead to medication reduction or elimination.

Contraindications

Neurofeedback may be contraindicated due to the nature of the disorder or the limits of the treatment facility. During the initial interview (before QEEG analysis), it is essential to continue to assess clients' readiness to undergo the training process. They must have the time and the finances to complete the training process. Also, it is essential to determine if the clients have Axis II disorders. If the initial interview has revealed a pattern of inter-personal problems, then neurotherapy may be contraindicated. Dialectic behavior therapy (DBT) may be the first place to start treatment (Linehan, 1993). Neurofeedback training will not magically undo the "covert" nature of transference, countertransference, splitting, or distrust (Demos, 1995). Neither will the risk of suicidality, self-harm, or explosive anger melt away with neurotherapy. The cycle of overvaluation and devaluation may find its way into the training arena. The best time to start neurotherapy may be after the DBT program has been completed.

Cautionary remarks may also be made about clients with dissociative identity disorder (DID) who are prone to switch from one alter-personality to another. Scores of 25% or greater on the Dissociative Experiences Scale (DES) (Putnam, 1989) are often found in survivors of psychological trauma. Correcting EEG abnormalities may not be in the clients' first best interests. The experienced neurotherapist who has received appropriate training in both psychotherapy and neurotherapy may well be in a position to treat dissociative disorders and Axis II conditions. In general, trauma-based con-ditions require an eclectic approach to neurotherapy. Posttraumatic stress disorder (PTSD) is often the primary problem. Complex protocols to re-solve DID are for advanced neurotherapists who specialize in this disorder (Manchester, Allen & Tachiki, 1998).

What about clients with borderline personality disorder (BPD) who have been in psychotherapy treatment with you for a number of years? Likely, the transference is so potent for those diagnosed with BPD that only a minority of *your* clients will be able to make the transition from psychotherapy to neurotherapy. Also, it may be unwise to switch to neurotherapy if the client is doing well with talk therapy. Sometimes the old adage applies: "Don't switch horses in midstream." On the other hand, some may well respond to site-specific training or deep states training. For example, it may be possible to train within the dorsal anterior cingulate region and improve cognitive functioning (Posner et al., 2002). Training in the right prefrontal cortex may reduce fear and anxiety (Fisher, 2003). Deep-states therapy may help to resolve psychological issues and soften Axis II traits (Peniston & Kulkosky, 1991).

It is common for potential clients with underlying PTSD to request neurotherapy for depression, anxiety, chronic fatigue and other disor-ders. Eyes-open site-specific training for depression or anxiety or other abnormalities in the EEG are unlikely to remit symptoms. Even if the trainee expresses some relief they will likely relapse shortly after training has concluded. The first order of neurotherapy is to work through the trauma. Afterwards, the presenting symptoms may no longer exist.

Highly dysfunctional families may have members that would benefit from neurotherapy. What is the greater need family therapy or neurotherapy? Behavior problems cannot be simply labeled as ADHD until the problem is seen in context. Neurotherapy will not "fix" a family problem; it is not a silver bullet. In order for the treatment to be successful, the family must be ready to participate in the program. Building family structure includes changes in nutrition, better control over TV and video game usage, curfews, boundary setting, improved sleep patterns, and sometimes family therapy. Many families need coaching to make these changes. It may take several sessions before parents or guardians can combine their efforts to make it work. Families who are unable to make crucial changes may not be ready to participate in a neurotherapy program. The following issues usually need to be resolved before commencing neurotherapy: child custody problems, family arguments and screaming, an impending egregious divorce, inadequate family structure, excessive strife associated with a newly combined family, bullying at school, daily interpersonal struggles, and so on. The life of our adult and child clients must have a measure of stability.

Preadolescent children often accept the authority of adults. In just a few short developmental years, however, that acceptance may fade. Adolescents who view neurotherapy as mind control are unlikely candidates for training. Parents who view neurofeedback as a way to stop conduct disorder will likely be disappointed. Teenagers who succeed in training are most likely motivated from within. They have parents who are a steady source of support. Teenagers who fail in training have one or more of the following symptoms: sleep deprivation, poor lifestyle habits, poor choice of associates, permissive parenting, lack of attention from one or both parents, a pattern of defiant or criminal activity. You cannot force teenagers to train for their own good. They must see the need for change and be willing to put forth the effort. On the other hand, do not confuse conduct disorder with hyperactivity, impulsivity, and developmental delays. When communicating with parents, help them to understand the limitations of neurotherapy. Make sure they have come to you with realistic goals in mind.

Neurofeedback training may be contraindicated for those with severe learning disorders, psychotic behaviors, or mental deficits. The appropriate candidate must be able to learn a new skill in a relatively healthy and supportive environment. If you are a new provider, some problems will be over your head. Consult with your supervisor (mentor) and jointly determine if you are ready to take on a new challenge.

At the close of your initial interview consider the following questions: Do I feel capable of working with this client? Is it possible to set a few simple goals? Are there too many presenting problems? Does the client expect me to fix his or her life? Is this client truly motivated for training and willing to make lifestyle changes? Is he or she both willing and able to come to my office at least once, twice or three times per week? Does this case require a more experienced neurotherapist? Would supervision help? And, finally, is there evidence that neurotherapy can really help such a person? (Hammond, 2001). Invite the client to review Hammond's *Comprehensive Neurofeedback Bibliography* on-line at isnr.org. There are many situations that could rule out neurotherapy—the sooner you make this determination, the better.

9

General Assessments and Cognitive Testing

NEUROTHERAPY IN THE HANDS OF AN EMPATHIC health care provider promotes self-esteem. It has the potential to impart hope and remove labels. Clients have problems but they can never be defined by those problems. Keep that thought in mind when conducting interviews and obtaining data. Clinical interviewing does not have to be sterile and unfeeling. Do not get so absorbed in baselines, computations, and brain waves only to forget the demeanor of the caring psychotherapist. Neurotherapists work with brain structures that do many things just fine. It is the client's unique brain that has the potential to transform itself. The few neurological regions that operate poorly do not negate that which operates well.

That having been said, neurotherapists do far more testing than most psychotherapists. They are interested in any instrument that can help isolate problematic regions of the cerebral cortex. Computer-driven cognitive assessment tools are an excellent way to obtain a baseline. However, there are other useful assessment instruments that can add to the clinical picture. The psychiatric interview puts a human face upon the presenting problem. Each client's presenting problem is different and so not all tests apply. The evaluation process includes:

- The psychiatric interview and psychosocial history
- General health matters that can effect training

- Computerized assessment tests
- Neurological overview

THE PSYCHIATRIC INTERVIEW

The experienced health professional will develop tentative diagnoses based on usual and customary interviewing practices. Guidelines on psychiatric interviewing and writing a mental status exam are found in the Susan Lukas's book *Where to Start and What to Ask: An Assessment Handbook* (1993). Many potential trainees come in with specific diagnoses or test results from other institutions. It is preferable to have a *baseline score on a test(s) that can easily be readministered in your office.* It may be wise to have the prospective client come in early just to fill out forms. In some cases, I have a second party fill out the Amen questionnaire or the attention deficit disorder–attention deficit/hyperactivity disorder (ADD/ADHD) behavioral checklist; it may be a spouse, partner, parent(s), or teacher(s). There are many ways to determine a clinical baseline. But I have chosen instruments that can easily be readministered.

- Amen questionnaire (Amen, 2001)
- Toomin's questionnaire (Available from www.biocompresearch.org)
- ADD/ADHD behavioral checklist (Sears & Thompson, 1998)
- Beck Depression Inventory (BDI; Available from The Psychological Corporation)
- Burns Anxiety Inventory (BAI; Burns, 1999)
- Dissociative Experience Scale (DES; Bernstein & Putnam, 1986)
- Personality inventories (e.g., Millon Adolescent Personality Inventory)
- Dyslexia, mania, eating disorders, and addiction scales
- Custom-designed instruments

The following is a discussion of three items on the list that require further explanation: Amen questionnaire, Toomin questionnaire, and custom instruments:

The Amen Questionnaire

The Amen self-report questionnaire (Amen, 2001) provides cognitive, emotional, behavioral, and psychological information about the brain. Amen organizes ADD into six types that can be identified by a specific array of symptoms. Each of the six types has a different metabolic pattern in the brain that can be seen via single photon emission computed tomography (SPECT) brain scans. Moreover, Amen asserts that the questionnaire in his book has a high correlation with SPECT. Therefore, the neurological specificity of his questionnaire is yet another way to determine electrode placement. His book contains suggestions for neurofeedback training as well as dietary suggestions. Parents have a great deal of intuition when it comes to filling out the Amen questionnaire. Sometimes I suggest that both parents and even a teacher fill out the questionnaire. It is especially helpful to have parents or guardians read the chapter that may apply to their child. Amen's book also reinforces the need to make changes in family structure. The Amen questionnaire is a behavioral checklist organized into categories. As such, it can also be used as a behavioral baseline. The questionnaire is not infallible; it should be used in concert with other instruments.

Toomim's Questionnaire

Hershel Toomim has published an online questionnaire (Toomim, 2003) to guide hemoencephalography (HEG) neurofeedback training, "Toomim's Cognitive Behavior Questionnaire: Directed to Specific Brain Areas." It is a series of questions designed to connect performance with neurology. I use his questionnaire to validate other tests. From time to time quantitative EEG (QEEG) brain maps lack specificity. Sensor placement and protocol decisions can become less complex when there is other supporting evidence. For example, consider the following sample questions and corresponding treatment recommendations taken from Toomin's online source, www.biocompresearch.org:

Question	Suspected Brain Area
Do you easily get lost?	T6
Did you bond with your mother?	Fp2
Are you uncomfortable sitting still?	Fpz, Fz

Toomim published another questionnaire to be used in conjunction with the MicroCog Assessment. It will be reviewed later in this chapter.

Custom-Designed Instruments

My psychotherapy supervisor taught me to say to the client who could not conceptualize wellness: "How will you know when you are better. What will be different?" In the same way, parents of children with pervasive developmental disorders or other problems can easily describe the problem but have greater difficulty knowing what wellness would look like. For example, the child or adolescent with Asperger's disorder may have difficulty with cognitive flexibility, interpersonal connections, and normal emotional displays. These characteristics can be transformed into a *daily* behavioral checklist:

1. How many times did he make eye contact?
2. When giving hugs, how stiff was his body, on a scale of 1 to 10?
3. How many times did he mention the name of a friend?
4. How much time was spent in repetitive activities?
5. How many times did he offer to help without being asked?
6. How much interest does he have regarding other family members, on a scale of 1 to 10?
7. How many times did you observe him in nail-biting behavior?

Customized questionnaires can be typed out, copied, and *filled out each week.* They can be used to chart progress in a way that is similar to baseline comparisons.

Computerized Assessment Tests

If neurofeedback training is indicated, then further cognitive testing will be required. I administer the following computerized tests when appropriate. I usually do not train children younger than 7 or 8 years of age. The child must be old enough to participate in the assessment process. In a few cases children are not able to participate in a continuous performance test due to immaturity, hyperactivity, impulsivity, or oppositional behavior. One youngster before training refused to take the intermediate visual and auditory (IVA); later, after 12 HEG neurofeedback training sessions, he agreed to take the test because his oppositional symptoms had decreased. There were mitigating circumstances that moved me to start training without an IVA. I depended heavily on clinical experience and observations in making an assessment in his case.

THE FOLLOWING CHART APPLIES TO EACH COMPRESSED
SPECTRAL ARRAY (CSA) IN THE COLOR INSERT:

1. Amplitudes are in microvolts (μV) from 0 to 50 μV
2. Time is from 0 to 40 seconds—for data acquisition
3. Frequency bands are color-coded in 4-Hertz increments:

	Delta	1–4 Hz	Green
	Theta	4–8 Hz	Dark Blue
	Alpha	8–12 Hz	Light Blue
	SMR	12–16 Hz	Gray
	Beta 1	16–20 Hz	Purple
	Beta 2	20–24 Hz	Brown
	Beta 3	24–28 Hz	Salmon
	Beta 4	28–32 Hz	Brick

Each CSA is a graphic representation of the EEG that has been acquired from a single site referential montage. Neurofeedback providers make judgments based upon microvolt values as well as graphics that show the EEG in action. It is essential to understand the difference between a normal and an abnormal bandwidth distribution of the EEG at any given location on the scalp. Not all providers use CSAs during the initial evaluation of the EEG. Not all neurofeedback-training systems will produce picturesque CSAs. Figure 5.1.c is a 2-dimensional graphic representation of the EEG with eyes-closed at Cz. Many clinical decisions stem from observing 2-dimensional graphics. Figures 5.2c–5.8c are CSAs.

FIGURE 5.1C
2-DIMENSIONAL EYES CLOSED NORMATIVE RECORDING AT CZ

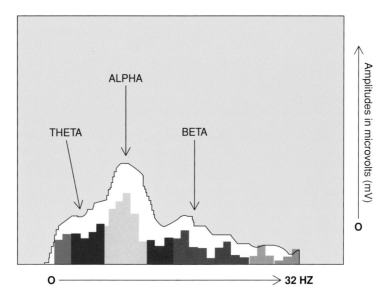

Figure 5.1c is a 2-dimensional display of the EEG at Cz; it represents a spit second in time. The EEG reflects a normal distribution of bandwidths with eyes-closed. Alpha amplitude exceeds all other bandwidths. Notice that alpha > theta > beta. Use this diagram as a template for future comparisons. The 2-dimensional graph is common software feature in most EEG training systems. It is yet another tool to guide training because it compares bandwidth distribution in the moment.

For example, after beginning alpha enhancement training (Pz) for one client I observed very high amplitudes of alpha at 11–13 Hz and low amplitudes of alpha at 8–11 Hz. The 2-dimensional graph clarified my training protocol. I needed to reward 8–11 Hz alpha and inhibit 11–13 Alpha. That made sense to me since this client was anxious and had an elevated posterior dominant rhythm (PDR). The 2-dimensional EEG graphics isolated the problem.

See Table 5.1 on page 92 for a numeric presentation of the data.

(Acquired by Model 2E made by BrainMaster Technologies, Inc.)

FIGURE 5.2C
3-DIMENSIONAL COMPRESSED SPECTRAL ARRAY EYES OPEN NORMATIVE RECORDING AT CZ

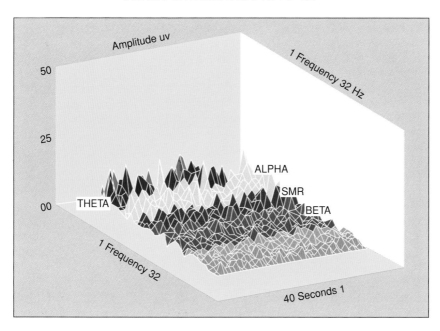

Figure 5.2c is a 3-dimensional cascading CSA; it represents 40 seconds of time. The EEG reflects a normal distribution of bandwidths with eyes-open. Alpha and theta amplitudes are nearly the same. Normally, alpha amplitudes drop when the eyes-open—this change in alpha activity is called alpha blocking. *That is why Figure 5.2c alpha is lower than Figure 5.1c alpha. CSA graphics can be used diagnostically; they provide a clinical overview of the client's EEG at one location.*

Figure 5.2c is an adult not a child. Expect higher slow wave amplitudes in younger children.

See Table 5.1 on page 92 for a numeric presentation of the data.

(Acquired by single-channel Capscan-80 developed by Expanded Technologies, Inc.)

FIGURE 5.3C
CLASSIC HIGH THETA-TO-BETA RATIO FOR 10-YEAR-OLD WITH ADHD
(Client A)

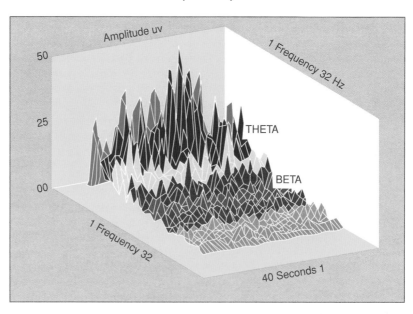

Client A CSA is an eyes-closed recording at Cz. This is the classic ADHD pattern because theta (dark blue) amplitude far exceeds beta (purple). Slow wave disorders are very common in the ADHD population. Delta as well as theta are elevated so the slow wave inhibit filter was expanded to 2–8 Hz. Abnormal EEG patterns are often found along the cingulate gyrus (Cz, Fz, and Pz).

PROTOCOL
Eyes-open, Cz referential montage:

- *Inhibit 2–8 Hz and 20–30 Hz*
- *Reward 16–20 Hz*
- *Ratio training 2–8 Hz/16–20 Hz*

Parents will especially appreciate this graphic because it will help them to see if their child has a slow wave disorder.

(Acquired by single-channel Capscan-80 developed by Expanded Technologies, Inc.)

FIGURE 5.4C
BETA EXCEEDS THETA AND ALPHA: OCD, ADHD, ANXIETY DISORDERS
(Client B)

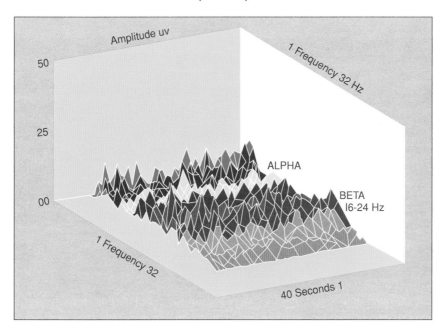

Figure 5.4c of client B is an eyes-closed recording at Cz. Beta (brown) exceeds both alpha (light blue) and theta (dark blue). Fast wave disorders are very common in ADHD, OCD, depression, and anxiety.

PROTOCOL
Eyes-closed, Cz referential montage:

- *Inhibit 16–24 Hz and Reward Alpha 8–12 Hz*

Clients with fast wave disorders will benefit greatly from diaphragmatic breathing. They may have a great deal of muscle tension. During training it's important to remind them to relax, drop their shoulders, breathe slowly, and limit facial movements.

(Acquired by single-channel Capscan-80 developed by Expanded Technologies, Inc.)

FIGURE 5.5C
LEFT HEMISPHERE RECORDING AT C3 FOR DEPRESSED ADULT CLIENT
(Client C)

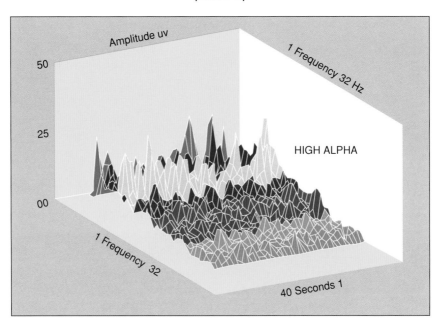

Figure 5.5c is an eye-closed recording of client C in the LH at C3. Compare alpha (light blue) amplitudes in Figures 5.5c and 5.6c. Alpha (light blue) amplitudes in the LH are much greater than the RH—alpha asymmetry patterns are common in depression:

(C3) LH alpha > (C4) RH alpha

(Acquired by single-channel Capscan-80 developed by Expanded Technologies, Inc.)

FIGURE 5.6C
RIGHT HEMISPHERE RECORDING AT C4 FOR DEPRESSED ADULT CLIENT
(Client C)

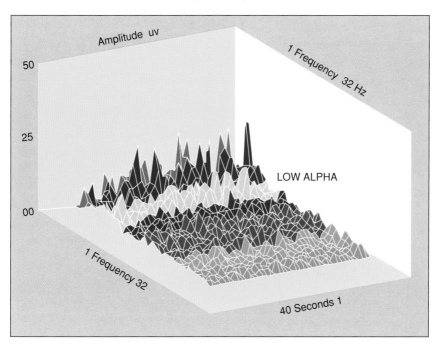

Figure 5.6c is an eyes-closed recording of client C in the RH at C4. Central, anterior, and posterior alpha asymmetries are found in many clients with depression.

PROTOCOL

Eyes-open for 25 minutes at C3:	*followed by*	*Eyes-open 5 minutes at C4:*
• *Inhibit 3–10 Hz and 20–30 Hz*		• *Inhibit 4–8 Hz and 20–30 Hz*
• *Reward 15–18 Hz*		• *Reward 12–15 Hz*

Client C responded to the training protocol and his depression remitted within a few sessions. LH slowing is common to many people with depression. LH slowing is not limited to anterior sites such as F3 or F7. It can also be found in central and posterior scalp locations.

(Acquired by single-channel Capscan-80 developed by Expanded Technologies, Inc.)

FIGURE 5.7C
RECORDING AT CZ FOR CLIENT WITH PTSD (Client D)

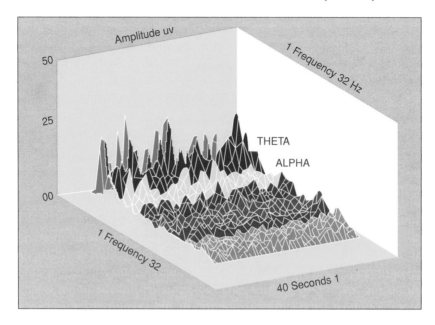

Figure 5.7c *is an eyes-closed recording of client D at Cz. Compare alpha (light blue) and theta (dark blue) in Figures* 5.7c *and* 5.8c. *Central (Cz) alpha and theta are significantly higher than posterior (Pz) alpha and theta. Furthermore, posterior (Pz) beta (purple) is higher than central (Cz) beta. Client D has PTSD. This is an example of a gross posterior to anterior imbalance:*

- *Cz slow waves > Pz slow waves*
- *Pz fast waves > Cz fast waves*

(Acquired by single-channel Capscan-80 developed by Expanded Technologies, Inc.)

FIGURE 5.8C
RECORDING AT PZ FOR CLIENT WITH PTSD (Client D)

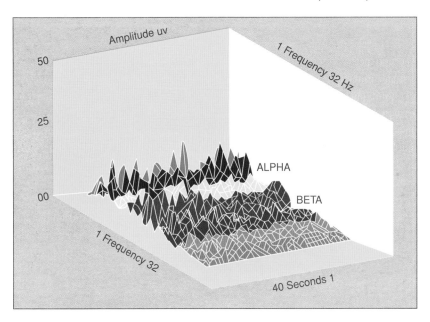

Figure 5.8c is an eyes-closed recording of client D at Pz. PTSD is the diagnosis.

PROTOCOL

Eyes-open at Cz for 20 sessions: followed by   *Eyes-closed at Pz for 30 sessions:*

- *Inhibit 3–10 Hz and 20–30 Hz*
- *Reward 15–18 Hz.*

- *Reward 8–12 Hz and 4–8 Hz*
- *Inhibit 15–30 Hz*

Figures 5.7c and 5.8c represent one of many manifestations of PTSD in the EEG. When a client is a survivor of trauma the first order of business is safety and grounding. Clients with dissociative disorders will benefit from eyes-open slow wave inhibition. This form of training promotes grounding. Not all survivors of trauma have central or anterior slowing. Some have widespread beta.

(Acquired by single-channel Capscan-80 developed by Expanded Technologies, Inc.)

FIGURE 6.1C
THETA MORPHOLOGY IN PREFRONTAL LOBES (Client E)

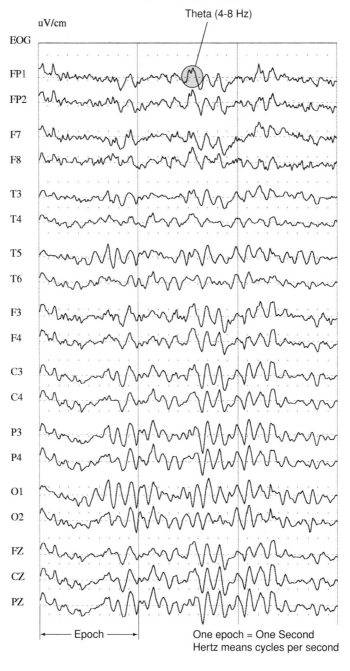

ANTERIOR EEG SLOWING

Theta (4-8 Hz)

uV/cm

EOG

FP1

FP2

F7

F8

T3

T4

T5

T6

F3

F4

C3

C4

P3

P4

O1

O2

FZ

CZ

PZ

|←— Epoch —→|

One epoch = One Second
Hertz means cycles per second

FIGURE 6.2C
NxLINK: PREFRONTAL-EEG SLOWING (Client E)

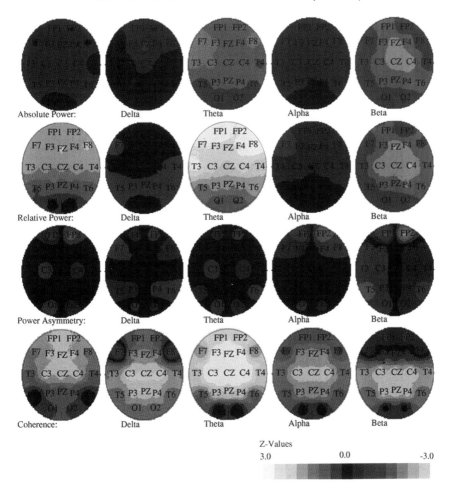

Z-Values
3.0   0.0   -3.0

Figure 6.1c (left) is a quantitative electroencephalograph (QEEG) for client E. Figure 6.1c is an eyes-closed referential recording coming from 19 scalp locations according to the International 10–20 system. Theta morphology or waveform can be located at Fp1, Fp2, F7, F8, and T3. It, along with other accepted epochs of data, was used to create the topographical brain map in Figure 6.2c.

Figures 6.1c and 6.2c come from the same EEG data. Figure 6.2c (above) is the NxLink topographical brain map. Remember, you are looking down at the head, the nose is at the top and the left hemisphere is to the left and the right hemisphere is to the right. (Black is normative.) The first line of heads in NxLink is called Absolute Power whereas the second line is called Relative Power. The Relative line takes into consideration the physical characteristics of the skull; it is more accurate than the absolute line. For example, anterior Relative Power theta bandwidth has a Z-value of 3.0, whereas anterior Absolute Power theta has an approximate Z-value of only 1.5. Client E responded slowly to EEG-neurofeedback. HEG-neurofeedback training in the pre-frontal lobes was more effective.

FIGURE 6.3C
BETA MORPHOLOGY (WIDESPREAD) (Client F)

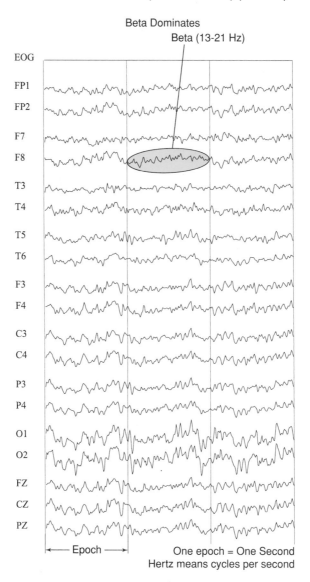

Beta Dominates
Beta (13-21 Hz)

EOG

FP1

FP2

F7

F8

T3

T4

T5

T6

F3

F4

C3

C4

P3

P4

O1

O2

FZ

CZ

PZ

|← Epoch →| One epoch = One Second
Hertz means cycles per second

Figure 6.3c is a quantitative electroencephalograph (QEEG) for client F. It is an eyes-closed referential recording coming from 19 scalp locations according to the International 10–20 system. It, along with other accepted epochs of data, was used to create the topographical brain map in Figure 6.4c. Brain wave morphology clearly demonstrates widespread beta. Compare the posterior EEG slowing and central EEG fast waves with the brain map in Figure 6.4c.

FIGURE 6.4C
NEURO GUIDE: SINGLE HERTZ BINS (Client F)

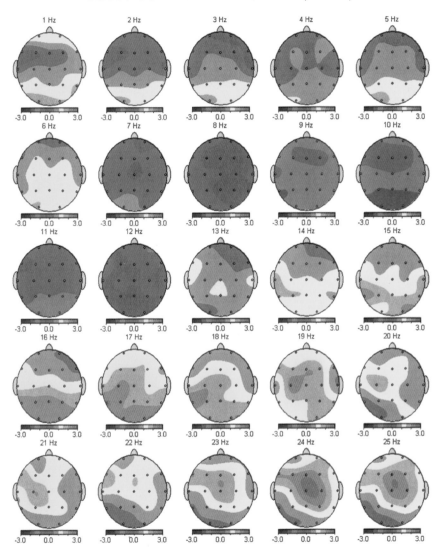

Figure 6.4c is a linkears, relative power, and single hertz bins brain map processed by NeuroGuide normative database software. Red color-coding defines the locations that vary the most from the norm. (Green is normative.) Beta morphology or waveform can be located throughout the scalp except at O1 and O2. Figures 6.3c and 6.4c come from the same EEG data.

FIGURE 6.5C
ALPHA MORPHOLOGY (WIDESPREAD) (Client G)

Posterior Alpha Asymmetry
T-5 Alpha Amplitudes > T6 Alpha Amplitudes

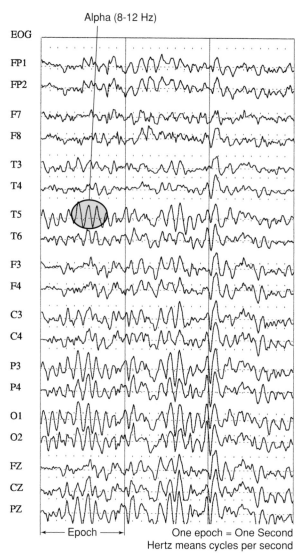

One epoch = One Second
Hertz means cycles per second

Figure 6.5c is a quantitative electroencephalograph (QEEG) for client G. Figure 6.5c is an eyes-closed referential recording coming from 19 scalp locations according to the International 10–20 system. Notice the presence of central and posterior alpha morphology or waveform.

FIGURE 6.6C
NxLINK: POSTTRAUMATIC STRESS DISORDER (Client G)

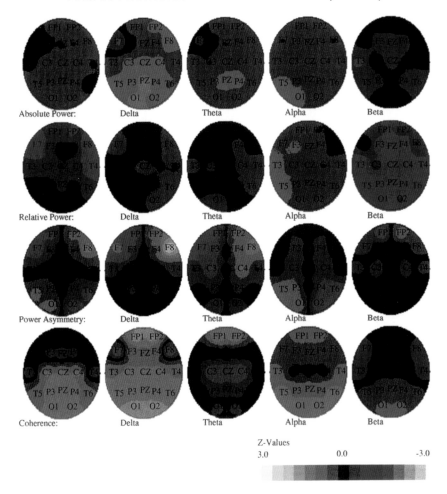

Figure 6.6c is the NxLink topographical brain map. The Relative Power line shows the evidence of posterior RH theta and posterior LH alpha. Client G has major depression that is reflected by the posterior alpha asymmetry.

Client G to responded poorly to EEG-neurofeedback. Site specific training for this client's global posterior slowing did not produce desired results. Client G quickly relapsed after EEG-neurofeedback training ended. HEG-neurofeedback was also contraindicated because anterior theta-to-beta ratio is normal. Photic stimulation program for beta enhancement helped to limit symptoms of depression in this client. It likely helped to reduce slowing in the visual cortex. But more was needed. Deep states training with photic stimulation was effective at opening historic issues of trauma. Working through the trauma was the key to relieving depression.

FIGURE 6.7C
NEUROGUIDE: COHERENCE Z SCORES (Client H)

Intrahemispheric: LEFT

	DELTA	THETA	ALPHA	BETA
FP1-F3	0.34	0.36	0.52	0.87
FP1-C3	-0.10	0.67	0.86	1.01
FP1-P3	-0.64	0.58	-0.26	0.25
FP1-O1	-1.38	-1.58	-0.83	-1.19
FP1-F7	-0.66	0.20	0.34	1.02
FP1-T3	-0.24	0.78	0.33	1.38
FP1-T5	-1.59	-1.44	-0.57	-0.72
F3-C3	-0.16	0.49	0.52	0.48
F3-P3	-0.18	0.15	-0.27	-0.02
F3-O1	0.01	-1.10	-0.84	-0.96
F3-F7	0.31	0.90	0.79	1.27
F3-T3	0.55	0.90	0.45	1.06
F3-T5	-0.39	-0.44	-0.30	-0.29
C3-P3	-0.42	-0.39	-0.10	-0.16
C3-O1	0.28	-0.76	-0.23	-0.43
C3-F7	0.31	1.11	1.01	1.50
C3-T3	0.93	0.88	0.73	1.16
C3-T5	-0.22	-0.69	0.23	0.37
P3-O1	0.83	-0.34	0.27	-0.01
P3-F7	-0.32	0.77	0.13	0.82
P3-T3	0.53	0.30	0.71	0.80
P3-T5	-0.16	-0.80	0.33	0.48
O1-F7	-1.57	-1.45	-0.93	-0.94
O1-T3	1.03	0.22	0.72	0.18
O1-T5	0.97	-0.24	-0.06	-0.25
F7-T3	0.49	1.15	0.70	1.42
F7-T5	-1.03	-0.23	-0.43	0.32
T3-T5	0.10	-0.20	0.41	0.68

Intrahemispheric: RIGHT

	DELTA	THETA	ALPHA	BETA
FP2-F4	0.00	0.74	0.85	0.98
FP2-C4	0.28	0.78	1.10	0.91
FP2-P4	-0.21	0.31	-0.81	0.06
FP2-O2	-1.09	0.28	0.43	-0.25
FP2-F8	0.12	0.56	0.80	0.88
FP2-T4	0.40	0.53	0.79	-0.73
FP2-T6	-0.63	-1.15	0.01	-0.75
F4-C4	0.57	0.28	0.84	0.48
F4-P4	0.09	-0.09	-0.76	-0.40
F4-O2	-1.08	-0.87	0.47	-0.36
F4-F8	0.56	0.93	0.90	1.19
F4-T4	0.91	0.66	0.90	-1.14
F4-T6	0.44	-0.56	-0.19	-0.71
C4-P4	-0.08	-0.26	-0.69	-0.43
C4-O2	-0.80	-2.08	-1.03	-1.68
C4-F8	0.13	0.22	0.78	0.66
C4-T4	0.44	0.09	0.59	-1.34
C4-T6	0.11	-0.84	-0.54	-0.23
P4-O2	-0.34	-1.52	-0.68	-0.67
P4-F8	-0.46	-0.26	-0.94	-0.31
P4-T4	-0.24	-0.59	-0.37	-2.16
P4-T6	0.40	-0.72	0.31	0.44
O2-F8	-0.30	0.69	0.76	0.00
O2-T4	-1.34	-2.30	-1.03	-1.71
O2-T6	-0.06	-1.71	-0.28	-0.39
F8-T4	0.28	0.18	0.37	-1.75
F8-T6	-0.62	-0.98	-0.19	-0.71
T4-T6	-0.39	-0.72	-0.99	-2.17

Interhemispheric: HOMOLOGOUS PAIRS

	DELTA	THETA	ALPHA	BETA
FP1-FP2	0.73	0.55	0.57	0.96
C3-C4	0.21	-0.26	-0.04	-0.10
O1-O2	-0.70	-1.26	-1.14	-0.90
T3-T4	-0.62	-1.25	-1.18	-0.52

	DELTA	THETA	ALPHA	BETA
F3-F4	-0.47	-0.19	0.43	0.65
P3-P4	-0.06	-0.71	-1.52	-1.15
F7-F8	-1.20	-0.21	0.36	0.75
T5-T6	-0.21	-1.80	-1.35	-1.42

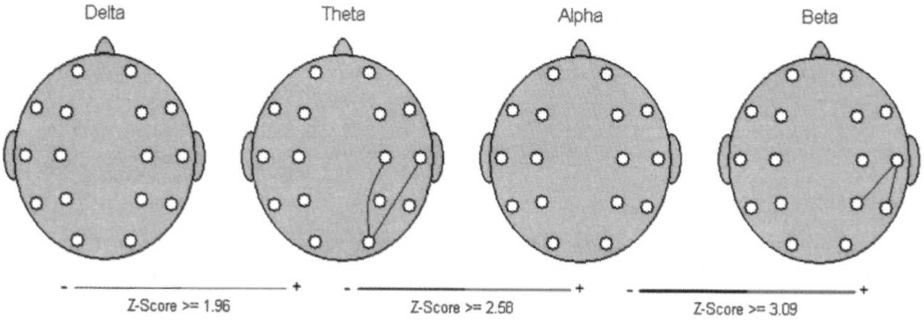

Delta   Theta   Alpha   Beta

Z-Score >= 1.96   Z-Score >= 2.58   Z-Score >= 3.09

Figure 6.7c of client H is an example of NeuroGuide's Coherence Z-Scores. Neuro-Guide shows both lateral and ipsilateral coherence scores called inter-hemispheric and intra-hemispheric, respectively. Figures 6.7c and 6.8c come from the same eyes-closed EEG data. The inter-hemispheric coherence between the homologous pairs T5 and T6 in the alpha range is 1.35 standard deviations below the norm—indicating mild/moderate hypocoherence.

FIGURE 6.8C
NxLINK: POOR ALPHA COHERENCE (Client H)

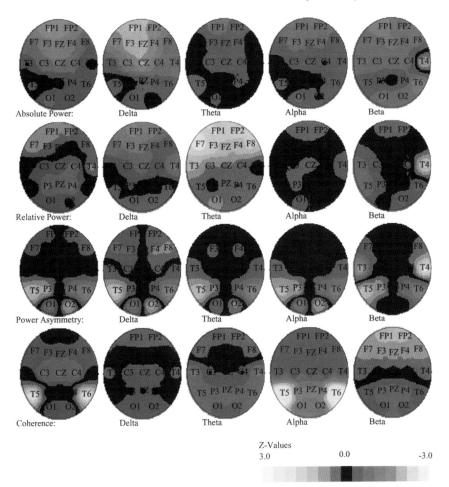

Figure 6.8c is an NxLink brain map that only shows lateral or homologous coherence z-scores for client H. T5 and T6 in the alpha range have a z-value of 3.0 standard deviations below the norm, which means that there is severe hypocoherence. Compare Figure 6.7c with Figure 6.8c. The NeuroGuide (Figure 6.7c) z-score is minus 1.35 whereas the NxLink (Figure 6.8c) z-score is minus 3.0. Why is there a difference? NeuroGuide and NxLink do not use the same normative database—nor do they process data in the exact same way. Consequently, even though the QEEG data is the same for Figures 6.7c and Figure 6.8c the results were different. It is up to the clinician to decide which map is more reliable in this case.

FIGURE 6.9C
NxLINK: DEPRESSION REFLECTED BY ANTERIOR ALPHA (Client I)

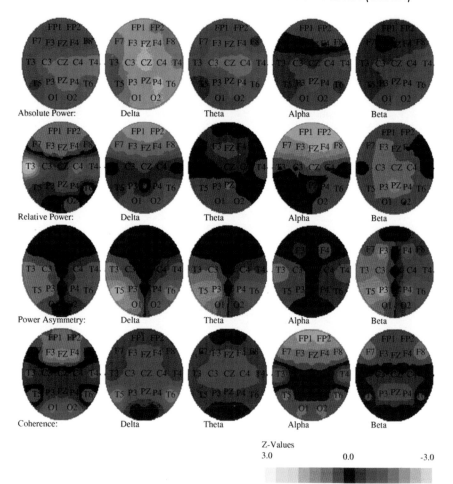

Z-Values
3.0   0.0   -3.0

Figure 6.9c of client I is an eyes-closed NxLink brain map. Relative Power line shows anterior slowing in the alpha range. This client's depression was reflected by widespread frontal alpha. Notice that the Relative Power line is more exacting than the Absolute Power line. Client I's learning disorder was reflected in the beta range of both the Relative Power and the Power Asymmetry lines. It responded well to EEG-neurofeedback. Alpha was downtrained at Fz and beta was downtrained at Pz/P3. HEG-neurofeedback was contraindicated because theta is not significantly greater than beta.

FIGURE 6.10C
NxLINK: ADHD REFLECTED BY ELEVATED CENTRAL THETA (Client J)

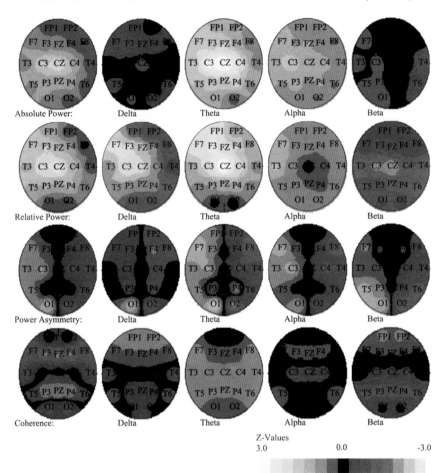

Figure 6.10c of client J is an eyes-closed NxLink brain map. Both the Relative Power and the Absolute Power lines agree—client J has too much theta. However, only the Relative Power line shows the dearth of beta. Client J responded well to EEG-neurofeedback downtraining theta and rewarding beta at Cz. However, J is also a fine candidate for HEG-neurofeedback because of the presence of frontal slowing. This is a classic example of attention deficit disorder that could have been readily diagnosed using a CSA or raw EEG data. Theta-to-beta ratios exceed 3:1.

FIGURE 6.11C
NEUROGUIDE: ADHD REFLECTED BY ELEVATED 10–17 Hz
IN POSTERIOR CINGULATE (Client K)

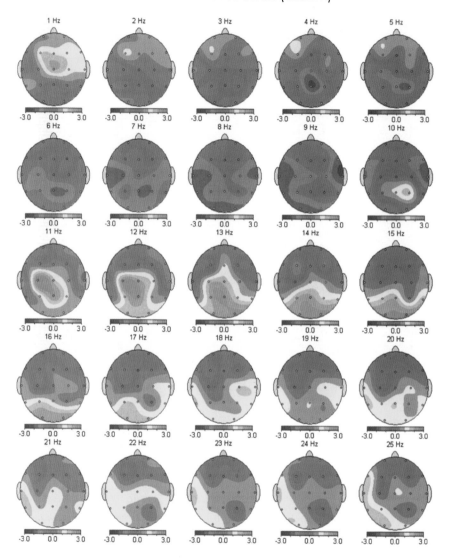

Figure 6.11c of client K is an eyes-open laplacian, relative, single hertz bins brain map processed by NeuroGuide normative database software. Posterior single hertz bins from 10–17 Hz are coded red. Client K has a "hot" posterior cingulate. Client K has symptoms of hyperactivity, mild insomnia and anxiety. Downtraining 10-17 hertz with a bipolar montage (Cz-Pz) was productive. The Appendix (Item #1) includes a diagnostic review of the raw data of 19 scalp locations.

FIGURE 6.12C
NxLINK: DEPRESSION REFLECTED BY ALPHA/THETA SYMMETRY (Client L)

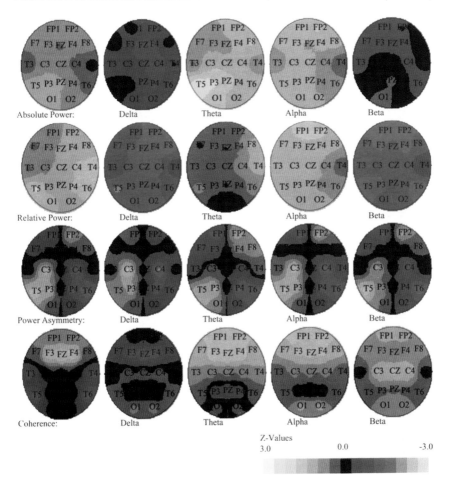

Figure 6.12c of client L is an eyes-closed NxLink brain map. The Power Asymmetry line shows a posterior alpha asymmetry common to depression. This adult client has widespread slowing and a dearth of beta. Figures 6.12c through 6.16c are additional brain maps that pertain to client L. The diagnosis is major depression, mild anxiety as well as an OCD spectrum disorder. The non-specificity of NxLink is a concern—single hertz bins would help to isolate specific frequencies. An eyes-open brain map would also help to round out the overall picture. NxLink in its written data format indicated that this client has an approximate dominant alpha frequency of about 9 Hz, which is below the norm.

The reader is encouraged to compare all 6 graphic presentations. The Appendix (Item #2) includes a diagnostic review of the raw data of 19 scalp locations.

FIGURE 6.13C
NEUROGUIDE LAPLACIAN MAP: DEPRESSION AND OCD SPECTRUM DISORDER (Client L)

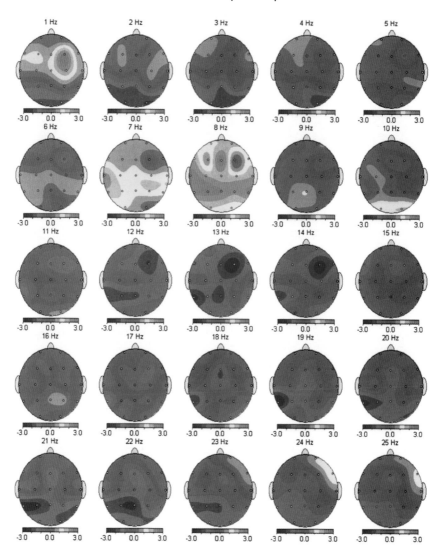

Figure 6.13c is laplacian eyes-closed single hertz bins map of client L processed by NeuroGuide normative database software. It isolates 6–9 Hz in the posterior LH. Thus, portions of both theta (4–8 Hz) and alpha (8–12 Hz) are contributing to the problem. Single hertz bins clarified the NxLink presentation in Figure 6.12c. Additionally, only this laplacian map, Figure 6.13c, makes it clear that Fz is a hot spot. Likely, client L's OCD spectrum disorder is reflected at Fz, which is part of the cingulate gyrus.

FIGURE 6.14C
NEUROGUIDE LINKEARS MAP: LESS SPECIFIC THAN 6.13C (Client L)

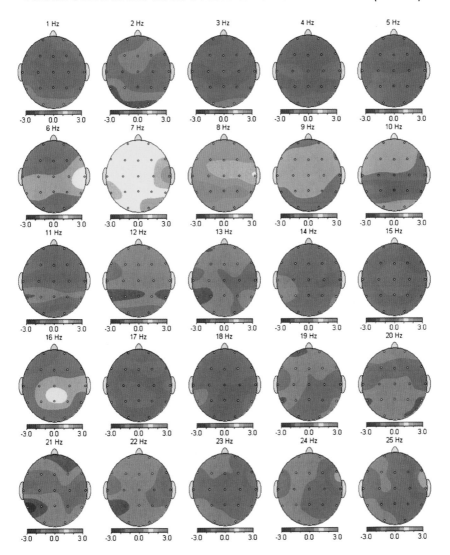

Figure 6.14c is a linkears eyes-closed single hertz bins map of client L. It is less specific than the laplacian map in Figure 6.13c. It does not isolate Fz as a problem area. But it does make it clear that 6–9 Hz are the problem frequencies.

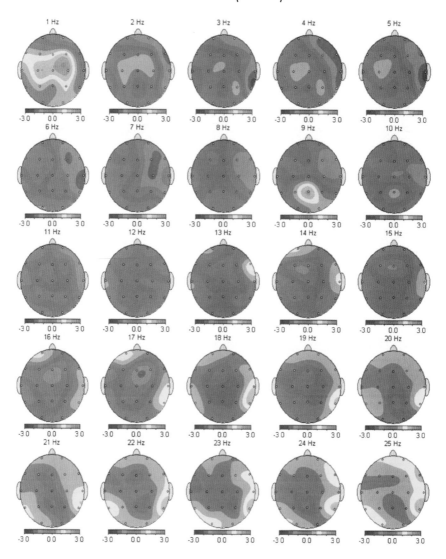

Figure 6.15c is a laplacian, eyes-open, single hertz bins map of client L. Other than 9 Hz at Pz the eyes-open map is relatively normal. Client L needs to do most of his training with eyes-closed. Client L's series of brain maps teach us that an eyes-closed map is not necessarily similar to an eyes-open map. However, sometimes eyes-open and eyes-closed maps are quite similar. All training for client L was therefore done with eyes-closed. No eyes-open training was attempted.

FIGURE 6.16C
NEUROGUIDE: TRAUMATIC BRAIN INJURY DISCRIMINANT ANALYSIS
(Client L)

TBI DISCRIMINANT SCORE = -0.69   TBI PROBABILITY INDEX = 75.0%

The TBI Probability Index is the subject's probability of membership in the mild traumatic brain injury population. (see Thatcher et al, EEG and Clin. Neurophysiol., 73: 93-106, 1989.)

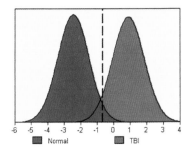

			RAW	Z
FP1-F3	COH	Theta	84.59	0.14
T3-T5	COH	Beta	57.89	0.74
C3-P3	COH	Beta	76.05	-0.07
FP2-F4	PHA	Beta	0.15	-1.04
F3-F4	PHA	Beta	0.05	-1.34
F4-T6	AMP	Alpha	-32.45	0.12
F8-T6	AMP	Alpha	-77.93	0.29
F4-T6	AMP	Beta	11.70	0.31
F8-T6	AMP	Beta	-20.19	0.99
F3-O1	AMP	Alpha	-108.99	-0.62
F4-O2	AMP	Alpha	-118.14	-0.68
F7-O1	AMP	Alpha	142.76	0.63
F4-O2	AMP	Beta	-82.51	-1.03
P3	RP	Alpha	67.35	0.68
P4	RP	Alpha	67.39	0.66
O1	RP	Alpha	74.20	0.79
O2	RP	Alpha	76.84	0.87
T4	RP	Alpha	44.18	0.22
T5	RP	Alpha	68.77	0.98
T6	RP	Alpha	68.52	0.64

TBI SEVERITY INDEX = 3.77

This severity score places the patient in the MODERATE range of severity.

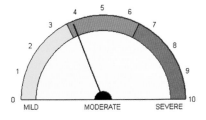

			RAW	Z
FP1-C3	COH	Delta	45.61	-0.76
FP1-FP2	COH	Theta	93.47	1.16
O1-F7	COH	Alpha	48.63	0.85
O2-T6	COH	Alpha	82.00	-0.39
P3-O1	COH	Beta	66.96	-0.93
FP1-T3	PHA	Theta	1.80	-0.39
T3-T4	PHA	Theta	-6.35	-0.56
O1-F7	PHA	Alpha	-45.11	1.06
F7-F8	PHA	Alpha	0.04	-1.73
T5-T6	PHA	Beta	0.24	-1.60
C3-F7	AMP	Delta	43.85	0.16
FP2-F4	AMP	Delta	21.80	0.73
C4-F8	AMP	Delta	11.36	-1.02
O1-O2	AMP	Theta	13.14	0.81
P3-F7	AMP	Alpha	130.13	0.50
FP2-P4	AMP	Alpha	-80.72	-0.08

The TBI Severity Index is an estimate of the neurological severity of injury. (see Thatcher et al, J. Neuropsychiatry and Clinical Neuroscience, 13(1): 77-87, 2001.)

*Statement of Indications of Use:
The Discriminant Analysis and Severity Index are to be used by experienced and qualified professionals for the post-hoc statistical evaluation of the human electroencephalogram (EEG). The Discriminant Analysis and Severity Index are to be viewed as an adjunct to the evaluation of the patient, and they do not serve as a primary basis for a diagnosis. Warning: Inclusion criteria of a history of traumatic brain injury and greater than 13 years of age must be adhered to.

Figure 6.16c is the NeuroGuide Traumatic Brain Injury (TBI) Discriminant Analysis for client L. It indicates a 75% probability of a mild traumatic brain injury. It suggests a reason for the low dominant alpha indicated by the NxLink map. The TBI analysis did not change the training but it can be useful for clients who want to know why they are having so many difficulties.

FIGURE 6.17C
EEG SIGNATURES FOR ADD

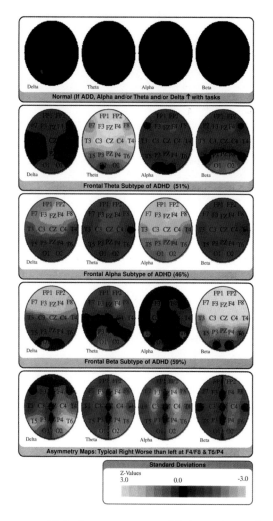

The EEG signatures are NxLink representations of Relative Power data. The first line is black and therefore normative. However each line indicates a different presentation for attention deficit disorder (ADD). Many therapists equate ADD with high theta-to-beta ratios but ADD is not limited to that configuration. It is unwise to assume EEG slowing. Data must confirm the rationale for protocol selection. QEEG data processed by normative database software have helped to create QEEG signatures to demonstrate typical EEG representations of specific disorders.

(Reprinted by permission of Robert Gurnee and the ADD Clinic of Scottsdale, Arizona.)

FIGURE 6.18C
EEG SIGNATURES FOR ANXIETY DISORDERS

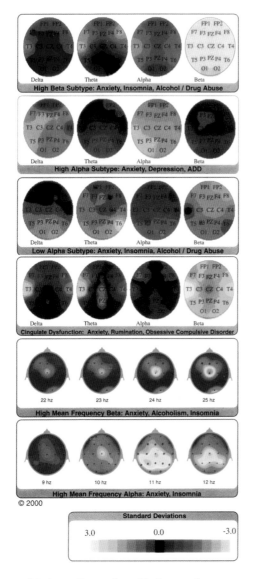

NxLink presentations of Relative Power data. High mean frequency topographical maps are also included. Notice that clients with anxiety disorder may have other comorbid conditions. The last two lines show the importance of knowing the high mean frequency or dominant frequency for both alpha and beta. High dominant alpha and beta frequencies are associated with anxiety and insomnia. Low dominant alpha and beta frequencies (not depicted here) are noted for poor cognitive processing, learning disorders and in some cases neurological dysfunction.

(Reprinted by permission of Robert Gurnee and the ADD Clinic of Scottsdale, Arizona.)

FIGURE 6.19C
EEG SIGNATURE FOR ADD

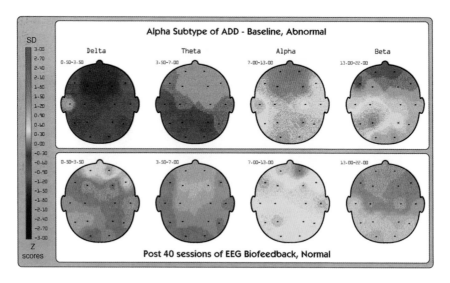

The following map is useful in showing the change that may come with neurofeedback training. This child's ADD was reflected by high amplitude anterior alpha. Forty training sessions transformed the unhealthy brain wave pattern into a healthy one. The corresponding IVA scores in Figure 6.20c verify that the change in the EEG was also accompanied by enhanced cognitive performance.

I invite the reader to compare this topographical brain map with the SPECT study that is shown in the book Healing ADD by Daniel Amen (2001, p.155). Both demonstrate the power of neurofeedback to transform cerebral metabolism without the use of medication.

(Reprinted by permission of Robert Gurnee and the ADD Clinic of Scottsdale, Arizona.)

FIGURE 6.20C
INTERMEDIATE VISUAL AND AUDITORY (IVA) TEST SCORES FOR CHILD
IN FIGURE 6.19C

Before:

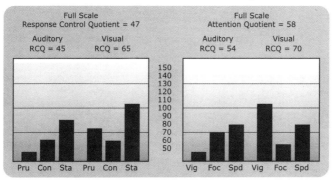

After:

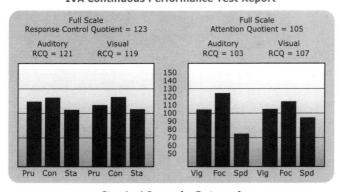

Standard Scores for Factors of
Prudence, Consistency & Stamina   +   Vigilance, Focus & Speed

These IVA score presentations demonstrate the change that so often comes with neurofeedback training to improve attention and focusing. Children and adults with attention deficit disorder typically receive a continuous performance test. Most neurofeedback providers use the IVA or the Test of Variables of Attention (TOVA).

(Reprinted by permission of Robert Gurnee and the ADD Clinic of Scottsdale, Arizona.)

FIGURE 6.21C
NEUROGUIDE: ARTIFACTS LIMITED THE VALUE OF THIS RELATIVE MAP
(Client M)

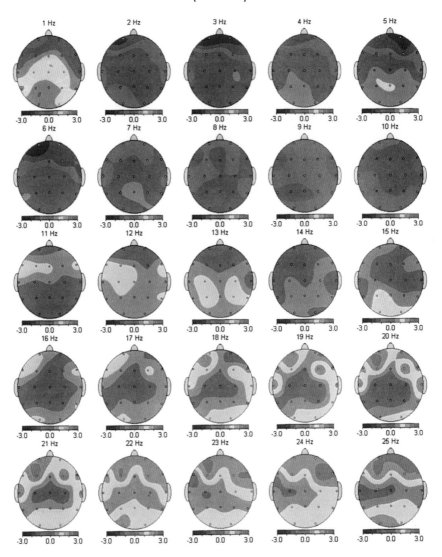

Figures 6.21c and 6.22c compare one linkears relative map with one linkears absolute map for an adolescent (client M). The relative map indicates excessive anterior (frontal lobe) beta whereas the absolute map suggests a combination of anterior theta as well as anterior beta. While acquiring quantitative electroencephalograph (QEEG) data I observed that this youngster had scalp and forehead tension. More was needed than 6.21c and 6.22c in order to determine if this was primarily a slow wave or a fast wave disorder. The deciding answer came from topographical brain map 6.23c identified a low dominant brain wave frequency.

FIGURE 6.22C
NEUROGUIDE: ARTIFACTS DID NOT LIMIT THE VALUE OF THIS ABSOLUTE MAP (Client M)

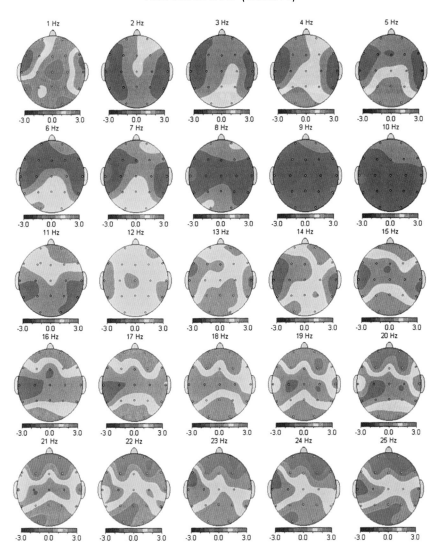

This absolute map, 6.22c, indicates prefrontal RH EEG slowing that is common with As-peger's disorder. Likely, client M also has a posterior fast wave disorder. HEG neurofeedback in the frontal lobes combined with the 2-channel training beta/SMR training at C3 and C4 helped to raise this adolescent's Intermediate Visual and Auditory (IVA) and MicroCog scores. Additional training was also done in the parietal lobes to reduce the evident posterior fast wave disorder.

FIGURE 6.23C
NEUROREP AQR AND LOW MEAN BRAINWAVE FREQUENCY (Client M)

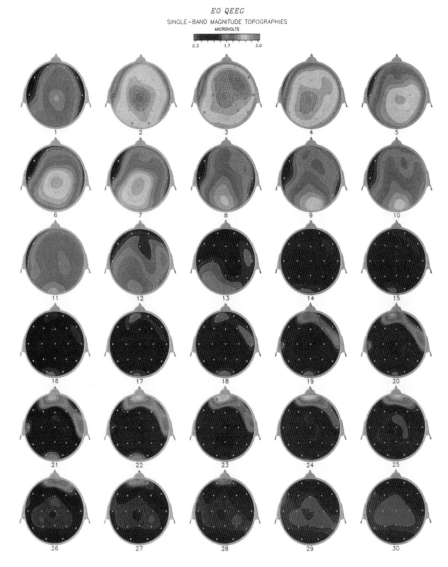

EO QEEG
SINGLE–BAND MAGNITUDE TOPOGRAPHIES
MICROVOLTS
0.3   1.7   3.0

Figure 6.23c is not derived from a normative database. It is a comparison of magnitude or amplitude readings from each of the typical 19 scalp locations. It shows that the mean (similar, but not exactly the same as dominant) brainwave frequency is well below 10 Hz. Figure 6.23c is an example of one of William J, Hudspeth's NeuroRep Adult QEEG Reference (AQR) Database reports. Knowing that this adolescent (client M) has a low mean brainwave frequency made it likely that this was a case of anterior slowing combined with a posterior fast wave disorder.

Some children have been given a battery of tests by the school or private psychologists. It's no wonder that many parents balk at the idea of more testing. I explain that, one of the purposes of testing is to establish a clinical baseline that we can use to monitor progress. If parents complain by saying that the school has already tested their child. I counter that the school will not reevaluate after every 10 or 15 training sessions. Furthermore, they rarely administer continuous performance tests that provide precise measurements of attention and reaction time.

Intermediate Visual Auditory. The Intermediate Visual Auditory (IVA), by BrainTrain (Sandford, 1995), is a continuous performance test that helps identify problems of attention, hyperactivity, and impulsivity. Written in a Microsoft Windows format, it is a tool to evaluate executive functioning. The test taker is instructed to click the mouse every time the number "1" is seen on the computer screen or heard through the speakers. Reaction time, accuracy, and consistency are all-important components of the test. The IVA identifies most children and adults who have trouble sustaining attention. Some individuals with ADD/ADHD, however, achieve an average to above-average score. Distraction and inattention in life are not the same as test taking. Test taking can be stimulating and challenging. Coping skills can be powerful enough to last for 15 to 20 min of testing. The entire computerized test including warm-up and cool-down cycles takes about 20 min. The results are ready for printing and review with the client immediately after the test ends. Scores are evaluated according to a normative database. After seeing the standard IVA printed report, I often hear a parent say something like this: "How could a 15-minute test describe my child so well?" Often that same caring parent had already spent large sums of money on psychological testing. Note: I don't show poor results to children. Figure 9.1 represents before and after results of treatment.

The IVA software produces a multipage written report and graphics. The graphics are straightforward and readily understood by adults and teenagers. They serve to confirm the existence of a problem. One sufferer of traumatic brain injury (TBI) questioned the seriousness of her problem—that is, until she saw her baseline IVA scores. Another adolescent questioned the value of neurofeedback training, until he compared his before and after IVA scores (Figure 9.1 reflects the benefit of just 15 sessions of HEG neurofeedback training). In most cases, the attention quotient (AQ) score improves faster than the response control quotient (RCQ) score. Typically,

FIGURE 9.1
IVA: PRE- AND POST-TREATMENT

BEFORE NEUROFEEDBACK TRAINING

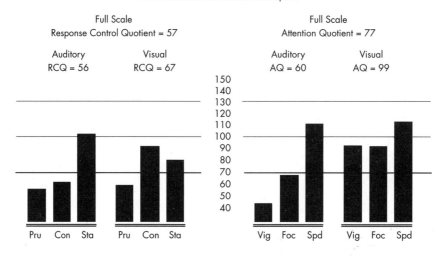

IVA Continuous Performance Test Report

AFTER NEUROFEEDBACK TRAINING (15 SESSIONS)

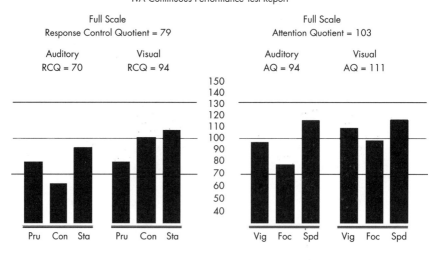

IVA Continuous Performance Test Report

The IVA continuous performance test is copyright by BrainTrain, Inc.

inattention improves somewhat faster than impulsivity. Major differences between auditory and visual scores should be factored into the neurological picture.

It's important to have a general understanding of the main heading and subheadings of the IVA. The RCQ has three measures that reflect general impulse control. The full-scale attention quotient has three measures that reflect attention and rate of response to stimuli. Scores are broken down into visual and auditory fields. In general a score of 80 or below suggests ADD/ADHD. The IVA interpretation manual provides the clinician with diagnostic guidelines to interpret test results. The test assesses attention and hyperactivity in a simultaneous auditory and visual format. Multipage reports can be given to school officials, insurance companies, and state agencies. One standard deviation is 15 points. A score of 100 generally relates to an IQ of 100. IQ scores that are 20 points greater than IVA scores suggest the presence of ADHD. IVA tests and retests can be used in a number of ways:

- Baseline measures for attention and hyperactivity
- Diagnostic support
- Treatment goals met (retest)
- Efficacy of treatment

If a child is on stimulant medication, there are different test-taking strategies. Some clinicians obtain all IVA baselines when the daily dose of medication has *not* been taken. Other clinicians, however, use the on-medication IVA score as a goal. Neurofeedback training continues until off-medication IVA scores equal on-medication scores. (Many neurofeedback providers use another continuous performance test called a Test of Variables of Attention (TOVA), but this test is not reviewed in this book.)

MicroCog. The MicroCog or PsyTest Assessment Management System by the Risk Management Foundation (MS-DOS Version 1, 1993) comes in a short and long format. Some potential clients are not able to endure the longer format. The MicroCog forms an excellent baseline for several areas of brain functioning, including working memory, math calculation, spatial abilities, cognitive processing, and speed. Although the database starts at age 18, I have had appropriate younger persons who are at least 11 years of age take the short form of the test. The goal is to establish a baseline of general cognitive performance. Taking the test a second time will demonstrate change. The younger test taker should be able to read and do basic math and have the maturity to follow written instructions. The MicroCog is a valuable tool in the assessment of TBI, ADD/ADHD, learning disorders, memory problems, reaction time, and general cognitive proficiency.

Herschel Toomim developed a questionnaire based on MicroCog results. It can be found online at www.biocompresearch.org. The Toomim MicroCog questionnaire brings the MicroCog to neurological life. It helps the clinician match poor test scores with discreet areas of the brain. For example, if the client scores poorly in the memory portions of the test, then two sites are recommended for training: T3 and F7.

THE PSYCHOSOCIAL INTERVIEW WITH A BRIEF MEDICAL HISTORY

Other issues may come up during the client's psychosocial evaluation. Important information may be gleaned from the family tree, such as how many people in the family tree have had bipolar disorder, ADD/ADHD, addictions, or chronic depression. Other data may be gathered from report cards (present or past) and school testing results. It is important to find out when the problem started and if it coincided with a particular event or change in the client's life. If there were head injuries, find out the severity of the injury: whiplash? unconsciousness? headaches or migraines? If seizure disorder is present, when was the last time the client had a seizure? Were the seizures generalized, petit mal (absence), or grand mal (tonic, clonic) seizures? How frequent and severe is the problem? Is the client recovering from a stroke? What symptoms are manifest: language problems, emotional problems, and/or paralysis? Hospitalizations, operations, or birth trauma may continue to affect the client's cognitive functioning. For example, some clients report that they have lost their cognitive edge after an operation, possibly a sustained reaction to the anesthesia. The brief medical history should cover the following:

- Prescribed medications
- Over-the-counter (OTC) medications
- Alcohol consumption
- Head injuries (auto accidents)
- Seizure disorder
- Stroke

- Learning disorders
- Developmental disorders
- Memory deficits
- Attention deficits
- Cognitive functioning
- Hearing problems (headphones needed during training?)
- Dissociative disorders, posttraumatic stress disorder (PTSD)
- Axis II disorders (*DSM-IV* checklists)
- Severe psychiatric or neurological disorders

The novice neurofeedback provider will think twice before training someone with any one of the following problems: head injury, seizure, stroke, psychosis, bipolar disorder, autism, fibromyalgia, and severe neurological problems. Typically, a QEEG and/or years of experience are needed to provide effective treatment. Discuss individual cases with your supervisor (mentor).

Alternative Treatments, Commonsense Health, and Neurotherapy

Diet, supplements, vitamins, herbs, lifestyle changes, and alternative treatments can influence our mental powers. Consequently, I introduce my clients to alternative approaches to wellness. I encourage my clients to do *research* on one or more of the following items: arnica, a homeopathic remedy, to heal the internal bruising that comes with head injuries and trauma (Weiner, 1996); alpha lipoic acid plus acetyl-L-carnitine to combat age-related cognitive decline (Nutt, 2003); sensory integration therapy to help the hypersensitive child to integrate the body and the brain (Smith, 2000); omega-3 oils to promote brain health; exercise to increase endorphins; natural progesterone cream and Vitex to reduce the symptoms of premenstrual syndrome (PMS); calcium (1,000 mg) plus magnesium (500 mg) for improved sleep and calmness (2:1 ratio).

Some clients may be referred to a naturopathic doctor (ND) for allergy testing and hormonal imbalances. Allergy or intolerance to milk and wheat is common to many of my ADHD clients. Sugar sensitivity may influence behavior in children and adults (DesMaisons, 1999). Consider pure white refined Stevia as a sugar substitute. Avoid carbonated soda drinks that are high in caffeine, sugar, and phosphates: Amen (2001) and Balch and Balch (2000) both included dietary recommendations and precautions for children with ADD. The articles written by Schnoll, Burshteyn, and Cea-Aravena (1999; 2003) will enlighten the parents of children with ADHD. The following 10 topics apply to many clients:

1. Sleep deprivation can result in symptoms of mental fog and depression.
2. Exercise (aerobic and resistance training) enhances CBF.
3. Eating a balanced diet and having adequate hydration are important; avoid junk foods.
4. Reduce caffeine intake (Hammond, 2003b, pp. 79–89).
5. Vitamins and antioxidants are necessary for brain health.
6. Food intolerance needs to be identified (simple test: Rector-Page, 1994, p. 347).
7. There may be thyroid problems (ibid.).
8. There may be hormonal imbalances (Keville, 1996; Lee & Hopkins, 1996; Martin & Gerstung, 1998).
9. Yeast overgrowth can contribute to mental fog and depression (Crook, 1986).
10. Flaxseed, omega-3, fish, and olive oil are beneficial for brain health (Stoll, 2002; Stordy & Nicholl, 2000).

Neurological Checklist

Psychiatric interviewing, test results, clinical diagnosis, and QEEG data fall under the umbrella of neurological functioning. During the initial interview I make a map based on the client's presenting symptoms. I draw a circle and divide it into four quadrants. I draw a circle at each suspected scalp location. For example, when I ask 12-year-old Peter, "What's 6 times 9?" and Peter snaps back, "54!" I say to myself, "Aha! His working memory just worked!" However, his quick reply caused me to tell him a story. "I know a man who was walking for 6 hours at about 9 miles per hour; I wonder how far he got?" If Peter fails to snap back, or if he looks confused, then I suspect the parietal lobes. Of course, if Peter had trouble doing the initial computation, then EEG slowing at Fp1, F7, and T3 may be the issue. If Peter's mother told me that he tends to worry too much and bites his fingernails, then I suspect the cingulate gyrus. Parents often describe in great detail their child's behavior and cognitive abilities. As they speak, I fill in the paper map. In this case, all suspected sites are marked (Figure 9.2).

FIGURE 9.2
CREATING AN ASSESSMENT HEAD DIAGRAM BASED ON SYMPTOMS

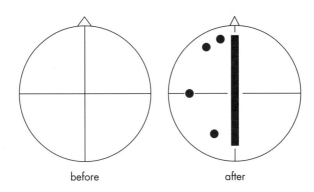

before   after

The reader may wish to consult the neurological checklist at the end of Chapter 2. Use that information to determine what areas of the brain may be functioning poorly. The Amen and Toomim questionnaires also contribute to the neurological picture, although these tests are relative and not absolute in nature—the brain is highly complex and the possibility of neuroplasticity is ever present.

10

Two-Channel Electroencephalograph Assessments and Case Studies

ACCURATE AND COMPREHENSIVE ELECTROENCEPHALOGRAPH (EEG) assessments guide neurofeedback training. They are essential to positive treatment outcomes. Consider some of the ways that EEG data can be gathered:

- single-channel assessments
- two-channel assessments
- nineteen-channel assessments

Single-channel assessments are done with single-channel EEG training systems that can take referential (monopolar) measurements from just one scalp location (see Figure 4.3). The compressed spectral arrays (CSAs) of Chapter 5 were all acquired with a single EEG channel. In order to acquire data from a second scalp location, it is necessary to move the head sensor to a new location and begin the data acquisition processes again. If you wish to obtain data from 10 different scalp locations, it will require 10 different recordings. This method is limited because it does not allow for simultaneous comparisons of contralateral scalp locations. It is also time-consuming.

Two-channel assessments are done with two-channel EEG training systems that can take referential (monopolar) measurements from two different scalp locations at the same time (see Figure 4.7). That means that examining contralateral scalp locations is greatly facilitated. It also means that five recordings can measure the activity in 10 scalp locations. Therefore, two-channel recordings are more efficient than single-channel recordings. (Some training systems have eight channels.)

Nineteen-channel assessments are done with 19-channel quantitative EEG (QEEG) data acquisition systems. That means that one single recording can acquire data from 19 separate locations. It also means that EEG morphology can be examined for the purpose of removing artifacts before the EEG data are processed. Furthermore, the clinician is free to take scalp measurements from fewer than 19 locations. For example, sensors can be mounted at 5, 6, 9, 11, or more locations in the quest for clean EEG data. Lexicor's NeuroSearch-24 has a breakout box that can limit the number of channels being used. This comes in handy for children who cannot sit still for the entire QEEG process. Later, the data from 5 or more channels can be artifacted and examined using Lexicor's V151 software. However, this software is written in DOS and is difficult to master.

WHY ARE TWO-CHANNEL ASSESSMENTS NECESSARY?

QEEG data acquisition is a comprehensive method of data gathering. However, not all clinicians own QEEG data acquisition systems. Thus, it becomes necessary to gather data with whatever equipment is available. Even when you have QEEG equipment, circumstances may hinder data acquisition from all 19 channels. For example, two children were unable to endure the $1\frac{1}{2}$-hr QEEG data acquisition process. On the other hand, they were able to endure a 25-min 2-channel assessment without having an emotional meltdown. The first child had frontal lobe slowing and the second had a gross beta asymmetry in the frontal lobes. The first child trained with hemoencephalography (HEG) neurofeedback and the second with EEG neurofeedback. Both children trained well under task using Paint, a standard Microsoft accessories program. On another occasion an adult wanting to continue treatment started by another reputable provider came to my office with a printed treatment plan in hand. Rather than saying "No map, no treatment," a simple 2-channel assessment came to my aid. It validated the treatment plan and added to it. A working knowledge of neurology plus a 2-channel assessment led to positive outcomes in all three cases.

It is so important to understand the meaning of data and not just the graphics presented by QEEG brain maps. To illustrate, even without a calculator, we have a general sense of the value of the contents in our shopping cart. Most of us know the difference between $60 and $200 worth of groceries at checkout time. We do not blindly accept the cash register's total. In the same way, the data from a two-channel assessment should support the Z-values presented by a topographical brain map (see Chapter 6). In fact, the data acquired by a two-channel training system should embrace the graphics. After all, the graphics are the byproduct of EEG data. Understanding the meaning of the EEG data will come to your aid when the graphics are in question. Topographical brain maps on occasion present a misleading picture. Data coming from a two-channel assessment may be used to verify or to refute brain map presentations. I am *not* saying that the QEEG data can be refuted; rather, I am saying is that the presentation of the data by normative database software may be skewed. Therefore, it must be understood that properly artifacted QEEG data are more accurate than the *un*artifacted data obtained from a two-channel assessment. Do not confuse QEEG data with topographical brain maps.

DATA GATHERING WITH TWO-CHANNEL EEG SYSTEMS

The assessment process is like putting together a jigsaw puzzle. Take it one piece at a time until the clinical picture becomes clear. After one or two evaluations, the step-by-step process will become more automatic. Practice data acquisition and EEG evaluations with cooperative friends and family—it's worth the effort. Good data acquisition and interpretation skills are the foundation for clinical success. Think about it: You are learning how to assess the electrical output of the brain. It is a skill worth learning. In the beginning, you will want to share the data with your supervisor (mentor).

The goal is to create an accurate estimate of cerebral functioning. Clean EEG data is a must. "Garbage in, garbage out" is true. The experienced clinician follows a method or a plan when taking recordings. Organization is the key. The more data acquired at the same time, the better. Many two-channel EEG training systems do not permit the removal of artifacts from the data. Therefore, if the data are questionable, repeat the recording. Furthermore, do not even begin recording the data if the computer graphics show a high degree of variability that reflects movement artifacts. Observe the filtered waves, the raw EEG, and the two-dimensional display for at least a minute. Do not begin recording data if the graphics are jumpy or highly variable. Wait until both the client and the graphics begin to settle down.

Data acquisition with two channels is the process of obtaining a series of 2–3-min recordings from several key scalp locations. Referential montages are used for both channels. Eyes-open and eyes-closed recordings are taken as needed—especially at Cz. The data are organized by predetermined bandwidths. When finished, the data are *printed* to facilitate comparisons. Methodology and neurology guide data acquisition procedures. That means that, to a certain extent, two-channel assessments are customized for each client. However, the first few recordings are the same regardless of the client.

If you have eight filters, set them as follows:

Delta	1–4 Hz
Theta	4–8 Hz
Alpha	8–12 Hz
SMR	12–15 Hz
Beta	13–21 Hz
Beta-1	20–25 Hz
Beta-2	25–30 Hz
Alpha-1	8–10 Hz

Follow the sequence as shown on the sample head (Figure 10.1). Recordings 1, 2, and 3 are mandatory. If they do not paint a clear picture, then take recordings at 4, 5, and 6.

1. Start at the vertex and fan out. Cz is the benchmark recording; it is your first clue. Acquire eyes-closed and eyes-open data to assess the quality of alpha blocking. Closely observe the bandwidth distribution at Cz for high theta-to-beta ratios or just the reverse, high beta-to-theta ratios. See Figures 5.1c, 5.2c, 5.3c, and 5.4c.

2. Take simultaneous anterior and posterior recordings at Pz and Fz, respectively. Normatively speaking, fast waves are anterior dominant while slow waves are posterior dominant. Eyes-closed Pz alpha amplitudes should exceed all other bandwidths. Frontal slowing often relates to depression or attention deficit disorder (ADD), whereas posterior fast-wave dominance relates to insomnia, anxiety,

FIGURE 10.1
PROTOCOL FOR A 2-CHANNEL EEG ASSESSMENT

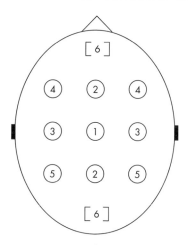

and obsessive-compulsive disorder (OCD). Review Figures 5.7c and
5.8c.

3. Take simultaneous contralateral recordings at the in-between sites
   T3/C3 and T4/C4. What did you find? Asymmetries? (See Figures
   5.5c and 5.6c.) Did the total amplitudes drop as you moved away
   from the vertex? Is theta relatively the same in both hemispheres?
   Normative eyes-open theta amplitude will be nearly the same as
   alpha. Normative eyes-closed alpha amplitude will be much greater
   than theta. Usually, beta amplitudes are higher on the left, whereas
   normative alpha amplitudes are equal to or are higher on the right.
   Remind the client to keep his or her jaw loose or relaxed.

Gross asymmetries or abnormal bandwidth distributions should be easy to
find. If not, then steps 4, 5, and 6 will be needed. Anterior and posterior
asymmetries are common. Remember, the data must be clean. Repeat any
recording that is suspect to high amounts of artifact. By this time at least
30–40 min have transpired.

4. Other contralateral recordings are also important. F3/F7 compared
   to F4/F8 will often show alpha and beta asymmetries. If RH beta is
   significantly higher than LH beta, the client likely has anxiety, stress,

or conditions like bruxism. If LH alpha is significantly higher than RH alpha, then the client is likely depressed and/or has ADD.

5. Lastly consider P3/T5 compared to P4/T6. Posterior alpha asymmetries are common in depression. Fast wave and slow wave asymmetries may be found in dyscalculia, learning disorders, or poor spatial processing. Posterior left is for word recognition whereas posterior right is for face recognition. Check the dominant brain frequency (also called the posterior dominant rhythm). Adult clients with age related cognitive decline and depression often have a dominant alpha frequency well below 10 Hz. Furthermore, the dominant brainwave frequency should be relatively the same in both hemispheres, if not suspect poor cognitive processing.

6. This is the last test. It relates to both HEG and EEG neurofeedback. Check the frontal poles (Fpz) and the occipital lobes (Oz) for EEG slowing. Look carefully at Lubar's chart in Figure 5.11 to determine ratios for anterior and posterior *ventral* slow-wave disorders—his chart is based on eyes-closed measurements. Whenever eyes-open recordings are taken at the frontal poles, muscle and eye-movement artifact must be minimized. If you wish to take an eyes-open recording, have the subject look down and stare at a singular object in the room. Instruct the subject to avoid eye movement.

By now over an hour has transpired and more time will be required to examine the data and come to conclusions.

In some cases an elevated theta-to-beta ratio can only be seen under task. Keep in mind that normative theta-to-beta ratios are lower at all *ventral* scalp locations including the frontal poles. The following is a summary of potential EEG abnormalities:

- Slow-wave disorder (ranging from 0 to 10 Hz)
- Fast-wave disorder (ranging from 13 to 32 Hz)
- High theta-to-beta ratio (greater than 3:1 or 2.5:1 for frontal poles)

  ○ hypoperfusion or inadequate regional cerebral blood flow (rCBF)

- Poor alpha blocking (alpha does not drop when eyes-open)
- EEG slowing under task (slow waves increase under task)
- Abnormal distribution of standard bandwidths

  ○ Theta > alpha (eyes-closed)
  ○ Beta > theta

- Gross contralateral asymmetry (BAT triad)

    - Right hemisphere (RH) beta > left hemisphere (LH) beta (depression, anxiety, etc.)
    - LH alpha > RH alpha (depression)
    - RH theta ≠ LH theta (depression, anxiety, ADD)

- Gross anterior-to-posterior imbalance

    - Posterior beta > anterior beta (insomnia, anxiety, hyperactivity)
    - Anterior alpha > posterior alpha (depression, ADD)

- Dominant alpha frequency

    - Alpha < 9.0–9.5 Hz (possible cognitive deficits)
    - Alpha > 11 Hz (anxiety/insomnia suspect)
    - Normative dominant alpha frequency LH = RH (approx.)

- Dominant or mean brain wave frequency

    - 10 Hz is normative

Several case studies will exemplify the method shown above. They have been simplified to demonstrate the power of two-channel assessments. They were customized to fit the client's diagnosis and neurological presentation. Consequently, not all of the regions listed on my chart were used. I stopped checking when it became apparent that the assessment had done the job. I felt confident that the EEG assessment was sufficient. Before and after IVA scores are provided in both cases.

Case Study #1

A 10-year-old child came to my office with the diagnosis of ADD. The ADD diagnosis was supported by an Intermediate Visual and Auditory (IVA) score response control quotient (RCQ) of 112 and attention quotient (AQ) of 46. The neurological checklist indicated that the problem was likely centered along the anterior cingulate gyrus. Three minutes of data were recorded in both the eyes-open and eyes-closed condition. Channel 1 records measurements at Cz, whereas channel 2 measures Fz. I have filled in Table 10.1 using actual readings. The theta-to-beta ratio was determined using power rather than amplitude or microvolts.

TABLE 10.1
High Theta-to-Beta Ratio

BANDWIDTH	EYES-CLOSED		EYES-OPEN	
	CHANNEL 1 (Cz)	CHANNEL 2 (Fz)	CHANNEL 1 (Cz)	CHANNEL 2 (Fz)
Theta (4–8 Hz)	29.5	26.0	27.4	21.3
Alpha (8–12 Hz)	25.3	19.1	17.0	16.3
SMR (12–15 Hz)	5.1	5.0	5.8	5.8
Beta (13–21 Hz)	12.9	14.0	12.1	12.6
High beta (20–30 Hz)	10.3	12.7	10.1	10.5
Power— theta/beta ratio	5.2:1	3.4:1	5.1:1	2.9:1
Dominant alpha Frequency	9.2	9.1	9.0	9.0

Discussion. Table 10.1 demonstrates a high theta-to-beta ratio that peaks at Cz. The theta-to-beta ratio exceeds 5:1, which places the subject in the ADD population (Figure 5.9). There is a sharp drop in the ratio at Fz, but it still reflects the diagnosis of ADD. Theta amplitudes are higher than alpha amplitudes, even in the eyes-closed state. Clearly, theta is the problem. This is a slow-wave disorder. Alpha blocking is normal because there is a sharp decrease in alpha amplitudes in the eyes-open state. My equipment allows for the assessment of dominant frequencies. Beta dominant frequencies were acceptable. Alpha dominant frequencies were low. Sometimes, I take a third recording to see if either theta or alpha increases under task. However, there was no need to do this since the theta-to-beta ratios met the criteria for ADD. Training protocols centered on theta inhibition at Cz. Training was conducted with eyes-open and under task (reading or playing solitaire).

Training with EEG neurofeedback was chosen over HEG neurofeedback due to the high theta-to-beta ratio at Cz. Theta-to-beta ratios were about 3:1 at Fz. Likely, the frontal poles also had high amplitudes of theta. Therefore, HEG neurofeedback was another possible training modality. This case study was an example of a classic EEG abnormality. There was a high theta-to-beta ratio along the cingulate gyrus. It was readily detected with a two-channel system. When LH and RH measurements were compared, no asymmetrical patterns were observed.

The chosen EEG neurofeedback protocol selection was to downtrain theta at Cz for 35 min with eyes-open while under task. Other protocols may have been selected:

- Ratio training (decrease theta-to-beta [4–8 Hz/15–20 Hz] ratio)
- Two-filter training (reward 15–20 Hz beta; inhibit theta)
- Three-filter training (reward beta; inhibit theta and high beta)

After 32 sessions the IVA AQ scores rose 49 points, from 46 to 95. Anecdotal reports from the family indicated better concentration and less school anxiety.

Case Study #2

Case study #2 is an example of an EEG assessment leading to a successful deployment of HEG neurofeedback training. The subject was in late teens. The ADD/ADHD symptom checklist and the Amen questionnaire were unrevealing. Math deficits (dyscalculia) were reported, although high school performance was otherwise average to above average. No hyperactivity, impulsivity, oppositional behavior, or conduct problems came out during the interview. School test anxiety was mild to moderate. The subject was motivated to increase the ability to sustain attention and improve reaction time and math competence. The IVA scores were as follows: RCQ of 101, whereas AQ of 70. Figure 10.2 shows the results of the MicroCog.

MicroCog and IVA results were quite revealing. Reasoning/calculation, reaction time, information processing accuracy, general cognitive proficiency, math, and numbers forward were all in the low-average to below-average range. According to the Toomim MicroCog Questionnaire, the following 10–20 positions were suspect: Fp1, F7, and T3. Fp1 and F7 were singled out because of their association with working memory, whereas T3 related more to long-term memory. Problems with math calculations are most likely a problem in the parietal lobes. However, the parietal lobes can't do their job properly unless the prefrontal lobes have zoomed on the problem and sent data back to the parietal lobes. The IVA scores supported the notion that the subject could not sustain attention. Most likely, this is a LH problem.

The next task was to see if site-specific EEG recordings would lend further support to the MicroCog report. Measurements were taken in multiple scalp locations using my 2-channel system. Cz, the benchmark recording was compared to Fz. The sites coming from the MicroCog analysis

FIGURE 10.2
MICROCOG SCORES

	Sum	SS	%ile	Sig Diff	95% Conf.	Reference Group Norms
						50 70 85 100 115 150
						Below Average / Low Ave. / Average / Above Average
LEVEL 1						
Attention/Mental Control	39	98	45	Y	83–113	
Reasoning/Calculation	29	77	6	Y	64– 90	
Memory	65	107	68	Y	96–118	
Spatial Processing	22	107	68	N	92–122	
Reaction Time	13	62	1	Y	51– 73	
LEVEL 2						
Information Processing Speed	60	100	50	Y	93–107	
Information Processing Accuracy	67	86	18	Y	75– 97	
LEVEL 3						
General Cognitive Functioning	186	91	27	N	83– 99	
General Cognitive Proficiency	44	83	13	Y	75– 91	

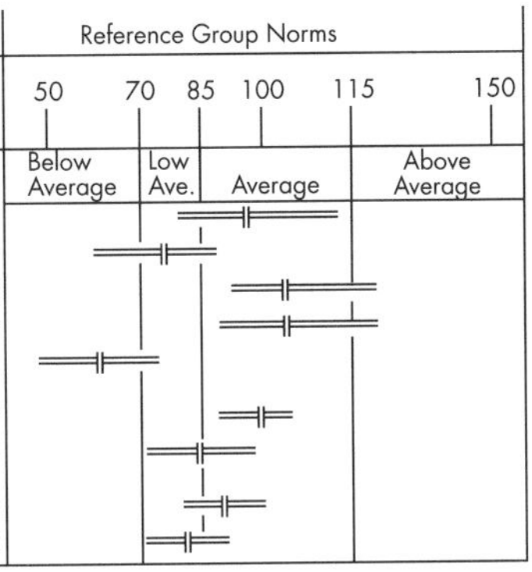

REFERENCE GROUP NORMS

PROFICIENCY SCORES	RS	SS	95% Conf.	Below Ave.	Low Ave.	Ave.	Above Ave.
Numbers Forward	7.7	6	3– 9		X		
Numbers Reversed	–	–	–				
Story Immediate Recall	4.2	8	5–11			X	
Story Delayed Recall	9.6	8	6–10			X	
Clocks	3.8	10	7–13			X	
TicTac	–	–	–				
Analogies	2.9	8	5–11			X	
Math	0.9	4	1– 7	X			
Object Match A	–	–	–				
Object Match B	–	–	–				

MicroCog: Assessment of Cognitive Functioning is sold by Harcourt Assessment, Inc. It is copy-write by the Risk Management Foundation of the Harvard Medical Institutions, Inc.

were checked in concert with their contralateral partners: Fp1 & Fp1–F7 & F8–T3 & T4. The results are posted in Tables 10.2 and Table 10.3.

Review of Table 10.2 and Table 10.3

LH theta-to-beta ratios were higher than RH ratios (e.g., F7 > F8). Anterior theta-to-beta ratios were higher than central ratios (e.g., Fz > Cz). Theta was equal to or greater than alpha in the eyes closed state. This case study represents a good example of LH slowing in general with an emphasis on the prefrontal lobes. I decided to train using HEG-neurofeedback at Fp2, Fp1, FP7 as well as T3. After 8 sessions the IVA Attention Quotient (AQ) scores rose 32 points, from 70 to 102. More importantly, there were positive changes in reaction time and schoolwork proficiency.

TABLE 10.2
Dorsal Theta-to-Beta Ratios

	EYES-CLOSED		EYES-OPEN	
BANDWIDTH	CHANNEL 1 (Cz)	CHANNEL 2 (Fz)	CHANNEL 1 (Cz)	CHANNEL 2 (Fz)
Theta (4–8 Hz)	20.4	20.2	15.8	15.9
Alpha (8–12 Hz)	20.5	16.8	17.5	15.1
SMR (12–15 Hz)	7.2	7.0	6.0	6.0
Beta (13–21 Hz)	8.2	7.8	7.6	7.1
High beta (20–30 Hz)	3.9	3.5	3.6	3.4
Power—theta/beta ratio	6.2:1	6.7:1	4.3:1	5:1
Dominant beta freq.	16.0	16.0	16.0	16.0
Dominant alpha freq.	9.0	9.0	9.0	9.0

TABLE 10.3
Ventral Theta-to-Beta Ratios

	EYES-OPEN					
BANDWIDTH	Fp1	Fp2	F7	F8	T3	T4
Theta	9.7	9.2	11.1	9.2	9.4	7.6
Alpha	10.0	9.2	10.2	9.1	11.2	10.4
SMR	3.9	3.9	4.0	4.1	4.2	3.4
Beta	4.7	5.2	3.4	5.5	4.9	4.5
High beta	3.6	4.2	3.4	5.5	2.6	2.5
Power—theta/ beta ratio	4.3:1	3:1	5.1:1	2.3:1	3.7:1	2.9:1

EEG data are drawn from three typical cases. The following three cases A, B and C will likely reflect some of the clients common to most neurofeedback practices. I have included microvolt readings, symptomatology as well as treatment options:

- Client A has a classic alpha asymmetry pattern common to depression. This is an eyes-closed example. Neurofeedback protocols will be designed to reduce left hemisphere alpha and increase beta: inhibit 8–12 Hz & 20–30 Hz but reward 15–18 Hz at F3/F7. Or, apply the alpha-asymmetry protocol.

TABLE 10.4
Alpha Asymmetry (Client A)

BAND	Fz	Cz	F3/F7	F4/F7
Theta	12	11	9	8.5
Alpha	13	15	14.5	12
Beta	7.5	7	6	6
H. B.	6	6.5	5.5	5

- Client B has a beta asymmetry pattern common to anxiety. This is an eyes-closed example. Neurofeedback protocols will be designed to reduce right hemispheric beta and increase beta: Inhibit beta 15–30 Hz at F4/F8; emphasize the need for diaphragmatic breathing.

TABLE 10.5
Beta Asymmetry (Client B)

BAND	Fz	Cz	F3/F7	F4/F7
Theta	13	15	9	10
Alpha	16	18	11	12
Beta	8	7	5	7
H.B.	6	6	4	6

- Client C has a pattern of anterior alpha slowing and elevated posterior fast waves. This is an eyes-closed example. The anterior alpha relates to depression and the posterior beta relates to a LD. I invite the reader to look at the topographical brain map-Figure 6.9 of the color insert.

TABLE 10.6
Anterior Alpha Slowing and Elevated Posterior Beta (Client C)

BAND	Fz	Cz	Pz	C3	C4
Theta	14	13	11	10	9
Alpha	12.5	14	14	11	11
Beta	12	12	12	9	7.5
SMR	4	5	6	3.5	3.5
H.B.	8	8	7.5	9.5	8

Detailed Discussion of Client C. Deciphering Table 10.6 (Client C), we note the following:

- Normative alpha travels along the cingulate gyrus in the following way with eyes-closed: Pz alpha > Cz > Fz. However, for Client C, Fz alpha rivals Pz alpha.
- The eyes-closed theta-to-beta ratio (Cz) is nearly 1:1 instead of 1.6:1 suggesting that there is too much beta (Montgomery et. al, 1998).
- Normative beta should yield the following pattern: Fz beta > Pz beta. Clearly the data shows Fz beta = Pz beta.
- On the other hand, this client has the normative theta pattern because Fz theta ≥ Cz theta.

Also, C3 (LH) theta is nearly the same as C4 (RH) theta, again within normal limits.

The successful treatment protocols were as follows: Inhibit eyes-closed alpha at Fz for 15 minutes followed by inhibit eyes-open 13–25 Hz beta at Pz/P3 for 15 minutes. This client made a number of positive changes: depression remitted. Needless to say, this client was *not* a candidate for the alpha asymmetry protocol. *Nor* was HEG-neurofeedback indicated. Clearly, the topographical brain map (6.9c) was much easier to interpret than the simple unprocessed microvolt data.

Common EEG Problems and Neurological Functions

The following list is a brief summary of EEG problems and neurological concerns. It is a partial list:

EEG
- Theta-to-beta ratios, especially at Cz
- Compare Fz with Pz

  - Anterior slowing? (1–10 Hz)
  - Posterior fast wave problem (10–30 Hz)

- Compare LH with RH

  - BAT triad irregularities

Neurology
- LH relates to poor cognitive processing and depression
- RH relates to social skills, anxiety, and spatial processing
- Z line relates to flexibility, attention and worry.

CONCLUSION

2-channel assessments can be valuable guides when assessing clients. If you would like more practice, feel free to consult the appendix. I have included peak-to-peak microvolt data for two of the topographical brain maps in the color insert. It is the same kind of data that would be acquired from a 2-channel assessment. 19-channels of artifacted-data are given for each case. Compare the manual EEG data assessment with the graphics of the topographical brain map. Two channel assessments have great value. They can find gross abnormalities, lateral asymmetries, posterior-to-anterior differences as well as theta-to-beta ratios. However, the following items are likely beyond the reach of the method shown above:

- Hot spots (Single hertz bins)
- Hypocoherence
- Hypercoherence
- Less-than-gross EEG abnormalities

QEEG recordings with normative database software will show hot spots that may elude 2-channel assessments. They can reveal mild-to-moderate, moderate and gross problems. In preparation for this book, I reviewed over a dozen cases with topographical brain maps. The original QEEG data was artifacted and processed with peak-to-peak microvolts within the common bandwidths such as theta, alpha, beta, etc. Thus, the EEG data was now in a form that resembled the data I ordinarily acquire from my 2-channel training system. All this had to be done because normative database software does not provide the user with simple amplitude readings. So, this was the first time, I had seen the original raw QEEG data. Quite frankly, in some cases, the raw data microvolt data did not present a clear picture. Topographical brain maps can isolate specific problems within specific frequency ranges. QEEG recordings produce 19-channels of simultaneous coverage of the cerebral cortex that can display both numbers and wave morphology. Artifacts can be removed from the raw data resulting in a better recording. However, maps can be misleading at times if you do not understand the meaning of the data. The next chapter will review guidelines for reviewing maps as well as options for protocol selection.

11

Quantitative Electroencephalograph Assessments, Montages, and Protocol Selection

TOPICAL BRAIN MAPS BASED ON normative database software are the most comprehensive means of identifying electroencephalograph (EEG) abnormalities. Clinicians can treat a wider range of problems with a greater degree of confidence. *Quantitative* EEG (QEEG) means that data are acquired from 19 sites—typically. QEEG leads to the production of topographical maps that can be studied by the clinician and shared with the client. QEEG promotes the study of wave morphology. QEEG gives the clinician the opportunity to artifact the data. QEEG, like any other test, is subject to flaws. For example, the process of removing artifacts from QEEG data is an art and not a pure science. Topographical brain maps are only as good as the data are clean. Each software package processes data differently. Each is based on a different sample population. Each has inherent flaws. That is why, it is often necessary to examine more than one software rendition of the same QEEG data.

A MAP IS ONLY AS GOOD AS THE PERSON READING IT

A Training Plan is based on much more than a topographical brain map. It requires information from at least three clinical areas: Diagnosis, EEG data, plus an understanding of Neurology. Hence, TP = D + E + N or DEN. This formula is exemplified by Figures 6.12c and 6.13c. This client's depression is reflected by excessive amounts of 7–8 Hz. Both topographical brain maps indicate EEG slowing in both the left hemisphere (LH) and the right hemisphere (RH). Davidson (1998) asserted that depression often relates to *hypo*activation of the LH, whereas anxiety often relates to *hyper*activation of the RH. Typically, slow waves are inhibited in the LH and fast waves are inhibited in the RH. Neurology guides protocol selection. Therefore, one region of the brain may be chosen while another is ignored, even though both have abnormal Z-values. In this case, EEG slowing in the LH was suppressed, whereas EEG slowing in the RH was ignored.

The ideal brain map locates a few discreet hot spots, or scalp locations with the highest abnormal Z-values. These are the scalp sites that are first chosen for training. Figure 6.13c suggests the following training sites: P3/T5 and Fz. Two specific regions were trained and this first depressed client responded well. (Baseline Beck Depression Index [BD] = 34: after 10 training sessions, BDI = 1.) Depression was the Axis I diagnosis. Obsessive-compulsive disorder (OCD) spectrum disorder was the Axis II diagnosis. The depression went into remission while the characterological disturbance remained. The order of events parallels the cognitive therapy tradition that describes the swing from Axis II to Axis I and then back again (Beck, Freeman & associates, 1990). In this case, posterior LH slowing (P3/T5) related to depression, whereas anterior cingulate (Fz) slowing related to the OCD spectrum disorder. Thus my first goal was to reduce depression. Consequently, 7–9 Hz were inhibited at P3/T5 for 20 min and at Fz for just 10 min. After 10 sessions, this client was no longer depressed, but there was a need for counseling and psychotherapy. After one lengthy talk session, we resumed neurotherapy, but this time Fz and P3/T5 were both trained for 15 min. The new goal was to address the Axis II condition. It would require a combination of counseling and neurotherapy. In fact, the training opened this client up to insights about the self and others. Theoretically, the client could be protected against future swings back into depression, the Axis I condition.

Maps Can Be Misleading

Chapter 6 explained the difference between absolute and relative power. It asserted that relative power maps are more accurate unless the presence of artifact artificially increases amplitude totals. For example, increasing the total amplitude with EMG mixed with beta will have the effect of decreasing the value of slower waves such as alpha 1 (8–10 Hz) and theta (4–8 Hz). Thus, the absolute recording may be more valuable. Figures 6.21c and 6.22c depict one linkears eyes-open single-hertz bins absolute and one linkears relative map for an adolescent. The relative map indicates excessive anterior (frontal lobe) beta whereas the absolute map suggests a combination of anterior theta as well as anterior beta. While acquiring QEEG data I observed that this youngster had scalp and forehead tension. More was needed than 6.21c and 6.22c in order to determine if this was primarily a slow wave or fast wave disorder. The deciding answer came from more than one source. First, psychiatric interviewing combined with my understanding of neurology pointed to a deficit in the right prefrontal lobe. Second, topographical brain map 6.23c identified a low dominant brain wave frequency. Figure 6.23c is not derived from a normative database. It is merely a comparison of magnitude or amplitude readings from each of the typical 19 scalp locations. It clearly shows that the mean (similar, but not exactly the same as dominant) brainwave frequency is well below 10 Hz. Figure 6.23c is an example of one of William J. Hudspeth's *NeuroRep Adult QEEG Reference* (AQR) Database reports. Knowing that this adolescent has a low mean brainwave frequency made it certain that this was a case of anterior slowing combined with a posterior fast wave disorder.

The treatment regimen was as follows. Three 8–10 minute segments of HEG neurofeedback at Fp1, Fpz, and Fp2 started each training session. The Brown and Brown (2000) three step protocol ended the session. Over the next 7 weeks of training at C3 and C4, I watched the mean brainwave frequency climb from an average of 5–8 Hz to an average of 9–10 Hz with bursts of 11 Hz. The parents of this adolescent reported a marked improvement in handwriting skills likely because the sensorimotor cortex governs fine motor skills. HEG neurofeedback training in the frontal lobes improved both social awareness as well as attention. Base IVA scores RCQ of 63 and AQ of 53. Fifteen training sessions over the course of 7 weeks yielded the following scores: RCQ of 104 and AQ of 90. Similar improvements were noted on before and after MicroCog scores. Additional training was required to address the posterior fast wave disorder: T6-O2 was chosen to improve eye—contact; P3 was chosen to improve math skills.

The above case study shows that topographical brain maps may not be enough to isolate a problem. Knowledge of neurology and general EEG characteristics are essential when putting together treatment plans. As you look at the topographical maps in the color insert notice that some maps do not present with an exact spot to train whereas others are very specific. The more specific a map is the easier it is to follow. The more general a map is the more difficult it is to follow. Consequently, choosing the right protocols requires more than just a topographical brain map. That is why, it imperative for the newcomer to the field of neurotherapy, who uses topographical brain maps, to seek out the advice of experts when attempting to artifact and interpret QEEG data.

Two maps are better than one. Experts in reading and interpreting topographical brain maps often examine several different software renditions of the same raw QEEG data before creating a list of protocols. For example, if one NeuroGuide's relative map leans heavily toward a fast-wave disorder while the NeuroRep AQR indicates a low mean brainwave frequency, then a flag should go up. This is but one example of the advantage of having more than one kind of map. Each different database has its own inherent weaknesses and strengths. The following is a list of 5 popular normative database options and their respective websites:

- NxLink (www.advancednts.com/nxlink/nxlink_qeeg_database.htm)
- NeuroGuide (www.appliedneuroscience.com)
- LORETA (www.NovaTechEEG.com)
- NeuroRep AQR (www.neurorep.com)
- SKIL (www.skiltopo.com)

Topographical brain map reports include maps and various data presentations. They do not, however, provide the clinician with raw amplitude data in peak-to-peak microvolts. If they did, then it would be easy to compare QEEG data with the data acquired by the typical two-channel training system. The relationship between the data and the graphics would be easier to discern. Furthermore, in some cases would expose the presence of EMG artifact. For example, it T4 beta was 18 μV while T6 beta was just 6 μV likely there is EMG contamination. Sharp differences in the beta range at ventral scalp sites (e.g., temporal lobes) are likely due to muscle artifact. If one of the reports included peak-to-peak microvolt readings within frequency bandwidths, it may explain why maps are sometimes misleading.

Maps Have the Edge Over Two-Channel Assessments

This case comes from a NeuroGuide, eyes-open, relative, single-hertz bins, Laplacian topographical brain map (Figure 6.11c). A 10-year-old came to my office with the diagnosis of ADD with the parental report of

hyperactivity, insomnia, and mild anxiety. The Amen Attention questionnaire and the Toomin questionnaire were nonspecific. Intermediate Visual
and Auditory (IVA) scores were low: response control quotient (RCQ)
83 and attention quotient (AQ) 74. The general attention deficit disorder
(ADD) behavioral checklist indicated impulse control, inflexibility, worry,
and hyperactivity. Perhaps the cingulate gyrus would reflect the problem.
I took several recordings with my 2-channel system but I could not get a
clear picture. However, I will admit, when I later saw the artifacted peak-
to-peak microvolt data for all 19 channels I could see the problem; it was
clearly identified by the NeuroGuide map.

The eyes-open, relative, Laplacian map indicated excessive 10–17 Hz
in central and posterior locations. The posterior cingulate gyrus was "hot."
This case does *not* resemble the classic hyperactive child who needs *more*
12–15 Hz along the sensorimotor strip or the cingulate gyrus. I definitely
needed the map for this case—one session had already been lost due to
an inadequate 2-channel assessment. With map in hand, my first protocol was 10–17 Hz inhibition with a bipolar montage Cz-Pz. The first
10 training sessions were 27 min long and under task. The 10-year-old
either played Microsoft's Solitaire or read picture books. I kept varying
the task to prevent zoning out or boredom. The IVA score after 10 sessions: RCQ 86 and AQ of 107. The AQ had increased by 33 points or
2 standard deviations. Parents reported improved sleep, better cooperation, and less anxiety.

I chose this case for a number of reasons. It clearly shows the value of
topographical brain maps and the potential flaws that may come with two-
channel assessments. But, I also chose this case because a bipolar montage
was chosen. Montage decisions require a degree of clinical finesse. Topographical brain maps are guides but not leaders in the protocol selection
process. (The appendix includes the artifacted peak-to-peak microvolt data
for this case.)

REFERENTIAL VS. BIPOLAR MONTAGES

More than one correct protocol can be decided in any given situation. But
in the above case study, I had to decide between a referential montage
and a bipolar montage. The most likely place for a referential montage
would have been Pz. Frequency bandwidth selection would have been the
same: 10–17 Hz. But I chose a bipolar montage. Why? The first reason was

logistics. This child was mildly hyperactive. I knew that two electrodes on the scalp would optimize common mode rejection. Bursts of common muscle (EMG) activity would tend to be canceled out. Therefore, the child would be training with more real-time EEG data with less EMG artifact. The second reason requires a longer discussion. The following comments come from experts and writers in the field of QEEG and neurotherapy:

1. Lubar and Lubar (2002) have a straightforward method for deciding between referential and bipolar montages. The following guidelines are made with reference to neurofeedback training for ADHD. Lubar records the theta-to-beta ratio at Cz using a referential montage. Next, a bipolar recording is taken with both active sensors placed on the scalp at locations CPz and CFz. These two locations were not standard 10–20 locations (CPz is midway between Cz and Pz, whereas CFz is midway between Cz and Fz). *The montage that yields the greatest difference* between theta and beta is chosen. Lubar presents one cautionary remark: If you train with a bipolar montage, monitor progress with a bipolar montage. Referential montages may fail to show a change in microvolts. Therefore, check the EEG in the same way that you did the training. For more information consult Lubar's (2001) article in the *Journal of Neurotherapy*.

2. Gunkelman (personal communication, July 9, 2003), a QEEG expert, considers referential montages to be accurate about 60–70% of the time. Bipolar montages have advantages and disadvantages. For example, if the two scalp locations chosen in sequence record alpha from the same local alpha generator (a local pool of neuronal activity) in the brain, then there is a redundancy of effort. On the other hand, if the two scalp locations record different local alpha generators, then there may be a distinct advantage to using a bipolar montage. He agrees with Lubar's approach to choosing montages: Find and use the montage that produces the largest readings, be it referential or bipolar. If a bipolar montage renders larger numbers than a referential montage, then *more than one local pool of neuronal activity* has been tapped into.

3. Ayers (personal communication, Jul. 7, 2003) examines the EEG at specific sites looking for abnormal wave patterns, amplitudes, and spikes. All training protocols employ bipolar rather than monopolar [referential] montages. She asserts that bipolar training is the only way to eliminate artifact and obtain a true recording. For example,

the prevalence of delta found in monopolar montages [referential] is simply a manifestation of artifact. If high-amplitude delta were truly present, normal functioning would be impossible. Bipolar montages are usually done within the confines of the RH or LH, although on occasion she trains using F7-F8 bipolar montage. She asserts that training T3-T4 puts the trainee at risk for seizure disorder.

Training with bipolar montages may be a form of coherence training (Walker, Norman, & Weber, 2002). Choose sites that are 2–3 standard deviations below the norm. For example, one adolescent with Asperger's disorder had poor eye-contact and made few verbal responses. NeuroGuide indicated poor coherence between O2 and T6 in two bandwidths. The posterior RH is involved with facial recognition and social connectivity. The bipolar montage revealed high amplitude beta and low amplitude alpha. I suppressed the beta and rewarded the alpha. Within three sessions his family communication skills and eye-contact had improved and he responded to my comments and humor. Bipolar montages may be chosen in accord with symptomatology, topographical maps and the Lubar method. Bipolar montages may be used with dyslexic trainees. The active and reference sensors connect Wernicke's and Broca's areas.

REVIEW OF NEUROFEEDBACK TRAINING
METHODS AND MODALITIES

EEG data may be acquired from 2 channel or 19 channel systems. Protocol decisions are based upon the findings. Consider the training options reviewed in this book:

1. Anterior EEG slowing at ventral lateral sites (F7 and F8) and the frontal poles (Fp1, Fp2, and Fpz) are excellent candidates for hemoencephalography (HEG) neurofeedback. Posterior slowing in the occipital lobes may also qualify for HEG—sometimes a small rectangular patch of hair needs to be shaved. Anterior and posterior slowing is usually reflected by high theta-to-beta ratios.

2. EEG slowing at dorsal sites and the temporal lobes are best downtrained with EEG neurofeedback. Electrodes can easily be mounted in the hairy regions of the scalp. High theta-to-beta ratios may be transformed by ratio training, beta/SMR protocols, or a single bandpass filter.

3. *Anterior* fast-wave disorders are often trained with just one bandpass filter. For example, if beta (13–25 Hz) is present in the frontal lobes, then it is appropriate to downtrain beta alone with no reward. On the other hand, *posterior* fast-wave disorders may qualify for more than one filter. For example, the data may indicate that alpha can be rewarded while theta, along with excess beta (13–25 Hz), is inhibited. When appropriate, alpha may be rewarded in posterior and central locations, but seldom in anterior locations. Do not reward theta in anterior regions of the scalp.

4. Coherence training may be done with two channels that both use the same frequency bandwidth. Uptraining coherence often increases amplitudes at both sites. Some consider bipolar (sequential) montages to be another way to remedy poor coherence between two sites—more than one bandpass filter may be used (see Figure 6.7c).

5. Hot spots indicated by single-hertz bins that are very well defined by the brain map may be trained alone or in combination with other bandwidths. Sometimes the trainee learns better with just one bandpass filter, and sometimes the trainee learns better with two or three. Watch the training results, compare the normal distribution of banded frequencies (Montgomery, Robb, Dwyer, & Gontkovsky, 1998), and study the map in order to make a clinical decision.

6. Eyes-closed training works just as well as eyes-open training—in theory. On the one hand, some children refuse to train with eyes-closed, some survivors of trauma have frightening images with eyes-closed. Some trainees fall asleep with eyes-closed. Eye-closed training reduces EMG artifact in most cases. On the other hand, eyes-open training permits the trainee to perform a cognitive task. Eyes-open training increases the risk of prefrontal EMG artifact. When possible, let the data guide the decision to train with eyes-open or eyes-closed.

7. Alpha asymmetry training is conducted with two channels, each channel utilizes a bipolar (sequential) montage. This training is to correct a discreet pattern of alpha asymmetry, it will not correct a general pattern of anterior alpha slowing.

8. If neither the EEG data nor the topographical brain map presents a clear picture, then consider the two-channel (C3 and C4) dynamic Brown and Brown (2000) protocol. Training the sensorimotor strip with two channels allows the clinician to track and correct problems with the BAT triad. Forty-hertz synchrony training may also help the brain to organize better with improved alpha blocking.

THE HISTORY OF PROTOCOL SELECTION

The widespread use of QEEG normative database software has revolution-
ized protocol selection. Corrective EEG neurofeedback training, however,
was done before the birth of normative databases. Regarding the evolution of beta/SMR protocols—remember, C3 is in the LH and C4 is in the
RH—initially, Barry Sterman set the stage for training along the sensorimotor strip. Sensorimotor rhythm (SMR) was rewarded at C3 for sufferers
of epilepsy—it worked! Margaret Ayers did much of her early training
along the sensorimotor strip. She emphasized the use of bipolar montages.
Her work with coma victims became legendary. She introduced Siegfried
and Sue Othmer to neurofeedback. After gaining some experience, they
promoted the use of single-channel referential montages at C3 and C4.
Beta (15–18 Hz) was rewarded at C3 (LH) while SMR (12–15 Hz) was
rewarded at C4 (RH). Theta (slow wave) and high beta inhibition were
part of the standard protocol. Beta/SMR protocols became the standard for
many clinicians (Ayers, 1999; Budzynski, 1999; Othmer, Othmer, & Kaiser,
1999; Robbins, 2000a).

The Othmers taught clinicians how to *balance* the time spent training at
C3 with the time spent training at C4 during a single session. For example,
10 min of training at C3 might be followed by 20 min of training at C4. In
theory, LH training promotes mental clarity and improved mood, whereas
RH training promotes calmness and may lead to an emotional release. The
Othmers presented the following caution: Training too much in the LH
creates tension or spatial defects, whereas training too much in the RH
creates mental fog or depression (Othmer & Othmer, 2000).

Joel and Judith Lubar emphasized training along the cingulate gyrus:
Fz, Cz, and Pz. Younger children were trained in the posterior cingulate
region, whereas older children were trained closer to the anterior cingulate
region. Referential or bipolar (sequential) montages were selected. The
Lubars' protocol combined theta (slow wave) inhibition with either a beta
or SMR reward. Beta was rewarded to improve attention, whereas SMR was
rewarded to decrease hyperactivity (Lubar & Lubar, 2002).

Another person of import was Michael Tansey. He trained along anterior cingulate gyrus near Cz. He published several papers that showed
the efficacy of this approach. He only rewarded 14 Hz—that's it (Robbins, 2000a). The expression *Tansey's Protocol* has come to mean training
at Cz that rewards just 14 Hz while inhibiting both theta and high beta
(Sabo & Giorgi, 1998). All of the above clinicians have had success stories.

Research papers have explored the efficacy of training with all of the above models.

The brain can be divided more or less into four quadrants. The dividing lines are the sensorimotor strip and the cingulate gyrus. It looks like a cross. Training along those dividing lines was the central theme of early neurofeedback training. From an anatomical point of view Cz, the vertex, is the most central scalp location. Neuronal generators from the thalamus target central regions of the brain. Consequently, it was held that training along the sensorimotor cortex would generalize to the entire cerebral cortex.

The Yonkers project mentioned in the Introduction made use of just two training sites: C3 and Cz. Beta/SMR protocols were used (Carmody, Radvanski, Wadhwani, Sabo, & Vergara, 2001). Evidently, many of the students who participated benefited from the training. In view of history, it is no surprise that many eclectic practitioners will start training along the sensorimotor cortex. I, too, came from that tradition. I found some clients who definitely benefited from that approach. However, others did not benefit—more was needed.

The acquisition of EEG data is central to corrective neurotherapy treatment. Brain maps derived from QEEG locate and define the nature of problems. QEEG is not the only way to assess the EEG. A two-channel training system is capable of taking multiple recordings from the scalp. Absolute microvolt readings from key scalp locations demonstrate gross asymmetries and other classic problems. Diagnostic tests, observations, and neurological clues help to guide the way. It's up to each neurotherapist to decide how clinical data will be obtained. One way or another, the neurotherapist must locate the problem *before* treatment begins. In many cases, clients are motivated for treatment when they see the nature of their problem depicted by multicolored brain maps. Brain maps make the job of being a neurotherapist easier—even though the brain maps have certain intrinsic flaws.

12

Creating and Executing Treatment Plans

TREATMENT PLANS ARE the byproduct of a great deal of clinical work. They are the net result of testing, interviewing, and EEG data acquisition and processing. They give clients concrete evidence that there is a plan of action. No treatment plan can take into account all the variables that will arise during the training process. Certain decisions are made while the client is training. Those decisions are seldom outside the parameters set forth in the treatment plan. Treatment goals govern the flow of each training session. In all cases, the quality of the training session is enhanced by good communications between therapist and client.

TREATMENT PLANS

I want each adolescent and adult client to understand the rationale behind my treatment protocols. I do not want them in the dark. Healthy minds are interested in the welfare of their brain. Motivation is the key to participation. Treatment plans may be presented in a formal or informal manner. Clients can be given a brief *written* or *verbal* report that includes two necessary ingredients:

1. What you intend to do and why you have chosen to do it.
2. What you expect from the client or parents/guardians.

For example consider the following report given to a parent.

Cognitive testing supports the diagnosis of attention deficit disorder. The ability to govern attention and impulse control is often managed by the midline of the frontal lobes, also known as the cingulate gyrus. Excessive EEG slowing was found along your child's cingulate gyrus and especially at the center of brain or Cz. Neurofeedback training will reward him each time his brain is more alert. After 10 to 15 sessions our clinic will readminister the IVA continuous performance test to check for progress. Your child's rate of progress will determine the total number of sessions needed to obtain a satisfactory score on the IVA. Many children have completed training between 20 and 40 sessions.

   Training will take place two times per week. Please bring a book to read and water to drink. A good night's sleep improves performance. Avoid eating sugary snacks before training. Dietary changes and the addition of supplements are presented in Daniel Amen's book. Family structure contributes to the overall success of neurofeedback. Generally, homework completion precedes pleasurable activities in the evening. Please consult my handout for further suggestions.

   I look forward to training your son and seeing his advancement. He already has tremendous potential and many fine qualities. Thank you for your participation in the training program at out clinic.

FAMILY STRUCTURE AND SELF-REGULATION

Implementing family structure is a challenge—counseling may be needed. Some parents are able to read handouts and follow through; other parents require coaching. The initial interview has *already* determined the parents' willingness to work with the program. Treatment was indicated because the parents were willing to make the necessary changes. Children with special needs require quantity time—the expression *quality time* is misleading. If there are two parents or guardians, then they must present a united front of discipline and concern. An emotionally and/or physically absent parent may promote feelings of abandonment or rejection. An overly kind (indulgent) parent may not truly understand the meaning of loving discipline and structure. Family systems theory is always at work; the child's behavior can be a symptom of the family's dysfunction (Boscolo, Cecchin, Hoffman, & Penn, 1987). Neurotherapy will not fix that kind of symptom. But the neurotherapist can be instrumental in getting the caring family into treatment.

Training can be sabotaged if the trainee fails to get adequate sleep or indulges in the wrong foods (junk food, caffeine, or sugar) or alcohol. Training is also hampered by personal crisis, illness, and critical life changes such as divorce, serious accidents, loss of employment, death of loved ones, personal trauma, and legal problems. Training requires that you stay on task without becoming anxious or worried about progress. All forms of biofeedback training require self-regulation. Success depends on the client's cooperation. The training process includes both training in the office and activities or homework outside the office. When communicating with clients I emphasize the concept of "shared responsibility."

Neurofeedback training is a relatively safe treatment. There are no reported casualties or permanent scars. However, if someone was trained *incorrectly* for many sessions, cognitive functioning could be compromised. Neurotherapy is a process, not an event; permanent learning does not come after two or three sessions. Most clients tell the therapist when training is making them uncomfortable. I always check in on parents to make sure that things are going well. Neurotherapy is all about change. It can effect the threshold dose of psychotropic medications. It can open up emotional issues that had been laid to rest. Thirty training sessions of eyes-closed alpha enhancement training can even cause an allergic reaction to alcohol which will be discussed in Chapter 13. Having said the above, it becomes obvious why most neurotherapists require clients to sign an informed consent document that reviews the above issues. I have included guidelines for creating a client release form in Appendix 4.

THE TRAINING SESSION

The client arrives and is welcomed into the office. The client is seated in a comfortable chair. Pillows are used if necessary, to make sure the younger client is not slouching. Legs may be crossed at the ankle level only; the yoga or half yoga position also works. It is important to explain each step of the sensor montage process to the client. Children often want to see the different color pastes and even smell them. Cleaning or preparing the scalp is done to remove natural oils and not because of poor personal hygiene. The term *sensor* is less intimidating than the term *electrode*. Do not hesitate to double-check the montage with an International 10–20 chart or the Styrofoam head used as a prop. A headband may be needed to secure scalp sensors at some posterior or anterior ventral locations. Placing a small tubular pillow behind the trainee's neck may prevent posterior sensors from moving.

Make sure there is a good electrical hookup. An impedance meter is used to check the quality of the connection. The raw electroencephalograph (EEG) should resemble a singular line that is free from distortions. Demonstrate electromyography (EMG) activity to the client. Reinforce the idea that facial movements must be kept to a minimum. Gum chewing is forbidden. If eye blinking is a major problem, then train in central or posterior areas. Of course, eyes-closed training may also solve the problem. Remind the client to keep hydrated; it's okay to take an occasional drink water (sport bottle) while training. Hemoencephalography (HEG) neurofeedback requires less preparation. I wipe the forehead and the sensors with an alcohol wipe and dry with a tissue.

Younger children (7 to 9 years of age) may do well when parents are in the training room. However, most children do very poorly when a parent is in the room. Parent/child dialogues should be limited during training— stop the training if necessary. Most children 10 and older do not require parental presence. Children who are old enough to train alone should train alone. Parents can be invited into the office on occasion, at the end of the session, to show them a graphic presentation of progress on the computer screen. On occasion I prefer to print it out and have the child hand it to the parent like a report card.

I try to make training an enjoyable experience. I give children a lot of support. For the children who use Microsoft's Paint program, I let them print out their creations (draft quality to save on the ink!). Some of those drawings are hanging in my hallway; others are at home. Children express emotional issues with art. You may wish to explore the basics of art therapy (Malchiodi, 1998). If the child is playing Microsoft's Solitaire, I turn it into a learning experience. I say to child, "Your mind is faster than your mouse!" because children will test out a move with the mouse. Actually, just watching a child play Solitaire is a window to their cognitive process. In every case, I try to make coming to my office a pleasant experience. All you need is a little imagination.

Keep the conversation focused on the neurofeedback process—this is not psychotherapy; do not review the client's week. Time is at a premium. The client's first training experience should be limited to 10–20 min. During that period, introduce the trainee to computer sounds and graphics. Set the volume for an appropriate level of comfort. *The most important part of the feedback is usually the sound!* Ask each trainee if the sound is okay. If there are sound

options, let the trainee hear each one and choose. Introduce the trainee to
the interactive games that are included in the software. Help the trainee appreciate how the movement on the computer screen and sounds correspond
to training goals. Having finished the introduction, train for the remainder
of the session.

When the first session has ended, I double-check with the client? Are
you okay? How is your balance when standing or walking? Are you feeling
different in any way? Please, monitor yourself closely for the rest of the day
and tonight. If your usual pattern of sleep changes, I would like to know. If
you have any concerns, do not hesitate to call the office. Or, please monitor
your child's behavior closely and call if needed.

What activity or task is best for the trainee? The one that keeps the
trainee engaged in the process. Trainees that zone out, lose interest, or
become bored are disengaged. It is very easy for someone with a slow-
wave disorder to mentally leave the training room. Consequently, I provide trainees with options. The trainee may have the option to read, do
homework, play solitaire, watch neurofeedback graphics, or do some other
mental activity. However, the activities may lead to artifact—watch out for
eye, hand, and facial movements. Some trainees will participate in two or
three activities in a 20-min period. Remember to *choose a task that fits the sensor location*. Posterior locations may indicate the need for viewing pictures,
picture books, or simple computer graphics. RH locations may indicate
the need for spatial tasks such as Microsoft's Solitaire or Paint program.
LH locations may indicate the need for cognitive tasks such as reading or
doing homework.

Trainees often ask what is expected of them during training: Should I
try to focus harder? What do I need to do? How does this work anyway?
Help the trainee appreciate that progress depends on maintaining *passive
awareness*. Diaphragmatic breathing often helps to keep the trainee relaxed.
Neurofeedback training is an unconscious process that requires the participation of our conscious mind. The brain responds to the feedback tones
because it becomes aware that they relate to specific brain wave actions.
The brain actually knows that the feedback tone relates to a different state
of mind. On the other hand, HEG neurofeedback works best when the
trainee is focused, alert, and engaged in a cognitive task. However, HEG
neurofeedback training in the occipital lobes calls for more of a relaxed
frame of mind combined with a visual task.

The clinician monitors the trainee's progress in accordance with the
software being used. An increase in slow-wave activity indicates zoning

out, whereas an increase in fast-wave activity relates to mental or muscle tension. Do not hesitate to stop training if necessary. Monitoring the client's peripheral nervous system with simple biofeedback equipment may be helpful. Training progress can be shared with the trainee during and after the session. Help the trainee to make the connection between zoning out and slow-wave activity on the training graph. "Wow, five minutes ago you were really focused—look at the slow-wave reduction!" After a while, the client will be able to tell you when there are positive and negative shifts in the training graph—even before the client sees it. Show the training graph at opportune moments—when it will help motivate the client. Do not make the trainee nervous.

How long should a session last? I have had success with a few clients by training 30–40 min at one site for each session. I pause training midway to give the trainee a break. Other clients seem to benefit from training at two or three different scalp locations, 10–15 min each. Each client is different in the amount of time needed. Watch the trainee's progress and body language. Stop and ask questions if necessary. How long to train and how many sites can be trained during one session may be more of an art than a science. Getting to know the trainee will help. However, there is no substitute for experience. HEG neurofeedback training is different. It is usually broken up into shorter segments of 10 min at three (or four) scalp locations. Doing some training in both hemispheres may be advisable.

Can trainees be left alone? Most trainees benefit from your presence, especially during eyes-open training. Very few children will make progress without your active presence. They need verbal feedback or mild coaching. I don't leave the room during the first session. New trainees need reassurance because electrodes are placed on their head and connected to a strange machine. Veteran adult neurofeedback trainees who have good training habits need less attention. In general, it's best to stay with the trainee—or at the very least, check in periodically to make sure that training is progressing well.

Listen to Your Client

The training session is a time to execute protocol decisions, make minor adjustments, and, most of all, listen to the client. Some clients notice a change within a few minutes of training, whereas others require more time. If a client is shy about giving verbal feedback, then fabricate a progress form for them to fill out before each training session. Positive change usually revolves around mental clarity, personal insight, improved mood, or general relaxation. Negative change usually revolves around an increase of tension, anger, negativity, spatial disorientation, and mental fog. Watch the way the client is learning plus their reaction to the protocol. Ask questions like, Do you still feel focused? Do you still feel calm? How are the muscles in your neck? Sometimes it will help to modify the length of the session. Some clients can only tolerate 5 or 10 min at a time. Do not hesitate to train incrementally, that is, three or four 5-min training periods at the same site.

Help trainees to make self-referential remarks. Are they feeling more alert? Does their mood feel lighter? Are they feeling calmer? Are they more or less alert? *Scaling judgments from 1 to 10 can help the client to assess current state of mind*. Some, but not all, children have the capacity to make self-referential remarks. Sometimes a change in mood requires no comment. Be prepared for potential emotional releases. They may have a negative or a positive connotation. On the one hand, crying, sadness, or weepiness may indicate too much training in the RH. On the other hand, emotional releases may signal a readiness to work through psychological issues. Be ready to debrief the client and make the most of therapeutic moment. Do not hesitate to stop training when negative symptoms occur. Some clients have negative responses when training in the right hemisphere (RH) or the left hemisphere (LH). Others have negative responses when training in anterior or posterior locations.

Maps don't talk; clients do. Listen to your client. Be ready to stop or shorten a session based on your client's report. However, do not become alarmed if progress is slow. For example, downtraining theta may result in an increase of theta in the first session or two. Actually, that's what often happens when a child with attention deficit/hyperactivity disorder (ADHD) tries to concentrate at school—the theta goes up. After a while, you should notice a decline in theta. It may take several sessions before you see theta make the downward descent in the training graph. On the other hand, if the child is becoming bored or zoning out, change the task; keep the child invested in the process.

Homework

Homework assignments are designed to reinforce training goals. The child with ADHD can be assigned a daily reading assignment during school vacations. The child with dyscalculia can do simple problem-solving tasks each day. Music lessons are a wonderful way to promote the growth of neuronal connections. The adult with age-related cognitive decline works at crossword puzzle problems or other cognitive tasks (Budzynski, 1996). The brain thrives on novelty and dies with routine; stimulate the brain and it will create new and better neuronal pathways; education, learning new skills, and frequent social contact comprise most brain-building programs (Katz & Rubin, 1999). On the other hand, hours of TV watching and video game playing time are counterproductive. Parents of trainees may be assigned to monitor and scale behavior patterns or report on changes in family structure or school performance. They should be alert to the practice of giving their children rewards for a job well done. Some will appreciate the suggestions in the book *Brain Gym* (Dennison & Dennison, 1989).

Homework assignments may also revolve around mental health. Most *anxious* clients benefit from daily diaphragmatic breathing exercises. Temperature training combined with autogenics builds self-regulation skills. Physical exercise promotes the flow of endorphins; resistance training builds self-confidence and limits osteoporosis. Depressed and anxious clients benefit from cognitive therapy and problem-solving tasks or communication and assertiveness skills training. I have handouts for each basic mental health assignment. The first session provides diaphragmatic breathing lessons for the anxious client, whereas the depressed client is socialized to the cognitive model. *Relaxation and Stress Reduction Workbook* (Davis, Eshelman, & McKay, 1995) is another source of homework assignments. Almost any mental health homework assignment can be given that applies to the treatment plan.

It should not be necessary to spend more than 5–10 min reviewing homework assignments. If the client consistently requires more than 25 min of counseling per session, then neurotherapy may have to take a backseat. Either send the client to a counselor or stop neurotherapy and focus on the issues. There may be an underlying psychodynamic issue that is hindering progress. (Chapters 13 and 14 enlarge upon this topic.) Your desire to train the client may have nothing to do with the client's most pressing need. Even though the client has gone through the entire assessment process with a map, it is still possible that psychotherapy is the first step to wellness.

Training Issues When There is Progress

What indicates that a client is progressing? Test scores are improved; positive behaviors are observed; symptom reduction is apparent. The EEG is also subject to change. Slow waves in the 0–10 Hz range will often change the most. What is a significant change? 15–20% drop in baseline microvolts (personal communication, Bob Gurnee, July 17, 2003). For example, theta may average $32\mu V$ during the first training session and then drop to $26\mu V$ after 10 sessions. Or, theta may increase under task (e.g. reading) during the first training session but 5–10 training sessions later theta shows a reverse pattern. Or, the slope of the training graph may look better after several training sessions even though the average amplitude has not significantly changed.

It's important to observe the training graph closely for reversals. For example, slow wave amplitudes may descend for 10–15 minutes and then begin to rise. Once, this happens it may be wise to stop and move to another training site; or, to take a 3–5 minute break. Each trainee is different—there is no exact number of training sessions required to reach a desired goal. Most trainees have at least two or more potential sites that require training. Changes in behavior and the EEG often dictate when it's time to consider additional sites.

If you are training in just one hemisphere, it will be necessary to take a two-channel bilateral recording after 5–10 sessions. Overtraining in one hemisphere can cause an unwanted asymmetry. For example, inhibiting abnormally high alpha at T4 could result in an unwanted alpha asymmetry; always maintain T4 alpha $\geq$ T3 alpha. Monitor training progress by means of contralateral recordings with two channels of EEG. Measure for change and progress and avoid assumptions.

If you are training with two channels such as C3 and C4, then it is important to watch the BAT triad. Maintain the following normative balance: (a) Theta should be relatively equal at C3 and C4; (b) LH beta $\geq$ RH beta whereas (c) RH alpha $\geq$ LH alpha. If an unwanted asymmetry develops, then alter the protocol. For example, if RH theta becomes 15% higher than LH theta, then *remove* the LH theta inhibit until symmetry has been restored. With two channels of data, it should be easy to track and reverse unwanted asymmetries.

Train for about 10 sessions before readministering depression and anxiety inventories. Clients are often amazed when they compare before and after training scores. Baseline scores or weekly progress reports are essential. Training is only as good as the positive changes that it produces. Clients who have achieved adequate symptom reduction should be overtrained for several sessions. Thereafter, it may be wise to come in one time per month for the next few months. Relapse prevention is important.

Another issue that arises is when and how to reduce psychiatric medication. Encourage the client to return to the doctor who prescribed the medications. Send the client with the latest copy of the Beck Depression Inventory (BDI) or the Burns Anxiety Inventory (BAI) (along with the baseline test). Medication withdrawal often brings unwanted side effects. However, symptom-free trainees on medication may experience agitation. In order to prepare clients for either possibility, I show them passages from prescription drug manuals. *If the client's psychiatrist changes medications and/or dosages frequently, it will likely sabotage neurofeedback training.*

The Client Who Trains Poorly

1. If no progress is realized after 5 training sessions, then it may be wise to move to another site. (Soutar, 2004).
2. Eyes-open vs. eyes-closed: If the client trains poorly one way, then choose the other in concert with the QEEG or EEG data presentation. Work with the trainees' level of stamina.
3. Changing the number of filters: Figures 5.1c and 5.2c and the Table 5.1 from Montgomery, Robb, Dwyer, and Gontkovsky (1998) provide both a visual and numeric understanding of eyes-open and eyes-closed normative bandwidth distributions. If you are training with just one filter then consider adding other filters that will balance out the normative distribution. Test out your theory— add the new filter with a minimal training threshold of 10 or 20%. You will know in just 5–10 min if the additional filter is helping.

    Consider the following: Delta may be inhibited but never rewarded, whereas theta may be inhibited but only rewarded during deep-states training. Alpha (8–12, 8–13, and 9–13 Hz) may be rewarded at central and posterior locations but seldom in anterior locations. Beta rewards may range anywhere from 13 to 21 Hz. Commonly sensorimotor rhythm (SMR; 13–15 or 12–15 Hz) is rewarded in the RH and beta (15–18, 16–20, and 17–21 Hz) is rewarded in the LH. Note: SMR can improve calmness or increase sadness, whereas beta can improve alertness or increase tension. Consider making high beta (20–30 Hz) inhibition the third filter. Let the topographical brain map, EEG data and the 2-dimensional graph (e.g., Figure 5.1c) guide you in the decision to add or remove filters.

4. Changing the scalp location: Some clients will not train well in one hemisphere or another. They will report negative thoughts, feelings, or sensations. Do not force the issue. The same statement applies to the anterior/posterior balance.

5. Changing the montage: Good bipolar montages produce robust two-dimensional display graphics. Avoid them if the graphics are flat. Good referential montages have minimum surface electromyography (SEMG) artifact effects.

6. Changing the task: do not insist on training with a task that annoys or bores the client. For example, one client becomes sleepy when he looks at computer screen graphics, plays solitaire or reads a book. However, reading one of Gray Larson's "Far Side" books such as *The Prehisory of the Far Side: A Tenth Anniversary Exhibit* (1989) or *The Far Side Gallery* (1984) keeps him wide awake. Be careful with humorous books because reading them can lead to facial movements. This client was doing HEG neurofeedback training so the occasional smile did not undo the training. In general, it is important to choose the task that most closely matches the neuronal functions associated with that region of the brain: Logic and reasoning tasks for the LH and human interest, humor, spatial tasks for the RH.

7. Keep on top of the training graph. Check in with the trainee frequently. Is it truly a poor protocol or have they given up?

Termination When Progress is Truly Lacking

Do not expect perfection. Some trainees will not progress. Progress can be measured in three ways: (a) changes in the EEG training graph; (b) symptom reduction; (c) positive lifestyle changes. If after 10–15 training sessions no concrete progress has occurred, then consider the following:

1. Does the TP = DEN?
2. Was PTSD missed in the initial diagnosis?*
3. Does the client need deep-states training?
4. How accurate is the data or the map?

---

*For example, children with reactive attachment disorder (RAD) who suffer from PTSD are often treated with eye movement desensitization and reprocessing (EMDR) before beginning neurotherapy.

5. Is the training being sabotaged by one of the six areas?

- Motivation lacking
- Dysfunctional family dynamics
- Issues relating to adolescence
- Poor cooperation
- Unhealthy lifestyle practices continue
- Critical incidents have shocked the system

6. Does this trainee have the capacity to learn?
7. Has the tense trainee truly mastered diaphragmatic breathing?
8. Does the trainee need psychotherapy more than neurotherapy?
9. How many more sessions will I continue before terminating?

Sometimes client or clinician expectations are unrealistic. For example, one mother called me on the phone and complained about her son's poor manners. Neurofeedback does not teach good manners! Other parents may expect neurofeedback to teach reading or math skills. Neurofeedback teaches the self-regulation of brain waves. It opens the way for successful tutoring and learning by building brain flexibility and balance. For example, one client with traumatic brain injury suffered with dyscalculia. He bought and used a math workbook to augment neurofeedback training. It worked: his math skills improved. That is why it is so important to convey the message that neurofeedback training often requires additional effort by the trainee!

After 10 training sessions, a depressed client with hypertension said to me, "I don't see where the neurofeedback is helping me but the counseling has been great!" I always have psychotherapy to fall back on when progress is lacking. But, after considering the above, some clients have to be terminated, apologies have to be made, and life goes on. The ethical clinician never promises a cure and always makes it clear from the start that "not everyone responds." I have heard of children being trained for over 100 sessions without concrete progress. Evidence must accompany the decision to continue training. Most clients will need at least 20–35 sessions. Training beyond 35 sessions is justified if the client is making steady progress.

13

Deep-States and Alpha/Theta Training

ALPHA WAS THE FIRST BRAIN WAVE to be named and trained. It was the first wave to be explored. Alpha states are often associated with meditation or a deep sense of inner calm. Herbert Benson studied the body's response to deep relaxation. He learned that "alpha waves increase in amplitude and regularity during meditation" (Benson, 1975, p. 58). Previous to his research, the general public assumed that the ability of Zen monks to control their physiology was purely a religious practice with no scientific basis. However, the ability of Zen monks to control their physiology can be learned by the general public. A study of the Harvard Medical School (2004) found that mindfulness meditation results in "brain wave recordings [that] show a pattern of activity—greater in the left prefrontal cortex than in the right—that's associated with happiness and optimism." The immune system also benefits: "mindfulness students produced more antibodies than the controls, and the response was greatest in those who shifted the most strongly toward a left-dominant brain wave pattern." There were other benefits to mental health including "inner calm . . . the ability to tolerate upsetting thoughts . . . fewer binge eating episodes. . . . Brain imaging showed that mindfulness treatment dampened overactivity in brain areas associated with compulsive behavior" (2004, p. 1).

Neurofeedback training can lead to an increase in alpha amplitudes and robust alpha synchrony. The relaxation response and mindfulness meditation effects can be acquired in a relatively short period of time. Alpha/theta

(A/T) training, alpha enhancement training and alpha synchrony training also have many non-clinical applications, such as peak-performance training to improve cognitive flexibility, creativity, athletic control, hemispheric synchrony, and inner awareness (Mason & Brownback, 2001).

A/T training is a valuable tool in the clinical arena. It is more efficient than talk therapy for the treatment of personality disorders, substance abuse, and posttraumatic stress disorder (PTSD). The "talking cure" was first used in the treatment of psychological trauma coming from emotional, physical, and sexual abuse; it directly engages the cerebral cortex. Indeed, certain problems can be "talked away" (Freud & Breuer, 1966, pp. 55–82). But egregious trauma has the power to severely compromise cognitive processing. If that is the case, neurology and physiology will override the healing power of psychology. For example, calling to mind a traumatic event may fire up the limbic system and freeze up the left frontal lobe. Broca's area in the left frontal lobe is responsible for speech—the key ingredient in talk therapy. The body, for its part, has a physiologic memory that holds on to trauma (Baum, 1997; Sills, 2001; van der Kolk, McFarlane, & Weisaeth, 1996; Wylie, 2004). The physiology of the trauma survivor can have a deleterious effect on talk therapy.

Imagine a treatment that would reduce the amount of time needed to disarm the limbic system. Imagine a protocol that would open up the past without tearing down day-to-day functioning. Imagine a 5-year therapy being reduced to 2 years. A/T training holds out the promise of resolving past issues while the client remains in a fairly relaxed condition (Robbins, 2000a, pp. 158–192). It has been known to bring the client into a witness state in the quest to build a bridge to the true self. It can cool down the limbic system, allowing the trainee to process the trauma with the frontal lobes. It is an effective tool for the resolution of trauma and the building up of the human spirit (White, 1999, 341–367).

HISTORY

Early neurotherapists facilitated "twilight states" of healing. Kamiya, Green, Budzynski, and others, using stand-alone neurofeedback equipment, rewarded alpha, theta, or both. It worked; emotional issues were resolved while the client entered the depths of the psyche in a relaxed state. Later, Peniston, and Kulkosky applied A/T training to two separate disorders: PTSD and alcoholism. They used two small populations of veterans from the Vietnam War. Both experiments were done in an institution. Building upon their success, Scott, Brod, Siderof, Kaiser & Sagan demonstrated the efficacy of their model with much larger numbers of volunteers: 121 court-mandated poly-substance abusers participated. Scott and colleagues had the support of a major institution. A/T training was proven to be superior to talk therapy when it came to resolution of long-entrenched trauma and the recovery from substance abuse. This study, unlike the Peniston and Kulkosky studies (1999) assessed the EEG prior to training and subsequently trained with two different protocols: (a) alpha suppression and (b) alpha enhancement (Budzynski, 1999; Robbins, 2000a; Scott et al., 2002; White, 1999).

Nearly half of those who participate in a rigorous 30–40-session A/T training programs will experience the Peniston effect. It is an allergic reaction to alcohol or other psychoactive substances that comes with intensive A/T training (Peniston & Kulkosky, 1999). Participants in A/T training programs are informed of the possibility of losing drug-related effects and becoming allergic to the substance they have been abusing. It is a major issue; clients must sign a release stating their knowledge of the Peniston effect (see Appendix 4). However, the success of A/T training programs is not related to an allergic side effect. Peniston and Kulkosky (1999) described the following benefits related to their program:

> This procedure can produce profound increases in alpha and theta brain rhythms . . . prevent an elevation of serum beta endorphin levels during the course of treatment of alcoholism, and produce decreases in self-assessed depression and other fundamental changes in personality variables. The personality changes reported correspond to being more warmhearted, more intelligent, more emotionally stable, more socially bold, more relaxed and more satisfied. (p. 172)

Traditional addiction treatment programs tend to raise serum-beta-endorphin levels (measured by taking blood samples). Consequently, participants become more anxious and have more cravings. A/T training programs seldom add to the anxiety that comes with being in treatment. They often result in reduced cravings. Intensive programs are best managed on an institutional level. Neurofeedback training for addictions is likely to include 2 training sessions each day—14 sessions per week! A/T training programs have also been adapted to smaller private practices (White, 1999). There is a place for alpha enhancement training in most neurofeedback practices. A/T training is a valuable tool for the treatment of several clinical disorders.

WHAT MAKES DEEP STATES SO DEEP?

A/T training opens the door to healing and the reclamation of repressed feelings and memories. The healing activity takes place during the so-called twilight states that are a natural part of the sleep-awake cycle. Our wakeful hours are accompanied by a great deal of beta activity. Beta helps us to stay focused and on task during the day. The day eventually turns into night and our electroencephalograph (EEG) shows increases in theta and decreases in alpha (Rowan & Tolunsky, 2003, p. 29). Sleep is associated with higher amplitudes of delta. Our interest is in the transition from alpha-to-theta-to-delta as we go to sleep and then back again as we wake up. Hypnopompic imagery comes while we are waking up. Hypnagogic imagery comes while we are going to sleep. The transition into sleep creates a state of mind that mixes reality with subconscious images. White (1999) described the role of alpha and theta in the healing process:

> With a predominance of theta waves (4–8 Hz) focus is on the internal world, a world of hypnogogic imagery where an "inner healer" is often said to be encountered. Alpha brain waves (8–13 Hz) may be considered a bridge from the external world to the internal world and visa versa. (p. 344)

A/T training promotes twilight states that may evoke hypnagogic imagery. Some clients report striking imagery and/or deep insights about their life. Traumatic events may be safely reexperienced. Working through requires less assistance from the therapist. Others gain a broader perspective on life. Rigid character traits soften up and life takes on a new dimension. Thus, A/T training is more than a trauma resolution technique. The release of traumata and personal growth happen side by side. A/T training is empowering because the client is doing the work. The therapist serves as the empathic facilitator. Termination issues are reduced because the client is more self-sufficient and less therapist-dependent.

A/T training is primarily the process of rewarding both alpha and theta. Other bandwidths may be rewarded or inhibited. Alpha reinforcement ranges from 50 to 70%, whereas theta reinforcement ranges from 20 to 50%. Some clients go into a deeper state of consciousness with ease. The training graph shows a definite trend. Alpha amplitudes begin to decrease while theta amplitudes remain constant or begin to rise. When the theta amplitudes exceed alpha amplitudes, it is called a crossover. Clients who take the plunge into theta often report striking images of the past or the reclamation of repressed feelings or emotions. Not all agree with this concept: A recent study questioned the need for the theta reward. It clearly demonstrated that imagery can take place without having a crossover or a theta reward (Moore, et al., 2000). However, imagery is *not* the sole component of the healing process. If imagery were the only goal, then the theta component may have little value.

Memories are stored in four different planes: behavior, affect, sensation, and knowledge, known as the BASK model (Braun, 1988). For example,I ask you when you last had ice cream. You reply, "I can see myself having ice cream with my friends at an ice cream stand this past summer." Thus, you have the "K," or the knowledge of the event, because you can visualize the activity. But do you still remember the "A," that is, the feeling of *love* you had toward your friends? Or do you still remember the "S" that is the sensation of the *cold* ice cream going down your throat? Lastly, do you remember the "B," that is, the action of *licking* the ice-cream cone, tongue-to-hand coordination? If you can say yes to all of those questions, then you have a complete memory. Therefore, visualization alone does not comprise a complete memory of an event. I have treated many a trauma survivor who remembered the "K" events but continued to suffer from the symptoms of PTSD because affects and sensations were repressed.

The goal of treatment is healing. The therapist must create a protocol that fits each client. For some of my clients the theta reward was too much; it revivified the trauma. For others, training with just alpha reward did not bring them to a state of healing and recovery. It is appropriate to question the value of efficacy of either the alpha or the theta reward. For example, Scott, Brod, Siderof, Kaiser, and Sagan (2002) indicated that substance abusers had either too much or too little alpha. Protocols were adjusted according to the EEG data. The study concluded that "there was no significant difference in abstinence rates between the alpha augmentation and alpha suppression groups." Consequently, the decision to reward or inhibit or remove either *alpha or theta* from the treatment protocol is determined by the assessment process and client's response to the treatment protocols.

A/T TRAINING FOR SURVIVORS OF TRAUMA

Symptoms directly related to PTSD include: flashbacks, social withdrawal, anxiety, irrational fears, sudden angers, depression, emotional numbness, substance abuse, inability to experience simple pleasures, detachment, foggy thinking or confusion, exaggerated startle response, helplessness, and nightmares. Symptoms can be solutions or ways of coping with deeper problems. For example, neurotherapy for depression may fail if the client has underlying PTSD. At first the client may respond to corrective protocols, but relapse is likely. Neurotherapy for PTSD requires a thorough understanding of the therapeutic skills needed for "trauma and recovery" (Herman, 1992). Issues such as self-harm, eating disorders, and dissociative disorders may also be part of the client's distress. An understanding of borderline personality disorder (BPD) may also be required: Hodges's (2003) review of the literature showed a strong correlation between PTSD and BPD. Therefore the neurotherapist who desires to treat this population must also have the skills of a psychodynamic psychotherapist.

A/T training is not for the client in chaos who has a weekly crisis and a poor support system. Stabilize the client first, train later: Dialectic behavior therapy (DBT) may be the first order of treatment. The client should be able to make the commitment to train once a week or multiple times a week. Consistency is the key to success. Also, it is the rare client who can come directly from a highly stressful day at work to do effective A/T training. Some clients have to be reminded to shut off their cell phones, come in early, and do deep breathing exercises in an auxiliary treatment room before the official session begins. Otherwise, the first 10–15 min of training will be devoted to calming down from the day's activities.

A/T training sessions may run overtime because training opens up issues that require further debriefing. Former talk therapy clients find the process of being hooked up to a machine very impersonal. The transition from one modality to another may not work. On the other hand, additional talk therapy may not be in the client's best interest. Treating survivors of trauma takes much more than sensor placement and bandwidth selection; it requires a thorough knowledge of trauma and recovery. Treating those with addiction issues requires a general knowledge of addictions counseling. The first step is always safety: Clients need a list of coping skills, cognitive/behavioral skills, and grounding techniques. They need a support base of friends and confidants. Breathing skills and journaling habits are essential to success.

A/T training can be done several times each week for 30 or more sessions. Training multiple times each week has many advantages. It keeps the door to EEG flexibility wide open while the trainee maintains a state of psychological readiness. Some clients choose to participate several times per week in A/T training programs. Each session begins with a 3–8 min constructive visualization. A/T training is for approximately 30 min. Debriefing may take another 15–20 min. The client is expected to keep a log of each session. Intensive training is for those whose fiscal and personal circumstances allow them to resolve deep emotional issues in a relatively short period of time.

Other clients benefit in a more informal way. They come once a week and train for about 20–25 min. The training begins after about 10–15 min of counseling and debriefing. During training they often experience personal insights or reclaim repressed memories. In between sessions clients spend time reflecting and journaling. These clients have a secure base, steady employment, and a good support system. They are not at risk for suicide, nor will they decompensate in the office or at home. A/T in this way becomes an adjunct to talk therapy. Some weeks you may skip training to talk through issues. Informal A/T training will likely reduce the total number of psychotherapy sessions.

ASSESSMENT AND PROTOCOL SELECTION

There are several ways to do slow wave training: (a) Alpha synchrony training is a multiple-channel protocol that rewards alpha alone in at least two contralateral scalp locations. It has been used for peak performance training as well as psychological depth work. Peak performance training with multiple channels is a more advanced technique that sometimes includes four or more channels (McKnight & Fehmi, 2001). (b) A/T training is a single-channel protocol that rewards both alpha and theta. It can facilitate twilight states for the purpose of opening up and resolving psychological depth issues (Budzynski, 1999). Thirty training sessions are common. (c) Alpha training with one reward and optional inhibit(s) is a single-channel protocol often used to ameliorate anxiety. In some cases alpha is the only reward because theta amplitudes are already too high. Most forms of slow-wave enhancement are typically done with eyes-closed in a quiet room and in a reclined position. The number of training sessions needed to bring relief varies from client to client.

Slow-wave enhancement may be contraindicated in some cases. For example, clients with widespread EEG slowing may not be good candidates for this protocol. The attention deficit/hyperactivity disorder (ADHD) child with a central theta-to-beta ratio of 3:1 or greater would not be a good candidate for slow-wave enhancement. It would likely promote foggy thinking and poor concentration. Anxious clients with excessive posterior alpha would also be unlikely candidates for alpha enhancement training.

Many survivors of trauma need special preparation before A/T training can begin. Dissociation may be their primary coping mechanism. They quickly drop into a theta state and lose time. When I am interviewing clients with dissociative disorders, it is common to see them zone out for brief periods of time, even though I am engaging them in conversation. They lose eye contact and begin to stare into aimless space. This retreat into theta is a form of self-hypnosis that prevents the survivor from squarely dealing with life. Before beginning A/T training, this population must engage in theta-reduction training. Eyes-open training is needed. Cz is often chosen as the site to begin beta/SMR protocols; ratio training should also be considered. The client must be taught basic grounding skills. I often tell trauma survivors, "Hold on to your keys and stay in the present."

Case Study: Alpha Enhancement Training for Anxiety and Depression

Consider the eyes-closed EEG data recording for client (x) who suffers from generalized anxiety disorder, mild to moderate depression, compulsions and psychological depth issues. Table 13.1 outlines the EEG data for this case.

Client (x) complained of facial tension, it's possible that beta may be artificially elevated due to SEMG artifact. LH beta > RH beta which is normal. Posterior beta and high beta > anterior beta and high beta which is not normal. Pz alpha is marginally higher than Fz alpha suggesting a need for greater posterior alpha amplitudes. This anxious client had a posterior alpha asymmetry LH > RH. (10.8 > 8.5). Theta rivals or exceeds alpha. Theta enhancement is contraindicated. The BAT triad suggested the following protocol:

TABLE 13.1
Eyes-Closed EEG for Client with Anxiety and Depression (Client X)

BAND	Fz	Cz	Pz	O1	O2
Theta (4–8)	11.4	11.8	9.5	8.0	8.4
Alpha (8–12)	8.3	8.8	9.1	10.8	8.5
Beta (13–21)	7.4	7.4	9.0	8.7	8.1
High Beta (20–30)	6.0	7.0	7.0	6.8	6.8

FIGURE 13.1
SINGLE CHANNEL ALPHA ENHANCEMENT AT O2 (CLIENT X)

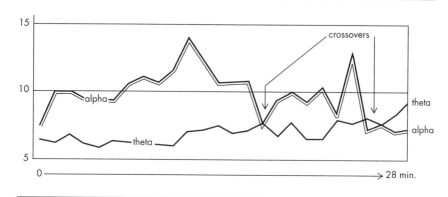

Reward alpha (8–12 Hz) for 28 min. at O2 (RH).

Observe alpha (8–12 Hz) at O1 (LH) in order to monitor changes in the BAT triad.

Headphones helped to limit outside noises and a simple tapping sound was the reward. A headband was needed to keep both posterior scalp sensors in place. After three training sessions, the client reported a lifting of depression and less anxiety but more training and counseling were needed. The client's overall training experience was positive. She said that during each training session, for a period of time, she let go and was unaware of my presence in the room—a unique experience for her. Training in the visual cortex may have contributed to her report of intense imagery. Enhanced muscle relaxation was another benefit of training. Decreases in beta were noted. Client (x) did not instantly open her eyes at the close of each training session—an indication of deep relaxation. Training ended with inhibiting theta for 5 min. at Cz for grounding purposes. Overall, she reported better sleep with more dreaming. This case demonstrates the power of simple alpha enhancement without other rewards or inhibits. It empowered this client to acquire the benefits of mindfulness meditation in a relatively short period of time.

The training graph for client (x) demonstrates deep relaxation. Although only alpha was rewarded it's helpful to see the course of both alpha (8–12 Hz) and theta (4–7 Hz). At first, alpha was rising and theta remained steady.

After peaking, alpha began to plummet and theta began to rise. Towards the end of the session the amplitude of theta exceeded the amplitude of alpha. This phenomenon is called a *crossover*. It is normal for alpha to decrease and theta to increase in amplitude during periods of drowsiness or deep relaxation. Delta, which is associated with sleep, however, did not significantly increase indicating that client (x) was experiencing deep relaxation rather than sleep.

SENSOR PLACEMENT FOR A/T TRAINING

Many clients benefit from both alpha and theta enhancement. Sensor placement is always in a posterior location, either at the midline or in the right hemisphere (RH) or left hemisphere (LH). Sensor placement follows the principles of the BAT triad. Do not train in a way that contributes to an already existing problem. If in doubt, chose a midline site such as Pz. Proceed as follows: Assess with two-channels, each with a referential (monopolar) montage, one scalp sensor at P3 and the other at P4. Consider the following six considerations:

1. If RH alpha $\geq$ LH alpha and RH theta $\cong$ LH theta then select a midline site for sensor placement such as Pz.
2. If LH alpha > RH alpha select P4 or O2 sensor placement.
3. If alpha asymmetry is normal but RH theta > LH theta then train at O1.
4. Pay special attention to the Putnam's (1989) Dissociative Experiences Scale (DES). Scores of 30% and higher strongly suggest the possibility of dissociative identity disorder (DID). Neurotherapy for DID is an advanced skill.
5. P3 placements are contraindicated for depressed clients.
6. Inhibit either alpha or theta in accord with the EEG assessment.

WHAT IS INVOLVED IN DOING A/T TRAINING?

Regardless of the method, standard psychotherapy practice always applies. The client must be emotionally ready and living in a supportive environment. Trauma survivors must be taught numerous skills: communication skills, cognitive therapy skills, assertiveness training, and general coping skills such as grounding, journaling, and exercise. It may take a few sessions or many sessions of coaching before the client is ready to proceed. ST training and diaphragmatic breathing are part of the A/T protocol. Qualified trainees can raise their skin temperature (ST) to 93–95 °F and hold it for 15–20 min. Daily practice is required for at least 1 week prior to the first A/T training session. I seldom begin A/T training unless the client can demonstrate both diaphragmatic breathing and the ability to raise hand temperature at will.

The client must be mentally and physically prepared for each A/T training session. The client arrives early enough to unwind, breathe, and remove muscle tension. Electronic communication devices are turned off. A few minutes later training begins. While the sensors are being mounted, it's time to review briefly the previous session and bring up any pertinent issues. The client assumes a comfortable position in a reclining chair. Next come sensor placement and impedance testing. The room temperature is made comfortable, noise level is at a minimum, and lights are turned off when ready. Many clients feel chilly or cold during deep-states training. Therefore, it is wise to have a light blanket available for use.

The client is instructed to do a 3–8-min constructed visualization. This visualization may take several forms: It may be an image of the ideal self. It may contain scenarios of the client entering into a potentially troublesome conflict. In the imagery the client handles the problem with nondefensive language or assertiveness. Or, the client is imagining being in a temptation scene, substances may be present, and the client walks away without using or purchasing. The therapist facilitates the process of choosing a constructed visualization. In most cases the client repeats one or more visualizations over and over again for the 3–8 min. In a few cases, the therapist does a form of guided imagery and walks the client through the process (Scott, 2000). Do not minimize the power of this technique. I have assigned it as homework for talk-therapy clients. It helps them build sense of self.

Once the visualization process ends, EEG training can begin. The trainee is instructed to "let go." I add a few gentle reminders to make sure clients understand what is expected of them: "Imagine you are getting a massage. What would you be thinking about? Remember that your problems will be there at the end of the session. If worry really helps, then why are there so many problems? Focus on your breathing. Imagine a safe place. Repeat supportive statements." The next step is to start the training. Alpha (8–12 Hz) is rewarded 50–70% of the time and theta (5–8 Hz) is rewarded 20–50% of the time. When two separate soothing tones comprise the feedback, the higher pitch is used for alpha and the lower pitch is used for theta. Inhibits may be added to the protocol. For example, inhibit 15–30 Hz if the client is struggling to relax. On the other hand, inhibit 2–5 Hz if the client is at risk for powerful traumatic images or sensations (Scott, 2000).

In some cases it is better to leave the room and allow the client to be alone. If it seems best to leave the room, keep track of the training with a baby monitor or some other method. Other clients request the therapist's presence. Trauma survivors often need the therapist's presence. Sometimes, just reminding clients to breathe slowly prevents relaxation-induced anxiety. It goes without saying that A/T training requires a good therapeutic relationship. If it is a clinic environment, make sure that all clients with emotional issues, regardless of the neurofeedback training modality, have the same therapist each week. Healing takes place within the therapeutic bond amid an arena of trust (Bowlby, 1988).

Many neurotherapists believe that the sounds in A/T training are more important than other forms of neurotherapy. For example, I have equipment that generates a separate feedback tone for each bandwidth. The theta has a lower pitch than the alpha. Both tones can resound at the same time and create a harmonious chord. When a client goes deep, the deeper theta tone can be heard more often than the higher alpha tone. Effective deep-states therapy can happen with many varieties of sounds including just a simple tapping sound. Rather than the sound, the key is having the correct scalp site(s) and set of filters that reflect the client's EEG data. Make sure the sounds are the correct volume and degree of pleasantness to suit the client's taste. In some cases headphones may be able to block outside noise. If the room is relatively quiet, the regular speakers are fine. Do not train in high-traffic areas.

FIVE RESPONSES TO A/T TRAINING

Not all respond to A/T training in the same way. One of the chief problems related to A/T training is the presence of busy thoughts that won't stop. When that happens, there are several techniques that will help. For example, the client can repeat the same word or words over and over again internally or name several objects in the room over and over again—"bore it to death" (Scott, 2000). Other clients find that repeating self-supportive statements over and over again helps. Imagining a waterfall or some other pleasant and safe scene may help. Above all, diaphragmatic breathing must be maintained.

In time the trainee falls into one of five patterns:

1. The client with negative experiences, such as painful imagery or body sensations.
2. The client with frustrations who remarks, "I just can't get deep."
3. The client who goes to sleep.
4. The client with no experiences but who reports a state of deep relaxation.
5. The client with excellent experiences, such as insight and the unlocking of repressed memories.

1. Once a client begins to reexperience painful trauma in a painful way, then it will become harder to make progress. Many therapists inhibit 2–5 Hz to minimize the pain (Scott, 2000). A/T training is supposed to minimize painful revivifications. However, teary eyes and deep sighs are common signals of relief. But sharp pains must be prevented. There are several ways to keep ahead of this problem. Watch the progress of the EEG and compare it to the client's body language. Sharp changes in delta or high beta may signal a change. Peripheral biofeedback equipment may also be helpful. Checking the client's pulse rate and/or breath rate is very important I have seen clients double their breath rate: Catch it before that happens and slow it down to within normal limits. If the above measures fail to work, turn off all theta feedback—only alpha feedback remains— and gently talk to the client, to make your presence known. Don't leave the room. Be ready to shut off the equipment. Don't let the client go into a painful abreaction.
2. Some clients can stop the busy thoughts by boring it to death, imaging a colorful waterfall, repeating self-supportive statements, or just concentrating on their breathing. For clients who do not see in colors, the goal is to see jet black. Seeing pure black is evidence of deep relaxation unless the client sees in color. Watch the training graph, it's easy to spot clients with busy thoughts; they are the ones with increasing beta and alpha that never dares to drop below theta. Many therapists inhibit 15–30 Hz to limit overthinking (Scott, 2000). After 10 sessions, if the client is still struggling with busy thoughts and never begins to feel deeply relaxed, then it may be time to stop the process. Go back to eyes-open training

with the emphasis on inhibiting beta. Clients who are anxious will have great difficulty doing A/T training unless they master the art of diaphragmatic breathing. Classes may be available locally that will help the client to learn stretching or movement therapy. The goal is to prevent feelings of frustration or failure. Carefully screen clients before the process begins.

3. When some clients begin to relax, they go directly into sleep. They have not mastered the ability to relax during wakeful states. This condition may be a defense mechanism to prevent working through issues. Regardless, watch the delta carefully. Remind the client to keep track of breathing. Ultimately, it is the client's responsibility to stay awake, not the therapist's. A/T training may be contraindicated.

4. Some clients report, after training for 30 min, "I felt relaxed, it was okay." The trainee's nonchalant way of describing A/T training suggests that it was the kind of relaxation that resembled lounging by the pool or the beach on a sunny day. Examine the EEG and look for evidence. Positive changes include decreases in beta or high beta, gradual alpha attenuation during periods of deep relaxation that may or may not accompany increased theta. If the EEG stays about the same, it is unlikely that the client went deep. Watch out for clients who opens their eyes the instant the session is over. If they were truly deep, it takes a little time to reenter the real world.

5. The client who is truly benefiting from the training often has much to say. It is the therapist's job to limit comments to open-ended questions such as:

   - What was your experience like?
   - Did you have any bodily sensations (floating, dizziness, hand tingling, myoclonic jerks*)?
   - Did you see any colors?
   - What was happening in your mind?

Notice that the client was not asked about imagery or memories or trauma. Clients who are asked about imagery after each session may come to believe that success depends upon seeing images. Allow clients to express themselves. Facilitate the process. If a significant

---

*Myoclonic jerks are sudden muscle movements that may occur during the first stage of sleep. Leg or arm movements are common as the client goes deep.

realization is uttered, then gently help them to work it through. Training logs or journal entries are made for each session. Some clients receive insights when doing journaling at home later that day. Others experience vivid dreams that will enrich the therapy process. But, do not assume that rich personal expressions are vital to the process. One former male trainee tells people in the community that his life was transformed by A/T training, even though he shared little with me during his training experience.

If the client reveals a traumatic memory, act as a facilitator and have the client do as much of his or her own work as possible. Consider the following questions: "If you could be there at the very moment the incident began, what would you do? What would you say to those present? What would you say to yourself? What words of comfort do you have for the part of you that survived the trauma? What does that part want from you now? Does that part feel safe now?" Remember that your *gentle* debriefing is not trying to dig up something new. However, it may be an opportunity to facilitate insight, self-esteem, and self-empathy and tear down the shackles of shame and toxic guilt. When all goes well, the relaxed client works through the deepest, darkest moments of his or her life. The symptoms of PTSD—flashbacks, startle response, paranoia, low self-esteem, fearfulness, depression/anxiety—will begin to fade as the number of sessions builds. After the program is ended, the client continues to get stronger. Most clients can complete the training in 30 sessions; sometimes more sessions are required. A/T training is a learning experience that is not limited to trauma resolution and recovery. It promotes inner growth, enhanced cognitive flexibility, and other intrinsic benefits.

After each session, make sure that the client is completely grounded. Some clients require theta inhibition at Cz for 5–10 min to restore a state of alertness. Other clients will feel more alert after the session than when they came in. Check out the clients' condition before they leave. Make sure they are okay to drive. Sometimes clients will call on the phone, complaining that they are still foggy. I direct them to listen to the Beach Boys or other kinds of upbeat rock-and-roll music. After 20–30 min of singing and listening to the foot-tapping, upbeat music of the oldies, theta begins to fade and beta gets stronger.

CASE STUDIES

Alice

Alice was a young single mother and a survivor of abuse. Her apartment was disorganized, messy, and unclean. Daily functioning was difficult. Treatment began by teaching her coping skills. The initial goal of neurofeedback was theta reduction to keep her grounded. Cz/SMR training rewarded 13–15 Hz, whereas theta and high beta were inhibited. Each session was divided between counseling and neurotherapy. Twenty-four sessions later, therapy ended. Her house was clean and organized. She was not overwhelmed by child care. She was able to return to college despite the fact that she had flunked out. The flashbacks had stopped. She stopped zoning out. A/T training was *not* begun.

Betty

Betty was a single, unmarried young adult. After 2 years of talk therapy she still suffered from panic attacks, flashbacks, and occasional depression. Talk therapy was ended. Two years later she returned for neurotherapy. Training started with 15 sessions of Cz/SMR. Next came twice weekly sessions of A/T training with Pz sensor placement, for a total of 30 sessions. Betty experienced the BASK for the first time in treatment. She worked through repressed memories and reclaimed more and more of her emotional self. Panic attacks and flashbacks were greatly diminished.

Cindy

Cindy was a married adult with adequate social and spousal support. She was an adult survivor of alcohol abuse, negative labeling, and toxic parenting. Her symptoms were depression, anxiety, codependency, passivity, and low self-esteem. The first session trained her to do diaphragmatic breathing. When she returned the next week, her level of anxiety had dropped 50%. Weekly sessions for several months were used to teach her assertiveness, cognitive, interpersonal skills, coping skills, and relaxation skills. Talk therapy was needed. Issues arose each week.

Eventually, Cindy felt safe enough outside and inside the therapeutic arena to commence neurotherapy. After 10 sessions of Cz/SMR training we began informal A/T training with Pz sensor placement. A pattern of

healing was noted in most 30-min sessions. After about 10 min her alpha dropped so low that no alpha feedback could be heard. For the next
5–10 min *only theta feedback could be heard*. Then, as she moved out of the
depth state, both alpha and theta tones could be heard. Painful issues were
discussed at each session without Cindy becoming overwhelmed. Issues
came up that had not been addressed in talk therapy. She squarely faced
both the cognitive and emotional reality of her upbringing. Training of
this nature proceeded for about 15–20 sessions. At that point A/T training
stopped. Cindy's reason for coming into treatment had been addressed.
Therapy was terminated.

Dorothy

Dorothy was a married adult with good social and family support. She
was diagnosed with DID. She specifically came to my office looking for
neurotherapy. Talk therapy had not helped; she could not trust a therapist
with her "stuff." It was difficult to know what was happening inside because
she made few self-disclosures to me. Weekly training started along the
sensorimotor strip: 10 min of C3/beta was followed by 20 min of C4/SMR.
While training in the RH (C4), she reexperienced repressed memories
but shared little with me. I was not sure if the treatment was working
until I received reports from the family that indicated major changes were
happening. Dorothy stopped training after 30 sessions. She returned a year
later. This time I suggested A/T training. The assessment clearly showed
RH theta > LH theta. Sensor placement at P3 was chosen. This decision
made sense to me, rewarding theta in the LH (P3) would be the mirror
image of suppressing theta in the RH (C4). Once-per-week eyes-closed
training commenced after the usual 3–5-min constructive visualization.
More traumata were worked through, but this time it was shared with me.
Dorothy developed more friends outside of therapy. Flashbacks stopped
and she reported an end of depression. Training stopped after 15 sessions.

The above case studies demonstrate the power of neurotherapy to enhance the therapy of PTSD. The clients learned grounding skills, diaphragmatic breathing, and basic coping skills before training started. Theta reduction was a key to zone-out prevention. Rewarding sensorimotor rhythm
(SMR) in the RH may lead to emotional releases. Deep-states training can
have many variations in the diverse world of trauma and recovery. The key
to success is prior assessment. Scott, Brod, Siderof, Kaiser, and Sagan (2002)
were successful because the Peniston and Kulkosky model was altered to fit

two different EEG patterns found in the experimental group. Some needed alpha suppression, whereas others needed alpha enhancement: "One size does *not* fit all."

IS DEEP-STATES TRAINING ALWAYS THE TREATMENT OF CHOICE?

The goal is to provide the trauma survivor with the best treatment available. I have trained a number of clients with A/T protocols in both formal and informal ways. In many cases it worked very well. The treatment for PTSD may require 50 sessions or more, that is, 20 sessions to reduce the EEG abnormalities and 30 sessions of A/T training (Figures 5.7c and 5.8c). Neurotherapy is an excellent way to resolve trauma. I have seen it repeatedly open up repressed memories and issues; I have no doubt of its power. But there are other power therapies that may be more economical (Wylie, 1996). EMDR has received the most press; it will be discussed in the next chapter because of its relationship to entrainment therapies.

Holographic memory resolution (HMR; Baum, 1997) is a power treatment for PTSD; it helps clients work through "somatic memories" (Wylie, 2004). It is an energy therapy that targets specific regions of the body. Trauma survivors often relive events on a daily basis. HMR teaches how to stop reliving the trauma in both their mind and their bodies. Clients must have an adequate sense of self in order to participate. I have had good results with short-term trauma resolution using this method. For example, after years of psychotherapy a survivor of childhood emotional and psychological trauma was looking for something better. She was motivated for treatment but her funds were limited. However, she made it clear: "I have had enough of talk therapy." Treatment began with five weekly sessions that included diaphragmatic breathing coaching, biofeedback ST training, cognitive therapy, assertiveness, and coping skills. My direct approach and the client's motivation resulted in Beck Depression Inventory (BDI) and Burns Anxiety Inventory (BAI) scores dropping to within normal limits. Reductions in the symptoms of depression and anxiety would not last unless the underlying trauma was worked through. Therefore, the next 7 sessions involved trauma debriefing with HMR. Repressed emotions and feelings were recovered and worked through by releasing them from the area of the body that experienced the most distress. The entire therapy took 12 sessions, the client was motivated and more than willing to do the homework

assignments. Neurotherapy was not the treatment of choice for the client
I just described. However, biofeedback for the body (hand warming) plus
diaphragmatic breathing were two of the ingredients needed to stabilize
this client. If HMR had not worked, I would have tried another power therapy that is used by many neurotherapists, brain wave entrainment (BWE)
or photic stimulation, which will be discussed in the next chapter.

CONCLUSION

Survivors of trauma or the substance abuser who participate in A/T, alpha
enhancement, or alpha synchrony programs get so much more than just
symptom relief. The successful trainees learn some of the physical and
mental control akin to Zen monks. They also gain a broader perspective
of life with enhanced cognitive processing. There is much more that could
be said about alpha training protocols. Clinicians who intend to specialize
in neurotherapy for addictions, PTSD, DID, or personality disorders will
want to read the Peniston and Kulkosky (1989, 1990, 1991) papers, the
Scott, Brod, Siderof, Kaiser, and Sagan (2002) report, the writings of White
(1999), and many others.

14

Entrainment Therapies

THROUGHOUT THE NATURAL UNIVERSE there is a tendency toward rhythmic alignment or entrainment. Striking an "E" tuning fork will cause other nearby "E" tuning forks to vibrate. Women who live in close quarters, such as in a college dorm, tend to have parallel menstrual cycles. Grandfather clocks placed in the same room will tend to swing their pendulums in sync with the dominant or largest pendulum. Crowds of people at a concert clap in unison to the beat of the music. Children shout, "Monkey see, monkey do."

Neurotherapists capitalize upon this natural phenomenon because of its potential to alter brain wave amplitudes and patterns. For example, music with a strong upbeat quality entrains faster frequencies, whereas music with a slow rhythm entrains slower frequencies. If you want to take the edge off a depressed state or a foggy mental condition, then listen to upbeat music. Brain wave frequencies tend to be influenced by the beat or rhythm of the music. Entrainment is not a biofeedback modality; it does not feed back biological signals to a trainee.

Brain wave entrainment (BWE) is induced by photic and audio stimulation. The literature refers to this modality in several other ways, including light and sound (L&S) and audiovisual stimulation (AVS). Photic stimulation entrains synchronous brain wave activity. Both brain hemispheres are stimulated. It serves as a stand-alone treatment for seasonal affective disorder (SAD), depression, anxiety, attention deficit/hyperactivity disoder (ADHD), academic achievement, age-related cognitive decline, and trauma resolution. Many neurotherapists use BWE to augment neurotherapy or to treat nonresponders. Another form of entrainment is also used for theta reduction: subliminal entrainment.

HOW DOES BRAIN WAVE ENTRAINMENT WORK?

Photic stimulation is the process of emitting pulsating light at a specific frequency. The pulses come from light emitting diodes (LEDs) mounted inside the lenses of darkened eyeglasses. LEDs come in different colors, such as red, blue, white, amber and green. Most entrainment systems require users to keep their eyes-closed to prevent damage to the retina. The intensity of the pulsating light is manually adjusted for individual comfort. Pulsating sound is the second component of most brain wave entrainment (BWE) equipment. Manual volume control is a standard feature.

Photic stimulation generates a series of repetitive flashes that reach the cortex via the optic nerve. Brain cells respond to visual and auditory stimuli by discharging electrical impulses known as evoked potentials. Visual and auditory evoked potentials can be measured by placing electrodes at the scalp at various locations. How long does it take the visual cortex to respond to a flash of light?

> When the stimulation is repetitive in nature, each stimulus follows the previous one by a short period of time (less than 500 milliseconds) and the successive evoked responses in the brain are found to overlap in time, so that the trailing end of one response is superimposed upon the beginning of the next. . . . In general, a repetitive flash produces an EEG response at the same frequency as the stimulation. (Collura, 2002, p. 49)

Consequently, the *repetitive flashes* of photic stimulation are programmed to pulsate within frequency ranges that are common to neurotherapy. For example, 5 Hz photic stimulation is in the theta frequency bandwidth and 20 Hz is in the beta frequency bandwidth. Frequency numbers are the same for both neurotherapy and BWE. If you have a basic understanding of neurotherapy, it can be generalized to BWE theory. Note: Photic stimulation entrains specific frequencies. The neurotherapy terms *reward* and *inhibit* do not apply.

BWE affects the brain globally; it is not site specific. The regions of the brain that process light or sound are likely the ones that receive the most stimulation. No sensors are placed on the head. The International 10–20 system is not used. In general, BWE does not differentiate between right (RH) and left hemispheres (LH). Both sides of the brain are entrained simultaneously. Only one frequency can be entrained at any given moment. Therefore, the theta bandwidth cannot be entrained as a whole 4–8 Hz, but it can be entrained one step at a time (4 Hz > 5 Hz > 6 Hz > 7 Hz > 8 Hz).

BWE software programs may be limited to just one frequency. What are the treatment effects when only one frequency is entrained? One study showed that BWE at a single frequency, 18.5 Hz, had a strong effect at Cz between 18.5 and 19.5 Hz and a weak effect throughout the beta bandwidth. "Variable-frequency stimulation might be more effective in the adjunctive use of AVS in neurofeedback therapy for ADD/ADHD, where activation of this broader range of frequencies is desired" (Frederick, Lubar, Rasey, Brim, & Blackburn, 1999, 23–27). Consequently, BWE programs often contain a series of changing frequencies.

BWE devices are programmed according to frequency and time. For example, a custom program can entrain 10 Hz for 2 min followed by 18 Hz for 2 min—the cycle can be repeated over and over again. The total length of the program is arbitrary, but most programs last at least 15 min and others go as long as 60 min. Rather than shifting from one frequency to another, it is also possible to create a program that increases frequency by 1/10-Hz steps. For example, a training session can start at 16 Hz and rise incrementally to 20 Hz for a 10-min cycle. In this case, the frequency would step up gradually, that is, 16.0, 16.1, 16.2, 16.3, and so on. The combinations are endless. Sophisticated BWE machines can also vary the way the sound is output—that is a study all by itself.

BWE has several potential benefits. It can cause a general increase in CBF (Noton, 1997; Siever, 2003). Theoretically, brain wave synchrony and lateral coherence improve at the programmed frequency. Increasing the amplitude of a particular frequency has the potential to influence mood or stress levels. For example, 20 min per day of 14-Hz entrainment leaves me feeling slightly depressed. I feel better with beta entrainment that steps up from 16 to 22 Hz. On the other hand, 14-Hz entrainment promotes calmness in some of my anxious clients. Neurotherapy and photic stimulation have much in common. Both neurotherapy and entrainment therapy have similar viewpoints about beta and sensorimotor rhythm (SMR): Beta is for mental clarity, whereas SMR is for calmness. However, there are numerous differences between the two modalities.

BWE poses danger to clients who have had or are at risk for seizure disorders. Ruuskanen-Uoti and Salmi (1994) examined a patient with a photoparoxysmal response (seizure) induced by photic stimulation. They came to the following conclusions:

Intermittent red light has reported to be particularly provocative, although green may be more so. The most common frequencies causing a photoparoxysmal response in photosensitive patients are between 15 and 20 Hz. The prevalence of photosensitive epilepsy is about one in 4,000 children and young adults, lesser in older adults, and higher in females. (p. 181)

Clients who buy, rent, or loan BWE equipment should have their first experience in the clinician's office and not at home alone. They should be made aware of the dangers. Never use BWE when there is a risk or history of seizure disorder. BWE is contraindicated for immature children who cannot be trusted to keep their eyes-closed. I have introduced dozens of clients to photic stimulation without a serious incident. However, a few adult clients were too light-sensitive for photic stimulation. One younger (anxious) client became jumpy within the first few seconds of stimulation: Entrainment was immediately stopped—no serious incident precipitated.

BWE machines usually come with canned programs designed to promote calmness, alertness, sleep, or an altered state of consciousness. A good machine can also be customized; software is included; programs can be created on a PC and downloaded via the communications port (RS 232 port). For clients who rent or purchase BWE equipment, I provide them with custom programs. I usually have three or four machines in stock ready for rental. Some clients choose to purchase a system after they have used it at home for a few weeks.

BWE Assessments

BWE equipment can be purchased by the general public—the Internet lists a number of distributors. Warning labels that declare the risk of seizure come with each unit. BWE can be guided by clinical assessments. EEG neurofeedback sensors can monitor the effect of L&S therapy. In other words, while the client is receiving photic stimulation, the clinician can graph the effect on the EEG. Sensors are mounted at the scalp locations of greatest interest using two channels. Check for changes in coherence, dominant brain wave frequency, and standard bandwidths.

BWE is not designed to correct lateral asymmetries. On the other hand, if the client suffers from a global problem such as general slowing or widespread high beta, then BWE may have clinical utility. The subjective report of the client is the most important feature of your assessment. After 3 days of consecutive training, many clients notice a difference.

Positive changes include improvements in mental clarity, uplifted mood, and greater calmness. If the client feels wired, use lower frequencies. If the client cannot tolerate the flashing lights, BWE is contraindicated.

BWE as a Stand-Alone Treatment

BWE can be a beneficial stand-alone treatment for many disorders. It produces changes within a few treatment sessions and can be used at home. Neurofeedback is a learning process; it teaches the trainee to govern certain aspects of the EEG or rCBF. BWE is not a learning process because it drives the EEG. Consequently, it is ideal for clients who are poor candidates for neurotherapy due to lack of funds, inability to learn, or distance from a provider. It is a way for some clients to stimulate their EEG during absences from therapy. But, for other clients, BWE is the therapy of choice that will make the needed changes with or without the added benefit of psychotherapy. The following list presents 6 possible ways that BWE can be applied to clinical disorders:

Depression, Seasonal Affect Disorder, Anxiety, and Sleep

1. Mood disorders may improve with beta entrainment.
2. The symptoms of seasonal affect disorder (SAD) may be lessened with 20-Hz entrainment (Berg & Siever, 1999).
3. Clients with clinical disorders may be benefited by 14-Hz entrainment. Some have reported greater calmness and less anxiety.
4. Sleep deprivation may result in symptoms of depression and poor concentration. Many BWE machines have programs to induce sleep. A program for sleep starts at the lower end of the beta band and then gently drops into the delta band. It is appropriate to entrain slow frequencies late at night because they are part of the sleep cycle. There is always some concern when delta is entrained. Assess for mood stability and attention periodically.

Attention Deficit Disorder

5. Joyce and Siever (2000) published a promising study in the *Journal of Neurotherapy* presenting BWE as an effective treatment for childhood attention deficit disorder (ADD) and learning disorders. They were able to train several children simultaneously with one piece of equipment and a special adapter hub. All training was done at

the school location. Entrainment began with 8 sessions that lasted 20 min each. The equipment was programmed to start at 7 Hz and gradually step up to 9 Hz. The first 8 sessions were designed to promote relaxation and reduce anxiety. Next came 27 sessions that alternated between 12, 18, and 10 Hz for approximately 2 min each, for a total of 22 min. Care was taken to gently ramp between frequencies in order to minimize potential seizure reactions. Since 18 Hz > 15 Hz, they chose white/blue LED lights rather than red—another precaution that may help to avoid seizure. Significant improvements were made in the experimental group, including attention, impulsivity, and reaction time. Ten students were trained simultaneously via a multi-user amplifier. The results of this study were excellent (pp. 9–25). David Siever is one of the leaders in the field of entrainment. For more information visit his Web site, www.mindalive.ca.

I reproduced the above entrainment protocol in my own equipment. The program cycles between 12, 18, and 10 Hz at 2-min intervals. I also have another program that cycles between 18 and 12 Hz at 2-min intervals. Currently, two former clients are using this protocol to improve their level of concentration without the use of stimulant medication. In their cases entrainment must be continued on a regular basis in order for it to continue working. I have not had a client who said that the change was permanent.

Posttraumatic Stress Disorder

6. BWE can be used to entrain deep states. It is an excellent alternative to A/T training for survivors of trauma. It brings repressed issues to the surface. I created a simple program that starts at beta (16 Hz), then gradually steps down to low theta (4–6 Hz). It dwells in theta for 15–20 min. The program ends by gradually stepping up and returning to 16 Hz beta—sometimes I dwell in beta for several minutes. The total program ranges from 25 to 30 min. I customize the program to suit the client's experience. The amount of time at lower frequencies may need to adjusted, as well as the cool-down time at the end when the client is returned to a normal beta state of wakefulness. Make sure the client feels totally grounded and alert when entrainment is finished. I follow the exact same order of events that was suggested in Chapter 13 for alpha/theta (A/T)

training, including breathwork and skin temperature (ST) training. Each session begins with 3–8 min of the constructed visualization before the entrainment process begins. Since there are no inhibits, the primary concern is to prevent client decompensation.

BWE has been known to trigger painful flashbacks with some survivors. It may be wise to monitor the client's physiology, including hand temperature, breath rate, and pulse rate. (I have seen breath rate double, whereas the pulse rate rose just four or five beats).

BWE, Eye Movement Desensitization and Reprocessing, and Alpha/Theta Training

Peterson (2000) explored the clinical effect of eye movement desensitization and reprocessing (EMDR), BWE, and alpha/theta (A/T) training. He admitted that "neurotherapy seems to have been losing ground in the treatment of PTSD in recent years, probably for two major reasons." First, he concluded that A/T training protocols may be incorrectly applied leading to treatment failure. Second, the "the advent and ascendancy of EMDR (Eye Movement Desensitization and Reprocessing) as a new wave psychological treatment for PTSD" (Shapiro, 1995). But how does EMDR work? "The bilateral stimulation employed in EMDR produces synchronous, slow-wave activity in the client." He concluded: "EMDR is an entrainment procedure." Consequently, it is better at *single-incident* trauma because it can "direct the client's attention to the specific target trauma and then induce the brainwave state needed to facilitate the resolution of that trauma." Peterson used a combination of neurotherapy and EMDR to process trauma. He cautioned that anti-anxiety medications may sabotage A/T training because these drugs suppress the limbic system. The most important ingredient is the "therapeutic alliance" and "EEG biofeedback is a catalyst for talk therapy, not a substitute for it" (Peterson, 2000, pp. 10–12).

Much of what Peterson said about EMDR *likely* applies to BWE for trauma resolution. BWE actively entrains the exact slow-wave states needed to gain access to traumata. It is more economical that A/T training because the goal is to open, work through, and bring closure. A/T training has much broader goals and a greater capacity to enrich the client's life—it may well take longer. A/T training, like all other protocols, must be modified according to the client's EEG data (Scott, Brod, Siderof, Kaiser & Sagan, 2002).

BWE and Neurofeedback Combined

Hammond (1999) reported on the "Roshi, a neurofeedback system utilizing photic stimulation which can be set so that the frequency of photic stimulation varies depending on the patent's existing dominant brainwave." His case study report demonstrated the efficacy of Roshi technology in the treatment of depression with frontal lobe alpha asymmetry. "After 5 sessions the patient was reporting that he didn't feel depressed any longer" (p. 63).

Roshi has several training components that combine to reduce frontal alpha asymmetry and enhance the dominant brainwave frequency. Photic stimulation drives the EEG while neurofeedback facilitates learning via auditory reinforcement. The Roshi's success suggests the importance of dominant brainwave frequency training which can also be accomplished with standard neurofeedback equipment and specialized software. Hammond's (1999) study also reinforces the concept that L&S treatment may be necessary for clients who are poor neurofeedback learners.

BWE as an Adjunct to Neurotherapy

Neurotherapy is an expensive treatment. If there is a way to shorten the overall number of sessions, then it should be considered. The program used by Joyce and Siever (2000) may help the ADD client progress faster. It has been reported that some parents use BWE first thing in the morning to help their children get started. Others use the program every day as an adjunct to neurotherapy—to reinforce current treatment protocols. If funds run out, then BWE can be used until neurotherapy can resume. Overall, some, but not all, report benefits from entrainment. I do not introduce BWE to all clients because it lacks specificity and seldom leads to permanent change. Some users report going to sleep during the entrainment process, even during fast-wave entrainment. However, clients who can afford only one neurotherapy session per week or those who are progressing slowly or not at all may benefit from BWE.

Case Study. Figures 6.5c and 6.6c depict a client with excessive posterior alpha and theta. This client suffered from endogenous depression, poor sense of self, and PTSD. Thirty sessions of quantitative EEG (QEEG) guided neurotherapy and cognitive therapy failed to bring positive results. Excessive posterior theta and alpha caused me to shy away from A/T training protocols. BWE was recruited into the clinical treatment plan. I created a beta entrainment program that cycled between 15 and 20 Hz. BWE each day—at home—resulted in an improved mood. Thereafter, homework was assigned to prepare the client for trauma and recovery. It included daily diaphragmatic breathing exercises and an appropriate constructed visualization to build a better sense of self.

The BWE program started in beta and gradually stepped down to 4–6 Hz theta. During the first entrainment session the client's breath rate began to increase while the program dwelled in theta. I intervened by reminding the client to slow down and breathe from the diaphragm. The client was perplexed. "Why the change in breath rate? Why am I thinking about a time in my childhood? What's going on?" I answered those questions in a general way: "Your body is trying to tell you something. Your job is to listen. Take an observer position and stand back. Whatever is being experienced is not happening now." Each new session brought the client directly to trauma recovery and resolution. Working through the traumata brought greater personal control, less depression, more insight, and a better sense of self. Since the program for trauma and recovery ended with beta, the negative effects that can come with slow-wave entrainment were prevented. BWE for the recovery and healing of trauma is an in-office program, and is not intended for home use. The recovery from trauma requires a therapeutic relationship. An understanding of systems theory also facilitates the resolution of trauma.

SUBLIMINAL ENTRAINMENT

Another adjunct to neurotherapy that some neurofeedback providers are recommending is subliminal entrainment via audiocassette or CD. Swingle (1996) discovered that listening to subliminal frequencies might influence brain wave patterns. Children with excessive theta may benefit while they are listening to subliminal entrainment sounds. It may help during homework times or when it's time to get up in the morning. There are no known side effects, but the entrainment effect is temporary.

Assess the child before sending the tape home. Establish a baseline at Cz for both theta and beta frequencies. Then begin playing the tape. After a few minutes and before the tape is over, take another baseline. If the amplitude of theta is lower, then encourage the parents to purchase the tape and use it every day. A tape is placed in the child's room. About 5 min before it's time to get up, the parents turn on the player and let one side of the tape play (for about 15 min). In a similar fashion, the parents turn the tape player on when the process of doing homework has begun. It is not necessary to play the tape loudly; it sounds like pink noise or a rushing stream. Play the tape just loud enough to be audible.

Parents report that the whole process of getting up and doing homework is just a little bit easier when the tape is used. Other parents have found it difficult to implement the process of playing the tape. This tape is not for the family; it should be limited to child or adult with elevated amplitudes of theta. It does not work with all slow-wave disorders. (10 Hz subliminal entrainment audiocassettes or CDs can be purchased from www.mindalive.ca)

PART III

THE NEUROFEEDBACK PRACTITIONER

15

Neurofeedback Education, Training, and Certification

MY FIRST INDIVIDUAL NEUROFEEDBACK TRAINING experience was at a workshop. The instructor used me to demonstrate alpha/theta (A/T) training. The class was watching for computer settings and sensor placement while I was experiencing deep-states training. The power and potential of neurofeedback was moving me into a different state of mind. I envisioned clients advancing farther and faster than they did with traditional talk therapy. I was ready for a change. Graduate school had opened up the psyche of the brain, but it soon became evident that counseling skills alone were not enough. Many of my clients were progressing slowly. Others simply did not respond to talk therapy. More was needed. I had a growing interest in alternative therapies. Eventually, this interest led me to neurofeedback; it would pool all of my interests and counseling skills into one unified package.

The practice of neurotherapy is relegated to the realm of professional health care providers. It begins with education. Formal training is available at a few universities and during weeklong workshops. It is not ethical to buy biofeedback equipment and set up shop without the proper credentials and training. Why? Neurotherapy is not a simple technique. It facilitates changes in the brain—each person's central processing unit. Health professionals who have a broad range of understanding of such topics as mental health, cognitive performance, and family dynamics best supervise its application.

213

Most *independent* neurofeedback practitioners already possess credentials in the health care system. Credentials may be formal licensing or certification that is granted by a duly authorized authority—usually the state, regional, or national government. For example, I am licensed by the state of Vermont as a clinical mental health counselor (LCMHC). Licensing requires a minimum of a master's degree, 3,000 hours of supervised practice, and a passing grade on two separate clinical tests. Forty continuing education units (CEUs) are required every 2 years. Other examples of independent neurofeedback practitioners include licensed social workers and professional counselors psychologists, marriage and family therapists, doctors, registered nurses, occupational and physical therapists, certified rehabilitation counselors and addictions counselors, as well as certain university professors. Qualified nonlicensed (noncertified) practitioners work in institutions or agencies that offer neurotherapy treatment.

I encourage the qualified professional to become certified by the Biofeedback Certification Institute of America (BCIA). Certification requirements are similar to most states' licensing requirements. Neurofeedback is a credible treatment because outcome studies and research trials have demonstrated its effectiveness. Although there are others, BCIA is considered by many in the field to be the primary certification organization. BCIA has certified individuals outside the United States, including Europe, the United Kingdom, and Australia.

BCIA is a certifying organization rather than a membership organization. Requirements include credentials in the health care system, special education, supervision, (mentoring) and passing a test. Continuing education units (CEUs) are required after certification has been awarded. CEUs acquired may be acceptable to both the state and BCIA. For example, I seek out biofeedback training that is approved by the American Psychological Association (APA) and BCIA. Furthermore, BCIA accepts CEUs from approved workshops in the field of psychology—biofeedback practitioners are counselors, too. Check the BCIA Web site for the most up-to-date requirements and recommended training programs: www.bcia.org.

A good training program provides an overall understanding of the history and clinical practice of neurofeedback. Each participant learns how to assess and train with one electroencephalograph (EEG) channel. Later, two-channel operation and protocols are introduced and demonstrated. A review of quantitative EEG (QEEG) is part of the program. Training programs usually provide participants with instruction manuals that are easy to read and follow. An effective manual is not merely a collection of published articles; it should serve as a written supervisor for the first-time neurotherapist.

Students will be introduced to at least one neurofeedback system. Several professional-grade models are available. (Visit the Web site www. futurehealth. com to make a few comparisons.) Do not immediately invest in the neurofeedback system that is recommended by instructors. First, learn the fundamentals of equipment operation; second, find out about other systems; third, interview someone who already owns the proposed system. Become an informed consumer of training programs and equipment before making the investment.

There are several approved training programs listed on the BCIA Web site. Each follows the blueprint for education outlined by BCIA. The blueprint consists of 40 hr of education that cover essential topics in neurotherapy. Make sure the training program will support you through the entire certification process. Pick two or three approved training programs from the list and ask the following questions:

- What percentage of your graduates passes the BCIA test?
- How will I be helped to pass the test?
- How will supervision (mentoring) be provided after training is complete?
- Are the supervisors (mentors) on your list BCIA-certified supervisors (mentors)?
- Will I receive an instruction manual for future reference?
- May I have the names and telephone numbers of two graduates?
- What brand equipment will be used during training?
- Do you sell and service the equipment that will be used?
- What is the cost of a two-channel EEG neurofeedback system?
- Can the equipment also be used for hemoencephalography (HEG) neurofeedback?
- Does your program qualify for CEUs?

After attending an official "blueprint" program with 40 hr of instruction, more training will be needed. For example, some training programs offer a partial fulfillment of BCIA's didactic requirement. A second exposure to neurofeedback instruction is probably needed. Totally different instructors will help to round out your understanding. They will not be wedded to the blueprint; other matters of significance can be covered along with the basics. In my case, I went through two complete programs and two shorter workshops. Later I attended workshops at conferences.

Get the most out of the training program. Neurofeedback training is typically a 5-day seminar. It's unlike any other educational experience you may have encountered at 2-day workshops for psychologists. Graduate school did not prepare you for neurotherapy! Many attendees feel overwhelmed with information the first time it's presented. Prepare for your first experience. Get more out of your first training experience. Ask better questions in class, and create a frame of reference: Read my book before attending your first workshop. *Getting Started in Neurofeedback* was designed (in part) to help the professional prepare. Another book that has generated great interest in neurotherapy is *A Symphony in the Brain* by Jim Robbins. His book was written for the general public. Many clients have read it. Reading these two books will give you a taste of what is to come. Education is the key to success. Expect to go to other seminars and conferences in the future. Becoming a neurotherapist is a mental, financial, and time-consuming investment—but it can be very rewarding.

Non-blueprint-oriented neurofeedback workshops are held throughout the year: Equipment manufacturers sponsor some, whereas experienced neurofeedback providers present others. Also, three different organizations hold conferences every year: Futurehealth, Association for Applied Psychophysiology and Biofeedback (AAPB), and ISNR. Some conferences offer BCIA approved training. Conference workshops may also award CEUs needed to fulfill state and/or BCIA requirements. The documentation of CEUs at conferences tends to be confusing. Make sure that statements made by conference representatives about CEU acquisition are crystal clear.

ISNR and AAPB publish journals. Keeping up with the latest improvements and innovations in neurofeedback is a challenge. Their literature has been an essential part of my learning experience. ISNR publications focus on neurofeedback, whereas AAPB publishes information about both neurofeedback biofeedback. I am a member of both organizations for a number of reasons:

- Journals are sent to members.
- Discounts are available for conferences.
- Networking with other professionals is promoted.
- Governmental laws and restrictions may be discussed.
- Support for the profession is enhanced.

SUPERVISION (MENTORING)

The staff at approved training programs will introduce you to BCIA-certified supervisors (mentors). After the 40 hr of training is complete, a brief internship with a BCIA certified supervisor (mentor) is the next step. The internship may start with a didactic presentation. Thereafter, you will be invited to watch and then participate in the entire process of sensor placement, impedance checking, artifact rejection, threshold setting, and monitoring the trainee's progress. Supervisors (mentors) will introduce you to assessment forms and other evaluation techniques. Equipment operation will be reviewed and practiced. Thus, you will be introduced to a viable neurofeedback practice. It will become a template or model for your new practice. After the face-to-face supervision (mentoring) is over, further contact may continue on the telephone or by e-mail. Hopefully, your client's training data can be transmitted via the Internet. That means, the supervisor (mentor) can look at the training progress of your client from a distance. Continue supervision (mentoring) until you are firmly grounded in neurotherapy. It may be necessary to consult with other experienced practitioners after the formal supervision period has concluded.

At this point in time, you have received 40 hours of blueprint training and have participated in a brief internship with a BCIA-approved supervisor (mentor). The next steps are as follows:

1. Purchase a neurofeedback system and supplies.
2. Purchase computerized assessment tests.
3. Practice using the system (with nonclients).
4. Choose an appropriate office (or rearrange an existing office).
5. Create a clinical vision for your practice.
6. Train your first client.
7. Advertise.

16

Purchasing a Neurofeedback System

I HAVE HAD MANY CONVERSATIONS with those who wish to purchase neurofeedback systems. There is no best system—there are drawbacks to every system. Most systems are easy to use once you become familiar with them. There are a number of factors that will guide your investment:

- Budget (how much money is available)
- Service (speedy repairs and technical support)
- Operating systems (DOS, Windows, or Macintosh)
- Optional two-monitor setup
- Built-in functions for assessment and operation
- Expandability to HEG neurofeedback and other biofeedback modalities
- Capacity for 40 Hz training
- Training programs to teach equipment operation
- Software features (sound, graphics, and flexibility)
- Internet transmission and long-distance training
- FDA clearance

Cash-flow management is essential to success. Many years ago my counseling supervisor said to me, "John, put on your business hat." He knew that unless I took certain financial precautions I would not make it in psychotherapy, regardless of my talent and abilities. His warning applies even more to neurotherapy. Beginning neurotherapists have gone out of business because they invested in a high-end system costing $10,000 or more. Unless money is no object, your first investment might have to be limited

218

to $2,000–$3,000, including a desktop computer (add another $500 for a laptop). The proposed system should be at least a two-channel system. Do not invest in a single-channel system! A single-channel system will not give you accurate symmetry comparisons. It will hinder the assessment process. It will eliminate the possibility of two-channel training.

At present, I have four training systems: two older single-channel units for backup, and two newer ones that are in daily use. Having a backup system is very handy, but if I had purchased a $10,000 system, it would be out of the question. Furthermore, some clients must be trained at home. How many people can afford a $10,000 home trainer? Actually, some neurofeedback providers do long-distance training. Professional-grade systems (for home use) can be purchased for less than $2,000. The trainee takes home a system and the trainer monitors progress. A few manufacturers have special software and hardware features that facilitate home training.

Purchase your equipment from a manufacturer who emphasizes service. All brands of equipment have breakdowns. When this happens, turn-around time for repair should be within a week. I have sent out systems on Monday and have had them returned on Thursday or Friday (with next day shipping both ways). Questions arise about software and hardware. Service means that your question will be answered the same day. Technicians are on board and ready to assist you with computer problems, software problems, and hardware connections. Make sure that service is available on a daily basis. Call for technical support before you buy a system; see what happens.

Advanced Windows and Macintosh operating systems (OS) are fundamental to the computer management scene in 2004. However, several older neurofeedback software packages are written in DOS. They work well with older computers and adequately with Windows 95 and 98 OS. DOS is less flexible than Windows. DOS is a reliable OS, but knowledge about DOS is fading. Consequently, it's best to purchase an EEG training system that operates with the latest version of Windows or Macintosh.

How computer savvy are you? I found it necessary to enlist local technicians who know a lot more about computers than I do. Each one of my desktops has been custom built—for about the same cost as a standard model. My computer guru stands ready to find the right driver or communications port, add special PC boards or sound cards to suit my needs. If the neurofeedback systems manufacturer builds you a computer, it could double the cost of a PC. Here is where service starts. Manufacturers should be willing to work with your computer guru if a special system needs to be built. On the other hand, most newer systems run on standard PCs purchased in the usual manner; they are compatible with the latest version of Windows and, in some cases, Macintosh.

Neurofeedback systems that are Windows oriented open up an entire new vista of training possibilities. Windows operation means that you can open and operate more than one software program at a time. (The USB port supports a secondary mouse.) For example, while the client is training, he can be engaged in educational games such as Tetris, Freecell, or solitaire, to name a few. The clinician decides what software game is appropriate. The 8–9-Year-old population enjoys drawing pictures on Microsoft's Paint accessory. It helps them to stop fidgeting and to focus on the activity at hand. Clients with learning disorders will at first be unable to win solitaire; cards will be missed. Progress in training will translate into better scores and wins at whatever educational game is played. Obviously, the chosen (educational) computer game cannot generate any sounds. It should help the trainee to stay focused. Action video games are never used. One client admitted to me that he zones out when looking at neurofeedback-driven graphics. He is not alone. Most neurofeedback-driven graphics are boring and repetitive. Fortunately, he no longer zones out because I instructed him to vary his training time between playing solitaire and reading a book.

Expandability is another issue. Some systems are capable of utilizing several modalities of biofeedback simultaneously! SEMG, galvanic skin response (GSR), and skin temperature (ST) can be monitored during neurofeedback training. Heart rate variability (HRV) training and hemoencephalography (HEG) neurofeedback modules can also be added. Some clinicians have skillfully used complex systems to their advantage. Clearly, having many options is of great value; just watch your budget. Most neurofeedback providers have more than one training system; if one system breaks, business continues with the remaining system(s).

HEG neurofeedback is essential to my practice. I evaluate with EEG and about half of my clients train with HEG. When purchasing a neurofeedback system training inquire if it can be upgraded to include HEG neurofeedback. Part I of *Getting Started with Neurofeedback* showed the relationship between slow-wave disorders and the quality of regional blood flow. Theta-to-beta ratios exceeding 2.5:1 suggest hypoperfusion—underactivation. Once electroencephalograph (EEG) slowing has been assessed, HEG neurofeedback training may be in order. This is especially true if EEG slowing is at prefrontal lobe sites of Fp1, Fp2, Fpz, F7, and F8. In many ways, HEG and EEG are interrelated neurological factors. In some cases it may be more cost-effective (Cost: $1700 includes hardware + software) to purchase a separate HEG training system rather than upgrading an existing EEG system. Contact www.biocompresearch.org for more information.

A double-monitor setup is popular with some neurotherapists. Having this feature may require the insertion of an additional video card inside the CPU. Engaging two monitors means that one screen is for the trainee and the other screen is for the clinician. It allows the clinician to check the trainee's progress and make changes when necessary, without disturbing the trainee. Single-monitor training means that the monitor will be rotated periodically into the clinician's visual field and then back to the trainee. Obviously, there are advantages to having two monitors. However, an additional monitor takes up more space. Furthermore, training success is not dependent upon a two-monitor setup. However, be prepared to swivel the monitor between you and the trainee. Single-monitor setups work well with automatic thresholding because the clinician is assured that feedback will remain constant.

At this time most clinicians train within the standard 0–32 hertz range. Most systems examine EEG data at 128 samples per second. In general, the ratio of sampling rate to maximum frequency output is 4:1. For example, if a system was monitoring 32 Hz, then a sampling rate of 128 would be adequate because $32 \times 4 = 128$. If a system was monitoring 64 Hz, then a sampling rate of 256 would be adequate because $64 \times 4 = 256$. However, accurate acquisition of EEG data is not determined solely by sampling rates. Furthermore, faster sampling rates are not always better than slower sampling rates. Good data acquisition is an engineering problem. Question manufacturers about product capability and make comparisons. I have raised the issue of sampling rates because high-frequency training is currently being researched. Parts I and II explored the value of 40-Hz training with two-channel scalp locations along the sensorimotor strip. However, many clinicians limit their practice to the 0–32-Hz range.

Not only do manufacturers have different sampling rates, but they also process raw EEG signals differently. Active bandpass filters, digital filters, and Fourier analysis are some of the ways that specific frequency ranges can be isolated. Each method has advantages and disadvantages. But even after the frequency range has been defined, there is yet another variable. Manufacturers have chosen different ways to output microvolt amplitudes. In *Getting Started with Neurotherapy* only peak-to-peak measurements—the full height of the wave from top to bottom—have been used (see Figure 4.2). However, amplitudes can be output in peak measurements that are half of the wave height. Lastly, there are the root mean square (RMS) measurements that output smaller microvolt numbers. Each of these three methods has clinical utility. However, if you transfer a client from one brand of equipment to another, a new baseline may have to be established.

Clinical-grade equipment can output various sounds and may have a variety of graphics. Sounds are very important, and a flexible system may be capable of outputting sustained, tapping, or pitch-variable sounds. Combinations of sounds may also be possible. Deep-states training works well with gentle sounds that invoke quiet inner states. If you plan to use an EEG neurofeedback system for deep-states training, find out what provisions have been made to accommodate this form of training. Some systems offer a variety of graphic presentations. Figures or images move on the screen when the trainee is rewarded. It's helpful to have more than one choice of graphics. It may be possible to purchase a custom graphics package for an additional cost. It may also be possible to create your own custom graphics presentation using media files. Early devices were simple; they displayed a green light when the trainee was successful. Do not buy a system based solely on its ability to create a variety of graphics.

FOOD AND DRUG ADMINISTRATION

The United States Food and Drug Administration (FDA) has created regulations that protect the public from unsafe medical equipment and medical practices. The FDA does not test or examine new hardware; it is up to the manufacturer to prove that their product is safe. Preventing electrical shock is a major issue. Some neurofeedback systems are powered by line voltage whereas others use batteries. All manufacturers of commercial-grade equipment must conform to good manufacturing practices (GMP) and in certain cases the FDA requires a 510(K) clearance. Commercial-grade biofeedback or neurofeedback systems may not be sold to the public for medical applications. A lay person may possess a system if a professional health care provider monitors its application. Manufacturers are not allowed to make statements about the effectiveness of biofeedback that have not been approved. Consider the following statement made by the FDA:

> Pre-Amendment biofeedback devices were used for *relaxation training and muscle re-education* [Italics added]. Any other intended use must be supported by valid scientific data. . . . If a new use raises new scientific issues, then the device is a new device. (USFDA, 1994)

What do these regulations mean for neurotherapists?

The FDA regulates the sales and manufacturing of medical equipment, including neurofeedback systems. Their primary concern is safety. Do not use a neurofeedback system that is powered by line voltage (e.g., 110 V AC) unless it has been cleared by the FDA. Never put a client at risk for electrical shock. I purchased a Neurosearch-24 for QEEG data acquisition from Lexicor Medical Technology, Inc. That system meets FDA standards. When the client is connected to the Lexicor with 19 scalp sensors and 2 ear sensors, there is virtually no risk of electrical shock. I decided not to purchase any QEEG brain mapping system powered by line voltage unless it had FDA clearance. Thus, I protected both the client and myself from electrical shock and potential legal action.

The FDA has approved biofeedback training for relaxation and muscle re-education—no more. Neurotherapists avoid dogmatic statements about the efficacy of biofeedback training. For example, Shannon (2000, July) wrote the article "Alternative Healing: What really works" for *Reader's Digest*: neurofeedback was listed as an alternative therapy with may positive applications, including the treatment of ADD. But that article does not mean that the FDA has approved neurofeedback for the treatment of attention deficit/hyperactivity disorder (ADHD). Therefore, do not assert that neurofeedback is an approved treatment for ADHD or any other disorder. Describe how neurofeedback works and its potential benefits. Share published articles with clients. Present case studies that stand on their own merit. Use the expression "focused relaxation" because the FDA has approved biofeedback training for "relaxation." Create a release form for adults and for the parents or guardians of minors (see Appendix 4).

One day the FDA may recognize neurofeedback as an approved treatment for one or more disorders, but, until that day arrives, avoid dogmatic statements. Furthermore, carefully supervise long-distance training. Do not allow clients who train at home to make treatment decisions. Follow FDA guidelines.

SUPPLIES

Manufacturers of neurofeedback systems provide sensor cups and leads. Make sure you get at least two with special earlobe clips as well as four that are mounted to the scalp. Buy extra leads—you will need them when one goes bad. Leads can be checked for continuity with an ohmmeter.

Buy an inexpensive ohmmeter from a hardware or electronic supply store. Continuity checking with an ohmmeter is simple. Place one probe on the sensor cup and insert the other probe into the plug that goes to the neurofeedback system. Good leads have practically no resistance from end to end. See Part I for instructions on how to use an ohmmeter.

Wire leads that extend from the neurofeedback system to the scalp may come as single wires with cups or as three wires inside a shielded cable that exit with one cup for each wire. (Other variations are also used.) Whether the wires are segregated or integrated, they must remain on the scalp during the training session. Some leads come with an alligator clip or a hairpin that can be attached to the collar of the trainee. Sensors that are loose tend to pull off the head when the trainee moves. When the wires are segregated, I bind them with tape and attach an alligator clip or hairpin. Never damage the casing that protects lead wires when fabricating a collar attachment device. Sensors must be cleaned and gently brushed in order to prevent corrosion—hot water is usually all that is needed. Sensors and lead wires need to be replaced when worn out or broken.

I clean the scalp and earlobes with NuPrep™ ECG & EEG Abrasive Skin Prepping Gel or with rubbing alcohol. I used 2-in.-square (50-mm-square) nonsterile gauze pads. Do not get the individually wrapped style; purchase it in bulk packaging. I cut up individual pieces of paper towels to place on top of sensors. I clean up the trainee's scalp and ears with nonscented wipes (sometimes called baby wipes). I purchase them in bulk from the supermarket. Sometimes I saturate the wipes with alcohol. Watch out for pierced earlobes; clean them thoroughly to prevent infection. I hand mature trainees a wipe and have them clean off their own earlobes. Sensor cups are filled with Ten20™ Conductive EEG paste. NuPrep and Ten20 paste can be purchased online from almost every biofeedback supplier.

Most clinicians check the quality of scalp and ear connections with an impedance meter. Approximately 5,000 Ω or less is acceptable for assessments. Impedance meters are an absolute necessity for neurotherapists. They can verify that both scalp sensors used in bipolar montages are relatively the same. For example, I have one child with thick hair and sensitive skin. I settle for about 10,000 Ω measurements at each scalp location. However, I make sure that the impedance to ground measurement at each individual scalp location is within 2,000 Ω of each other. Impedance meters start at approximately $300.

I have a Styrofoam head in my office, similar to the ones used by beauticians. International 10–20 positions are marked on the head. I check the head every so often to make sure my scalp positions are correct. I also show it to clients who have questions about the treatment. Optimit sells a harness that identifies each International 10–20 position; it can be used on clients or to ensure the accuracy of the 10–20 positions on your Styrofoam head. BrainMaster Technologies, Inc., sells Optimit Marking systems.

Purchase several indoor/outdoor digital thermometers. One can be used to monitor the client during neurofeedback training. The others can be distributed to clients for a small fee. ST training and diaphragmatic breathing can be taught at the same time. There are other more expensive home training instruments that are available. The use of light and sound (L&S) (photic stimulation) requires further training and investigation. Some neurotherapists make use of this technology. They rent or sell L&S sound equipment. Purchase brain wave entrainment (BWE) equipment that can create custom programs for clients. You may wish to check the following Web sites for different brands: www.futurehealth.com, www.mindalive.ca and www.syneticsystems.com.

COMPUTERIZED TESTS

The first step in the evaluation process is computerized testing. The following computerized tests are routinely administered in my office according to the need:

- Intermediate Visual and Auditory (IVA) (distributed by BrainTrain)
- MicroCog (distributed by The Psychological Corporation)
- QEEG

The above three tests assess various cognitive functions.

IVA is not the only continuous-performance test on the market. Many clinicians use a Test of Variables of Attention (TOVA). This fine testing instrument also works well. However, visual and auditory responses are divided into two separate tests. Some attend workshops to receive training in the administering and interpretation of TOVA or IVA. Both TOVA and IVA are costly. Individual tests must be purchased separately. Take the test yourself and see how your level of attention compares with the general population.

The MicroCog is a cognitive performance test for adults 18 years and older. It can be administered to adolescents as well, but they will be placed in the adult population category. A detailed report and graphs are

immediately available (on screen) when the test is concluded. The MicroCog is in DOS format and will not print easily—most printers will not
work. Tech support will give you suggestions. I print on a HP Deskjet 960C
with the standard parallel connection to my computer—it won't adapt to
USB. One day MicroCog will advance to a Windows system. MicroCog
operating software is less expensive than IVA's, but the individual tests are
more costly. MicroCog is sold only to qualified professionals according to
state regulations.

REVIEW OF INVESTMENT COSTS

Your investment thus far includes:

1 training program (and hotel expenses)

1 neurofeedback system and supplies

1 PC

2 computerized tests

Purchasing one commercial-grade system and supplies, two computerized tests, one PC, and one training program with hotel expenses for
5 days will cost at least $4,500–$5,000 in the year 2004. Obviously, prices
can go much higher depending on what neurofeedback training system
you choose. Fortunately, most training programs will award 40 CEUs for
the 40 blueprint hours of training. Many therapists already have a PC at
the office. Future expenses may include:

- Hemoencephalography (HEG) neurofeedback upgrade separate
  unit $1,400–$2,500
- QEEG data acquisition unit: $7,000–$9,000

QEEG data acquisition systems do not include normative database software packages. Software costs vary from $3,000 to $10,000. I do not own
any normative database software. I send out QEEG data to be processed
elsewhere. Novice neurotherapists send many of their clients to facilities
that have the equipment and software needed to produce brain maps.

The ideal QEEG system will have the following features: FDA clearance,
Windows operating system, multiple-channel training, smooth transition
between assessment and training, multiple-site monitoring during training,
easy-to-use artifacting software, instant results on coherence, symmetry,

dominant brain wave frequency, capacity to review wave morphology, compatibility with normative database software, expansion capabilities to other biofeedback and neurofeedback and entrainment modalities, capacity to both monitor and train using various biological signals, the ability to create custom macros to fit the individual style of the practitioner. Of course, this hypothetical system will provide owners with excellent service and technical support, all at a price that one can afford. My largest investment was in QEEG assessment equipment and supplies. Expect to pay over $8,000 to purchase a 19-channel assessment tool.

PRACTICE, PRACTICE, PRACTICE

Following supervision (mentoring), equipment will be purchased and the software to run that equipment will be loaded in your computer's hard drive. Make sure you are getting a good EEG signal. Practice placing sensors on family members. Take measurements and readings. Determine the theta-to-beta ratio at various positions on the scalp. Compare alpha, theta, and beta measurements at Cz to see if they are in proportion. If one of your family members has a high theta-to-beta ratio at Cz (or elsewhere), it may be acceptable to train them—check with your mentor (supervisor) and stay within the guidelines presented to you at the training program. Become very familiar with the new equipment. Practice over and over again, so that software operation becomes automatic. A personal experience with biofeedback is necessary. Understand what goes through the mind of a trainee—train yourself before you train others. Biofeedback Certification Institute of America (BCIA) requires personal training time, and this is a good time to start.

Take EEG recordings from family and friends. But avoid casual training experiences. Do not train anyone without an adequate evaluation or proper mentoring (supervision). Experiments in neurofeedback training can backfire. For example, psychotherapists do not counsel friends because there is a dual relationship. In the same way our judgment can be skewed when it comes to friends. On the other hand, it may be appropriate to train certain family members, especially when little or no counseling is involved. Read the ethics guidelines printed on the BCIA Web site for more information.

17

Finding the Right Office, Marketing, and Clinical Vision

THERE ARE MANY WAYS TO START a successful practice as a neurofeed-back provider. Some professionals limit their practice to one segment of the clinical population whereas others treat a variety of clinical conditions. A few have concentrated on peak performance training for athletes, business executives and others in search of improved mental power and flexibility. Choosing the best model for clinical practice and setting up an office can be a dauting task. Chapter 17 will help you to prepare for this challenge.

CHOOSING AN OFFICE

Your brief internship introduced you to an appropriate office setup. If you were to tour my office, you would find a waiting room, bathroom, hallway sink (for cleaning sensors), and three treatment rooms. My main treatment room is for neurofeedback training and evaluation. This is the room where I acquire data for brain maps. It is also the room where I do deep-states training because it tends to be quiet and the lights can be turned off or dimmed. The client sits in a nonrocking recliner chair. Cushions and back supports are useful for clients with back problems or for children who are too small for the chair. A colorful cloth or towel is draped over the back of the chair that can be changed as need be. The training computer sits on a computer desk with wheels. Next to the client is a small movable cart that holds supplies such as NuPrep,™ Ten20™ paste, paper towels, 2-in. square (50-mm-square) nonsterile gauze pads, rubbing alcohol, and baby wipes. Neurofeedback training systems are placed near the client on the same movable cart. I find it helpful to file brain maps in the main treatment room. My second treatment room is for peripheral biofeedback, BWE, and bodywork. My wife does energy work and reflexology in this room and a commercial-grade surface electromyography (SEMG) biofeedback system is there when needed. My third treatment room is for neurofeedback training, sit-down counseling, and interviewing and general office work.

Outside Electrical Artifact or Interference

Neurofeedback systems are sensitive to outside electrical interference. The client with scalp-mounted sensors is like an antenna. Therefore, an office space that is heavily bombarded by radio waves (radio frequency interference [RFI]) and other electrical signals (electromagnetic interference [EMI]) may be unacceptable. Close proximity to powerful electrical equipment or motors may also impede the data acquisition process. Shielding can be fabricated in the attempt to limit electrical interference. (In the movie *Enemy of the State*, Gene Hackman had a secret fortress that was protected by a grounded copper-coated wire fence. No outside signals could get in. It was an overgrown Faraday cage.) But how many practitioners really want to rip down their walls, floors, and ceilings to create a grounded wire mesh enclosure? Grounded shields can be made from silver paint (available in McMaster-Carr catalog) to prevent excessive outside electrical interference. Silver paint can be applied to the panels of a changing screen; however, RFI and EMI can come from the ceiling or the floor.

The real solution is to find an office that is not subject to excessive RFI and EMI interference. I prefer an office space on the lowest floor of a brick building. Before signing a 1-year lease, ask an electrician or a power company professional to check the proposed site with a commercial-grade gauss meter. Do not rely on hobby gauss meters that cost about $100. A highly trained technician can give a prospective office a clean bill of health. But there's more: the grounding in the building must be proper. An electrician can check this, or you can with a relatively inexpensive testing device; it looks like a plug with three prongs and light-emitting diode (LED) lights. It's available at the hardware store; it plugs into each outlet to check for proper grounding. Lastly, the intensity of fluorescent lights can also corrupt your readings. Fluorescent lights are a source of

60-Hz artifact. Remember, hertz means cycles per second. It does not matter if the electrical signal comes from muscles, brain waves, or fluorescent lights; they are all output in cycles per second. Fluorescent lights do not always cause excessive interference, but they do sometimes. Lastly, pay attention to the carpet—static electricity can damage some systems. Take precautions to reduce static discharges, which often increase during dry weather. An antistatic mat can be purchased from McMaster-Carr catalog service. To be effective, it is grounded to the wall outlet. Standing on an antistatic mat grounds both client and clinician before sensors are mounted.

Location, Location, Location

If the decision is made to dedicate the practice to neurofeedback, then an appropriate name may be in order, one that clearly identifies either neurofeedback or the clinical population you intend to treat. *Find an office that is on a well-traveled road.* Good visibility is a plus. New clients often come from referrals within the community or from those who keep up with the latest scientific developments. Some have read *A Symphony in the Brain* (Robbins, 2000) or another book that describes the potential of neurotherapy. Usually these folks ask intelligent questions and are willing to try high-tech solutions. Medication reduction or elimination may be one of their goals. Many locate me because of my professionally designed office sign. Somehow they missed the ads in the newspaper and the brochures I displayed at local health stores. They failed to attend the health fair and missed the article I had just written for the local health journal. But they did see my highly visible sign. Ultimately, it is the satisfied trainee who is your best marketing agent—especially *mothers* who have seen a positive transformation in their children. It is also important to network with other professionals and to give presentations to schools and large support groups.

The budget often dictates which office you choose and where it is located. It may be helpful to position your office near other alternative health care providers. Or, it may be helpful position your office near a hospital or other medical practice. Neurotherapy has one foot grounded in medical practice and the other foot planted in the alternative health care category. The location of your business may determine which foot is carrying more weight. Choosing an appropriate office must be in concert with your clinical vision—it may have much to do with the kind of office you choose to create.

CREATING A CLINICAL VISION FOR YOUR NEW PRACTICE

I have been in practice for a number of years. My mental health practice was at one time devoted solely to the practice of psychotherapy for individuals and couples. For that matter, I continue to do some mental health counseling. But now most of my new clients are seeking neurotherapy. The name of my business is Neurofeedback of Southern Vermont. I am not shy about declaring my specialty. Others have realized a vision different than mine. They do not see their professional life consumed with neurotherapy. For example, a group practice may choose to offer neurotherapy as one of many therapies offered at their clinic. An independent therapist may envision neurotherapy as an adjunct that is applied to specific clinical disorders.

Practice Models

If the decision is to make neurotherapy an adjunct, then avoid clinical diversity. For example, you may wish to specialize in neurotherapy for attention deficit disorder (ADD) and other related learning disorders. Or you may wish to limit your practice to the treatment of depression and anxiety disorders. Or you may wish to highlight neurofeedback and photic stimulation for the treatment of posttraumatic stress disorder (PTSD). Keep a simple focus. Avoid becoming overly diversified. Independent practitioners may find it advantageous to keep their professional name as the name of the practice. Avoid a business name that can label you as a neurofeedback provider. It may be a signal to the community that you are no longer providing counseling services for families, groups, or individuals.

Attention Model. Advertise to the community that you are specializing in attention enhancement and improved cognitive processing. Services include (a) family counseling and couples therapy, (b) coaching for ADD/ADHD (Schwiebert, Sealander, & Dennison, 2002), and (c) neurofeedback training for those looking for an alternative to medication. Assess new clients for attention processing with the Intermediate Visual and Auditory (IVA), MicroCog, and perhaps a simple IQ test. Many clients with attention deficits have an IQ test that is 20 points higher than the IVA test score. The computerized tests should show problems with sustained attention and cognitive deficits. At that point, some clients may choose neurotherapy, medication, or one of your counseling options.

Almost half of your potential clients with slow-wave disorders will improve with hemoencephalography (HEG) neurotherapy in the prefrontal
cortex. Theta-to-beta ratios determine the efficacy of regional cerebral
blood flow (rCBF) enhancement. Theta reduction training may also be appropriate at Cz. If you choose to train along the sensorimotor cortex, then
a two-channel protocol will make it easier to maintain the balance dictated
by the beta/alpha/theta (BAT) triad. In addition to excessive theta, anterior
alpha slowing and posterior fast-wave disorders are commonly found in
this population. The goal of this treatment is to enhance attention. Hyperactivity and impulsivity may also improve. Success comes with improved
IVA scores and better grades. Do not limit yourself to children. Adults are
good candidates. Neurotherapy to enhance attention is an important adjunct to couples therapy. Distractibility and inattention are communication
busters. Combine communication coaching with neurotherapy to improve
the quality of marriage counseling. The above model is not intended as
treatment for conduct disorder or traumatic brain injury (TBI).

Trauma and Recovery Model. Counselors, social workers, and psychologists
who specialize in trauma and recovery and other psychological depth issues
may wish to limit their practice to deep states training via neurotherapy
and brain wave entrainment (BWE). Perhaps they are already adept at eye
movement desensitization and reprocessing (EMDR), holographic memory resolution (HMR), or some other power therapy for the treatment
of PTSD.

Neurotherapy can be used to teach the client grounding skills. Eyes-
open protocols for single-channel theta reduction at the vertex may be
appropriate. Begin with the assessment process outlined in Chapter 10.
Anywhere from 5 to 20 sessions will be needed. BWE at 14 Hz or in
the beta range may also promote better grounding and an uplifted mood.
Thereafter, either BWE or neurotherapy can be used to recover repressed
memories and feelings. BWE is not for all clients; it will trigger flashbacks in
those who have not mastered diaphragmatic breathing and other grounding
skills. Neurotherapy takes longer but it may be more appropiate for the
client with Axis II traits or substance abuse issues. Neurotherapy also allows
for complex reward and inhibit protocol designs that utilize four or more
filters. Complex protocols for dissociative identity disorders require further
training and workshops to ensure proper application.

BWE is also a powerful tool to help psychotherapy clients who are
blocked. For example, after 12–15 productive sessions, the therapy for one

adult was waning. Comments were becoming more intellectual and less therapeutic. In order to change that trend, I arranged for the client to engage in BWE for the next 3 sessions. Combining BWE with talk ended the block and opened up significant issues that were soon worked through. BWE not only reduced the total number of sessions, but it may have made the difference between treatment success and failure.

Peak Performance Model. Peak performance for executives and others can take on many forms. There are several approaches to peak performance or cognitive enhancement. Its possible to begin with the goal of improving IVA or MicroCog scores. After 20 or more sessions to enhance cognitive performance, alpha synchrony, alpha enhancement, or alpha/theta (A/T) training can be used to provide the trainee with greater mental flexibility and a broader perspective of life. This approach requires good marketing skills. It targets leaders in the business world, athletes, and others who need to enhance creativity. Quantitative EEG (QEEG) assessments and topographical brain maps demonstrate the rationale for treatment designs. What makes this approach unique is its emphasis on positive growth and personal development rather than on symptom reduction and clinical disorders.

For more information on alpha synchrony training and peak performance training, read the papers by McKnight and Fehmi (2001), Norris and Currieri (1999), as well as Mason and Brownback (2001). Further information can be found in *Biofeedback*, volume 29, number 1 (2001). This issue heralds the theme: "The Pursuit of Optimal Functioning" (www.aapb.org).

CONCLUSION

Getting Started with Neurofeedback emphasizes the need for assessment before training commences. No list of canned protocols is provided for the reader because of the diversity and complexity of the cerebral cortex. "One size does not fit all." The same clinical disorder may have many neurological faces. The application of any protocol without prior assessment will result in needless treatment failures. The rationale for any treatment plan must be founded upon a clinical diagnosis, a careful analysis of the EEG, and a working knowledge of neurology (TP = DEN). Treatment protocol decisions, clinical methods, and theory vary from practitioner to practitioner. However, "the proof is in the pudding." Exit questionnaires and baseline

comparisons are the means to establish that proof and the value of neurofeedback training.

Neurotherapy is about helping others to help themselves. It empowers
the client to regulate the self by altering cerebral functioning at the cellular
level. Neurotherapy is an ever growing and expanding field. After your first
training experience is complete, keep up with current research. Organizations such as the International Society for Neuronal Regulation and the
Association for Applied Psychophysiology and Biofeedback publish excellent journals that keep abreast of current developments in neurotherapy
and biofeedback. Networking with other practitioners at one of the annual
conventions will broaden your scope of neurotherapy. The growth of neurotherapy is in no way limited to the United States. Clinical research and
development is a worldwide phenomenon. This book is designed to help
professionals enter into the international field of neurotherapy. More and
more seminars for professionals are highlighting the role of brain dynamics
in human psychology. Neurotherapy is a practical way to apply current
neurological discoveries.

APPENDICES

Appendix 1

TABLE A1.1
Eyes-Open Peak-to-Peak Microvolt Data*

HERTZ	DELTA (0–4)	THETA (4–8)	ALPHA (8–12)	BETA (13–21)	SMR (12–15)	H.B. (20–30)	A-1 (8–10)	A-2 (10–12)
FZ	13.1	11.1	7.8	9.4	4.3	8.2	3.9	3.9
CZ	12.7	9.9	7.8	8.2	4.0	5.5	3.5	4.3
PZ	13.3	8.7	10.9	9.8	5.7	6.0	3.9	7.1
C3	12.5	9.0	10.0	8.0	4.5	5.8	3.8	6.2
C4	11.5	9.0	7.9	8.7	4.2	6.4	3.4	4.5
T3	8.4	6.2	5.0	9.9	3.3	13.6	2.4	2.6
T4	9.1	7.0	4.4	9.9	3.4	12.1	2.2	2.2
T5	8.9	6.2	5.9	8.4	4.1	7.1	2.5	3.4
T6	9.3	7.0	6.7	8.8	4.2	6.1	2.9	3.8
F3	13.3	9.6	6.9	7.8	3.7	7.4	3.5	3.4
F4	11.7	9.6	7.2	9.6	4.0	9.6	3.3	3.9
F7	9.6	6.5	4.8	6.5	2.9	9.4	2.6	2.2
F8	8.2	6.7	4.7	6.7	2.9	6.5	2.3	2.3
P3	11.5	7.9	9.1	9.2	4.8	6.2	3.6	5.5
P4	12.2	8.7	11.0	9.8	5.3	6.1	4.5	6.5
O1	10.2	6.7	7.5	11.2	5.0	11.8	3.2	4.3
O2	10.4	7.3	8.2	10.1	5.3	6.8	3.6	4.6
FP1	8.8	6.9	4.7	6.6	2.7	9.1	2.4	2.3
FP2	9.0	7.3	4.8	7.8	3.0	12.2	2.4	2.4

*Dominant alpha frequency approximately 11.0 Hz.

Table A1.1 is rendered in peak-to-peak microvolt measurements of client K, a 10-year-old with anxiety and ADHD. The data were artifacted and

237

processed with Lexicor MS-DOS software. The following represents an analysis of the data. The reader is invited to look at the Figure 6.11c (client K) and compare it to the data. The topographical map facilitated the task of interpreting the data much easier.

Consider the following summary:

- Theta lateral symmetry (okay)—e.g., C3 ≅ C4
- Dominant alpha = 11 Hz (too high) possible anxiety, insomnia
- C3 alpha > C4 alpha, (concern, especially from 10–12 Hz)
- PZ SMR > CZ SMR
- PZ (10–12 Hz) excessive
- Temporal lobe beta/SMR/H.B. equals or exceeds beta at vertex or CZ (concern)
- Theta-to-beta ratio at CZ is 1.2:1 magnitude = 1.44:1 power ratio (lower than average)
- Posterior beta and SMR > anterior beta and SMR (concern)

Data derived training protocols:
- Downtrain fast waves at PZ from 10–15 Hz.

- Downtrain high alpha at C3 from 10–15 Hz.
- Downtrain 13–30 Hz at O1, T5, T3

Map derived training protocols:
Map and data very similar (10–17 Hz) is excessive and should be inhibited.

Training protocol: Downtrain with eyes-open 10–17 Hz at CZ-PZ (bipolar montage).

Results: Improved sleep, concentration and calmness.

FIGURE A1.1
CLIENT K: REJECTED SAMPLE OF QEEG WAVE MORPHOLOGY

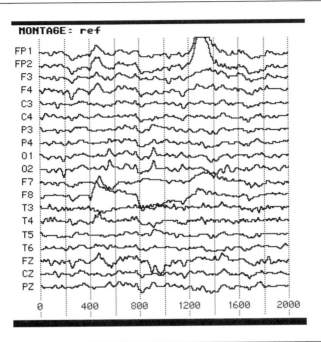

Wave morphology of data for client K as seen in Figure 6.11c. There is widespread artifact due to muscle and body movement. Eyes-open data acquisition is challenging due to the increased eye-blinking and forehead movement. Eye-rolling and blinking can readily be seen at FP1 and FP2.

FIGURE A1.2
CLIENT K: ACCEPTED SAMPLE OF QEEG WAVE MORPHOLOGY

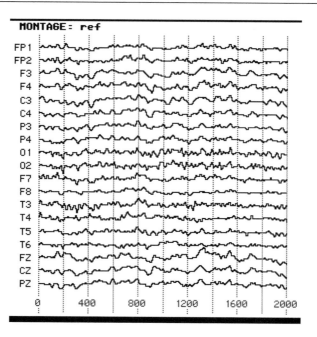

Wave morphology of data for client K as seen in Figure 6.11c. Figure A1.2 wave morphology is much cleaner than the morphology in Figure A1.1. It was one of many epochs that were used to process QEEG data and form the Figure 6.11c topographical map. The task of the technician artifacting the data is to reject the epochs with unsuitable data and to accept the epochs with clean data. The accepted epochs can be numerically processed by normative database software.

Appendix 2

HERTZ	DELTA (0–4)	THETA (4–8)	ALPHA (8–12)	BETA (13–21)	SMR (12–15)	H.B. (20–30)	A-1 (8–10)	A-2 (10–12)
FZ	6.7	7.0	9.8	5.3	2.0	3.9	5.8	4.0
CZ	7.2	7.5	11.8	6.7	2.6	4.7	6.9	4.9
PZ	6.8	7.3	14.8	7.3	2.9	4.5	9.5	5.4
C3	6.7	6.5	10.2	5.7	2.3	4.4	5.9	4.2
C4	5.5	5.9	8.9	5.6	2.2	4.1	5.1	3.8
T3	4.5	3.9	5.6	4.0	1.6	3.5	3.1	2.5
T4	5.1	4.0	5.2	4.4	1.7	4.1	2.8	2.4
T5	5.0	6.0	11.9	6.0	2.3	4.2	8.4	3.4
T6	4.4	5.2	10.1	5.0	1.9	3.8	6.6	3.4
F3	7.0	6.4	9.2	5.1	1.9	3.9	5.4	3.9
F4	7.2	6.4	9.1	5.2	2.0	4.2	5.4	3.7
F7	5.8	4.7	6.7	4.3	1.6	3.5	3.8	2.9
F8	5.9	5.0	6.9	4.3	1.6	4.4	4.1	2.8
P3	6.6	7.0	13.7	6.7	2.7	4.2	9.3	4.4
P4	5.6	6.4	12.5	6.4	2.5	4.3	8.1	4.4
O1	5.1	6.3	16.6	7.2	2.9	5.0	8.6	8.0
O2	5.0	6.1	17.1	6.8	2.7	5.3	8.5	8.6
FP1	7.1	5.8	8.1	4.3	1.7	3.5	5.0	3.1
FP2	7.2	6.1	8.4	4.6	1.7	3.9	5.2	3.2

TABLE A2.1
Eyes-Closed Peak-to-Peak Microvolt Data*

*Dominant alpha frequency approximately 9.0 Hz.

Appendix table A2.1 has peak-to-peak microvolt measurements of client L, an adult patient with major depression and mild traumatic brain injury (mTBI). The data were artifacted and processed with Lexicor MS-DOS software. The following represents an analysis of the data. The reader is invited to look at the Figure 6.13c (client L) and compare it to the data. The topographical map made of the job of finding the correct frequency much easier. Consider the following summary:

- Theta lateral symmetry (okay)—e.g., F3 ≅ F4
- Dominant alpha = 9 Hz. (too low) possible cognitive deficits
- Posterior LH alpha > RH alpha (major concern)
- PZ, P3, and T5 have high A-1 alpha
- Anterior LH and RH alpha symmetry (okay)
- Anterior LH and RH beta symmetry (okay)

Data derived training protocols:
  Downtrain Alpha P3 and T5

Map derived training protocols:
- Downtrain 6.5–9 Hz at P3/T5
- Downtrain 6.5–9 Hz at FZ (I also added a beta reward)
- Dominant frequency training (Peak Alpha frequency)

Response to training: Improved mood, alertness, and better interpersonal communication. The artifacted microvolt data did not clearly show that there was EEG slowing at FZ and the mild TBI. The topographical brain map's single hertz bins specified exact range. The topographical brain maps for client L also made it clear that this client needed to train only with eye-closed. The client responded rapidly to the exacting protocol suggested by NeuroGuide's eyes-closed Laplacian map. However, I later added alpha dominant brain wave frequency training to the protocol. According to the client's self-report 10 minutes of peak frequency training gave him more energy.

FIGURE A2.1
TRAINING GRAPH OF CLIENT L: EXAMPLE OF A GOOD LEARNER

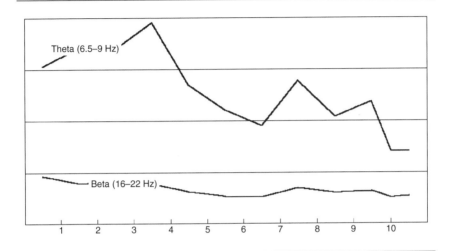

Brainmaster software training graph.

The training protocol was to inhibit 6.5–9 Hz and reward beta at P3/T5. Client L consistently responded well at each training session. This excellent training graph corresponded with his rapid recovery from depression. Client L had to reduce the 6.5–9 Hz at each training session. Slow wave activity did not permanently stay low, likely, client L's improved mood came from learning how to decrease slowing at will in the LH. Other clients will not be able to repeat client L's training graph. They may have lesser gains at each training session. Or they may be able to reduce the total amplitude of the specified frequency over the course of 5–15 training sessions.

FIGURE A2.2
CLIENT L: PEAK FREQUENCY TRAINING GRAPH

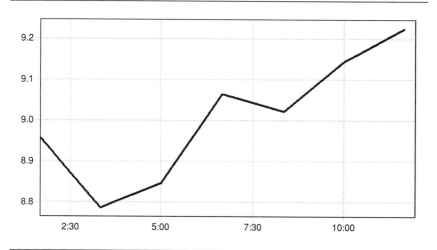

BioExplorer (© Cyber Evolution, Inc.) software training graph.

Client L was given the task of raising his posterior dominant rhythm (PDR). A referential montage was used and the scalp placement was at P3/T5, the same location used to downtrain 6.5–9 Hz. Client L remarked that this type of training produced increased energy and better mental clarity. Client L suffered from depression that was accompanied by a low dominant brain wave frequency. The goal of peak frequency training is to achieve 10 or 10.5 Hz. In the above graph client L achieve a modest gain.

Appendix 3

For Children Who are in Training

"The following handout can be given to the parents/guardians of children who are commencing neurofeedback training. It is a reminder to parents that successful neurotherapy requires the cooperation of the entire family. The suggestions contained in this handout cover such topics as diet, sleep, exercise, homework, and discipline. Most parents need more than just a handout to make family life style changes."

1. Sleep is critical; sleep deprivation will limit the effectiveness of training.
2. Diet may effect the training process. Limit or avoid sugary drinks, caffeinated drinks, candy and junk food, simple carbohydrate snacks, etc. Many children train poorly if their diet consists of soda, pizza, potato chips and other fast foods.
3. Amen (2001) recommended a higher protein diet. A well balanced diet with protein, vegetables, fruits and complex carbohydrates may help to reduce the symptoms of ADD.
4. Hungry children train poorly. If there is not enough time for a meal a high protein snack (sugar free) may improve the quality of training.
5. Some authorities claim that children with ADHD are prone to food allergy or intolerance. Wheat and milk have been sighted as common offenders. A naturopathic doctor (ND) may be able to isolate the problem.
6. How is food intolerance different than a food allergy? A child who is allergic to a food will likely have a same day reaction whereas a child who is intolerant to a food will likely have a delayed reaction. Symptoms of food intolerance may not manifest themselves until the problem food is ingested each day for 2 or more days. In some cases a rotation diet may be the solution. Rather than eliminate certain foods it may be beneficial to add them to your diet every third or fourth day.
7. Amen recommended certain supplements (2001, p. 274).
8. Children with ADHD do well with short term and immediate

rewards or consequences. That principle holds true at home and during training.

9. Motivation is essential. Children, who do not want to train, usually will not train. Teenagers cannot be forced to train. Some children will train if there is a reward system. Other children will not train—regardless of the reward.

10. The chicken and egg problem. Training may help hyperactive children to sit still more often. But how can they sit still to train if they are hyperactive? In some cases a small dose of Ritalin may help them to sit. In other cases vigorous exercise before training may help.

11. In general children with ADHD require more structure than those without ADHD. Family structure may include various rules such as homework first, fun second. TV programs are selected for content. Hours of consecutive unmonitored TV viewing and video game playing may undo training benefits and should be avoided. School sports cannot be played unless grades are maintained. Exercise is critical, aerobic exercise can be very calming—sometimes exercise comes before homework. Amen (2001) recommended a vigorous exercise program.

12. In some cases family therapy may be in order. A qualified therapist may be able to offer practical suggestions that go far beyond the scope of the above statements.

13. Training at the very minimum ought to be weekly, often children will train 2–3 times per week for the first few months, if possible.

14. Biofeedback is a self-regulation skill, unlike medications, it is not fast acting. After your child has consistently trained for 10–15 sessions it is essential to monitor progress. Daily charting of your child's behavior will help guide training protocols. The days immediately following the training will reflect the immediate benefits of the training. Teachers may also be especially helpful in assessing your child's progress.

Appendix 4

Suggestions for Creating a Release Form to be Signed by Clients, Parents, or Guardians

Neurotherapy clients who are training for purposes greater than relaxation training and muscle re-education may be requested to sign a release document. This document serves to inform the client that neurotherapy is an alternative treatment that is relatively safe but powerful. In some cases it may be wise to consult with a lawyer or an expert in medical practice when creating a release form. Consider the following four items.

1. Neurotherapy may change the threshold of medication effectiveness. For example, if a neurotherapy helps a trainee to ameliorate the symptoms of depression and that same trainee continues to take the anti-depressant wellbutrin then it may result in agitation or other overdose problems. Medication dosages may well have to be adjusted during the course of therapy and it is the trainee's responsibility to consult with his or her doctor to adjust medication dosages.
2. Neurotherapy may well be considered an experimental treatment despite the fact that there are hundreds of studies that support the efficacy of this treatment. Those studies do not constitute FDA approval. Neurofeedback and biofeedback are approved methods for general relaxation and muscle training and no more.
3. Neurotherapy may change one's mood or general emotional outlook. It may trigger sensations or memories of past events of trauma.
4. Trainee's who engage in eyes-closed alpha or alpha/theta training on a regular basis may well be at risk for the Peniston effect. This form of training is often used for survivors of childhood trauma and substance abusers. Almost half of those engaging in institutional studies who trained 5 or more times per week became allergic to alcohol, narcotics, or other addictive substances that had been formerly used. I have not personally seen this effect with my clients, who train only a few times per week, but nonetheless participating in deep states training puts individuals at risk for the Peniston effect and they must be informed. They have a right to know.

Trainees should be willing to sign a release that states that that will not hold you or your agency liable for any consequences that relate to the above mentioned concerns.

- Trainees need to understand that training may facilitate a neurological change.
- Trainees should not substitute neurofeedback for appropriate medical care.
- Neurofeedback providers do not make unsubstantiated claims.

Governmental laws and regulations may also need to be considered when creating a suitable release form for adult clients and another form for the parents and guardians of minors. Good communication with your client is probably the most important element in preventing potential lawsuits.

Make sure your adult client or the parents/guardians of a minor sign and date this consent form. In effect they are consenting and volunteering of their own free will to engage in neurotherapy despite the fact that there are possible negative consequences.

Appendix 5

Seizure Disorders (Epilepsy)

Neurofeedback providers are not neurologists. They are not expected to nor are they authorized to diagnose seizure disorders. However, since we are exposed to the EEG, it is best to be alert to the possibility of seizure disorder. First it's important to understand the some of the most common forms of seizure disorders and second it's important to know what to look for in the raw EEG or wave morphology.

1. Petit mal or absence seizures are mild generalized seizures. Episodes last from 5 to 30 seconds during which time the person stops activity and stares into space. Hence, the term absence means that the person is not longer consciously present. After the seizure episode the sufferers resume their former activity with little or no understanding of what has just happened. Several seizure episodes may happen each day or in severe cases there may be hundreds of episodes each day. Absence seizures or petit mal often occur in childhood between the ages of 6–12. Petit mal (absence) seizures are less dangerous than grand mal seizures.

2. Grand mal or generalized tonic-clonic seizures make their appearance in late adolescence or in adulthood. This type of seizure is often preceded by an aura or physical weakness, calling for help and/or unconsciousness. During a grand mal seizure the body becomes tonic or rigid for about a minute. Thereafter, the body goes into the clonic stage. Limbs begin to move in a jerking manner. The severe clonic response may continue for several minutes. After tonic and clonic stages are complete the victim may lapse into a deep sleep or feel disoriented.

There are many other types and designations for seizures including temporal lobe, partial (focal), nocturnal and febrile seizures. The key to identifying seizures in the EEG is the ability to recognize the morphology pattern of a spike that it is usually followed by a much slower wave. Hughes (1994) stated:

249

The sharp wave is the same as a spike, except for a difference in the duration of the event. Spikes are shorter in duration, usually <70 msec (approximately $\frac{1}{14}$ of a second), while sharp waves last from 70 to 200 msec ($\frac{1}{14}$ to $\frac{1}{5}$ of a second).

Another pattern related to the spike is the spike and wave complex, which consists of a spike followed by a wave. These complexes usually repeat themselves, especially at the frequency of 3/sec and at times under 3/sec or at 6/sec when bilateral. (p. 17)

FIGURE A5.1
IDENTIFYING SEIZURE SPIKES

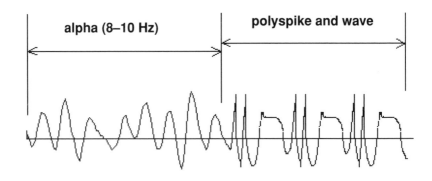

Normal alpha (8 Hz) wave morphology is shown in the left half of Figure A5.1. Compare the morphology of normal alpha with that of the polyspike and wave. Abnormal spikes have a sharp spear-like appearance which may followed a much slower wave that is 3.5–4.5 Hz. Seizure spike and wave patterns tend to repeat. They may be seen throughout the EEG or in just in one focal area. A polyspike (two or more spikes) and wave pattern is common to myoclonic seizures. *But a single-spike and wave pattern is more common to absence seizures.* If you observe a child or adolescent zoning out during neurofeedback training look for a single-spike and wave pattern in the raw EEG. Copy that pattern by pushing the print screen button on your keyboard so that it can be pasted to Microsoft Paint or to some other graphics program. A printout or an electronic file of the wave morphology pattern can be sent to your supervisor or mentor. It would also be wise to have the data examined by a neurologist. Sometimes a spike and wave pattern may be normal but that is not always the case. If your client has epilepsy then the treatment protocol will likely change.

Neurotherapy for epilepsy often takes place along the sensorimotor strip. SMR is often rewarded while theta is often inhibited. Protocols vary from case to case and with each seizure type. It must also be noted that slower spike and wave patterns may accompany brain injuries rather than seizure disorders. Furthermore, there are numerous other abnormal manifestations that have not been included in this brief discussion.

Appendix 6

TABLE A6.1
Medication Effects Upon the EEG

DRUG NAME OR CLASSIFICATION	EFFECT UPON THE EEG AND OTHER COMMENTS
Barbiturates	"Barbiturates produce an increase in the amount and amplitude of beta activity. The beta may reach high amplitudes and, although diffuse, it is often most prominent in the frontal regions" (Rowan & Tolunsky, 2003, pp. 81, 82).
Benzodiazapines	"Like barbiturates, benzodiazapines produce prominent beta activity. Even after the last dose of one of these drugs, excessive beta may persist for some days. Some diffuse theta range slowing may be seen along with attenuation of the posterior dominant rhythm" (ibid.).
Neuroleptics	"Phenothiazines, thioxanthenes, and butyrophenones at therapeutic doses cause slowing of the PDR along with diffuse slow waves" (ibid.).
Lithium	"Lithium may lead to diverse and prominent changes in the EEG. . . . One may see slowing of the PDR along with an increase in diffuse slowing. Intermittent rhythmic delta waves most prominent in the frontal or occipital regions may appear" (ibid.).
Tricyclic Antidepressants	"Tricyclic antidepressants such as imipramine, amitriptyline, doxepin, desipramine, and nortriptyline usually increase the amount of beta activity as well as theta activity in the record. The frequency of the PDR is usually decreased" (ibid.).
Cocaine	"Increased high frequency" (Hammond, 2001b, pp. 93, 94).
SSRIs	"The newer SSRI antidepressants such as fluoxetine (Prozac), venlafaxine (Effexor) and paroxetine (Zoloft) produce less delta and theta activity, decrease alpha, and increase beta" (ibid.).
Wellbutrin	"Antidepressant agents such as bupropion (Wellbutrin) have dopaminergic effects that tend to reverse vigilance impairment and drowsiness. Bupropion also decreases seizure threshold and produce epileptiform discharges in the EEG" (ibid.).

(continued)

	TABLE A6.1 (Continued)
DRUG NAME OR CLASSIFICATION	**EFFECT UPON THE EEG AND OTHER COMMENTS**
Stimulants	"Stimulants can decrease EEG slowing and increase fast activity. Topographically most medication effects are seen maximally over midline frontal or parietal cortex" (ibid.).

Appendix 7

Figures A7.1 and A7.2 are examples of gross asymmetries that can be easily identified in the raw EEG. Hughes states that the "background rhythm [raw EEG] can be considered as a general indication of the excitability of the central nervous system" (1994, p. 16). When we look at all 19 channels of the unfiltered background rhythm it gives us a general idea about the client's nature. But in Figures A7.1 and A7.2 we will examine only two EEG channels.

Figure A7.1 shows approximately 16 complete brain waves in approximately two seconds or 8 waves per second. Therefore the background rhythm of the EEG is 8 cycles per second or 8 Hz. The LH or T5 rhythm has greater amplitude than the RH or T6 rhythm. This is a case of alpha asymmetry common in depression. The LH alpha is greater than the RH alpha. However, the asymmetry is in the 8 Hz range. Training will be set between 7–9 Hz rather than 8–12 Hz. Downtraining 7–9 Hz helped relieve this client's depression. This is a case of a gross asymmetry that can be identified in the raw EEG. Only some asymmetries can be clearly seen in the raw EEG. Usually we have to examine the filtered waves.

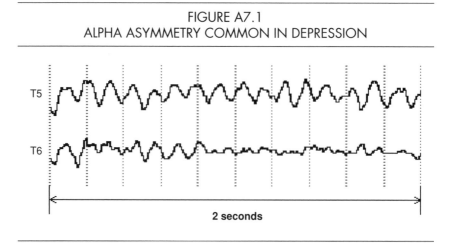

FIGURE A7.1
ALPHA ASYMMETRY COMMON IN DEPRESSION

T5

T6

2 seconds

FIGURE A7.2
BETA ASYMMETRY (AGGITATED DEPRESSION, PTSD)

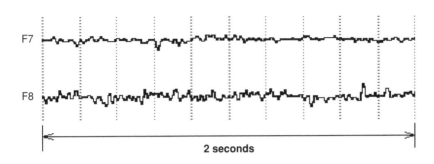

Figure A7.2 presents a very different background rhythm. This client has an agitated depression combined with PTSD. Simply downtraining beta will not resolve those symptoms. Resolution depends upon working through past trauma as well as being mindful of the prefrontal beta asymmetry. It would be very difficult to count the number of complete waves presented in Figure A7.2. But it is easy to see that the amplitude of RH or F8 beta far exceeds the amplitude of LH or F7 beta. Filtering the raw EEG indicates shows that the asymmetry includes both beta and high beta. Some clients respond well to anterior beta inhibition for limited periods of 7 minutes or as much as 15 minutes. I usually watch the training graph for reversals. As soon as beta begins to climb I stop the session. Other clients with excessive anterior beta may not respond to beta inhibition training. Alpha reward training in posterior locations may help to reduce excessive anterior beta. For clients with PTSD eyes-closed beta (15–30 Hz) inhibition at F8 may trigger a flashback.

References

Alexander, F. (1946). *Psychoanalytic therapy: Principles and application.* New York: Ronald Press.

Amen, D. (1998). *Change your brain, change your life.* New York: Three Rivers.

Amen, D. (2001). *Healing ADD: The breakthrough program that allows you to see and heal the 6 types of ADD.* New York: Putnam.

American Medical Association (1998). *Current procedural terminology: CPT 1999.* Chicago: Author.

American Psychiatric Association (1994). *Diagnostic and statistical manual of mental disorders* (4th ed.). Washington, DC: Author.

Atkinson, B. (1999). The emotional imperative psychotherapists cannot afford to ignore. *Family Therapy Networker, 23*(4), 22–33.

Ayers, M. (1999). Assessing and treating open head trauma, coma, and stroke using real-time digital EEG neurofeedback. In J. R. Evans & A. Arbarbanel (Eds.), *Introduction to quantitative EEG and neurofeedback* (pp. 203–222). San Diego, CA: Academic Press.

Baehr, E., Rosenfeld, J. P., Baehr, R., & Earnest, C. (1999). Clinical use of an alpha asymmetry neurofeedback protocol in the treatment of mood disorders. In J. R. Evans & A. Arbarbanel (Eds.), *Introduction to quantitative EEG and neurofeedback* (pp. 181–201). San Diego, CA: Academic Press.

Balch, J. F., & Balch, P. A., (2000). *Prescription for nutritional healing* (3rd ed.).New York: Avery.

Baum, B. (1997). *The healing dimensions: resolving trauma in the bodymind and spirit.* Tucson, AZ: West Press.

Beck, A. T., Freeman, A., & Associates (1990). *Cognitive therapy of personality disorders.* New York: Guilford Press.

Benson, H. (1975). *The relaxation response.* New York: William Morrow.

Berg, K., & Siever, D. (1999). The effect of audio-visual entrainment on seasonal affective disorder in a northern latitude. *Journal of Neurotherapy, 3* (3–4), 70–71.

Bernstein, E., & Putnam, F. W. (1986). Developmental, reliability and validity of a dissociation scale. *Journal of Nervous and Mental Disease, 174,* 727–735.

Blume, W. T., & Kaibara, M. (1995). *Atlas of adult electroencephalography.* New York: Raven Press.

Boscolo, L., Cecchin, G., Hoffman, L., & Penn, P. (1987). *Milan systemic family therapy.* New York: Basic.

Bowlby, J. (1988). *A secure base: Parent-child attachment and healthy human development*. New York: Basic.

Braun, B. G. (1988). The BASK model of dissociation clinical applications. *Dissociation*, 1(2), 16–23.

Brown, V. W., & Brown, S. (2000). The role of 40 Hz activity and training. (question 2). *The Journal of Neurotherapy*, 4(2), 100–101.

Budzynski, T. H. (1996). Brain brightening: Can neurofeedback improve cognitive process? *Biofeedback*, 24(2), 14–17.

Budzynski, T. H. (1999). From EEG to neurofeedback. In J. R. Evans & A. Arbarbanel (Eds.), *Introduction to quantitative EEG and neurofeedback* (pp. 65–79). San Diego, CA: Academic Press.

Burns, D. D. (1999). *The feeling good handbook*. New York: Plume.

Cantor, D. S. (1999). An overview of quantitative EEG and its applications to neurofeedback. In J. R. Evans & A. Arbarbanel (Eds.), *Introduction to quantitative EEG and neurofeedback* (pp. 3–27). San Diego, CA: Academic Press.

Carmody, D. P., Radvanski, D. C., Wadhwani, S., Sabo, M. J., & Vergara, L. (2001). EEG biofeedback training and attention-deficit/hyperactivity disorder in an elementary school setting. *Journal of Neurotherapy*, 4(3), 5–27.

Carter, R. (1998). *Mapping the mind*. Los Angeles: University of California Press.

Collura, T. (2002). Application of repetitive visual stimulation to EEG neurofeedback protocols. *Journal of Neurotherapy*, 6(2), 47–70.

Congedo, M., & Lubar, J. F. (2003). Parametric and non-parametric analysis of QEEG: Normative database comparisons in electroencephalography, a simulation study on accuracy. *Journal of Neurotherapy*, 7(3–4), 1–29.

Crane, A. (1998, October). *Modules A & B biofeedback training*. Ossining, NY: American Biotech Corp.

Criswell, E. (1995). *Biofeedback and somatics*. Novato, CA: Freeperson Press.

Crook, W. G. (1986). *The yeast connection*. Jackson, TN: Professional Books.

Damasio, A. A. (1994). *Descartes' error: Emotion, reason, and the human brain.*New York: Quill.

Davidson, R. J. (1998). Affective style and affective disorders: Prospectives from affective neuroscience. *Cognition and Emotion*, 12(3), 307–330.

Davidson, R. J. Abercrombie, H., Nitschke, J. B., & Putnam, K. (1999). Regional brain function, emotion and disorders of emotion. *Current Opinion in Neurobiology*, 9, 228–234.

Davidson, R. J., & Irwin, W. (1999). The functional neuroanatomy of emotion and affective style. *Trends in Cognitive Sciences*, 3(1), 11–21.

Davis, M., Eshelman, E. R., & McKay, M. (1995). *The relaxation & stress reduction workbook* (4th ed.). New York: New Harbinger.

Demos, J. N. (1995). Creating resonance within the therapeutic bond: Empathy and transference as covert transmissions. *Voices: The art and science of psychotherapy*, 31(1), 90–98.

Dennison, P. E., & Dennison, G. E. (1989). *Brain gym: Teacher's edition revised*. Ventura, CA: Edu-Kinesthetics.

DesMaisons, K. (1999). *Potatoes not prozac*. New York: Fireside.

Diamond, M. C., Scheibel, A. B., & Elson, L. M. (1985). *The human brain coloring book*. New York: HarperPerennial.

Fisher, S. (2004). Fear and FPO2: The implications of a new protocol. *Journal of Neurotherapy*, 8(1), 88–89.

Francina, S. (1997). *The new yoga for people over 50: A comprehensive guide for midlife & older beginners*. Deerfield Beach, FL: Health Communications.

Frederick, J. A., Lubar, J. F., Rasey, H. W., Brim, S. A., & Blackburn, J. (1999). Effects of

18.5 Hz auditory and visual stimulation on EEG amplitude at the vertex. *Journal of Neurotherapy*, 3(3–4), 23–27.

Freud, S., & Breuer, J. (1966). *Studies on hysteria.* New York: Basic Books

Glenmullen, J. (2000). *Prozac backlash: Overcoming the dangers of prozac, zoloft, paxil, and other antidepressants with safe, effective alternatives.* New York: Simon & Schuster.

Gurnee, R. (2002, September). *QEEG subtypes of major depressive disorder and implications for treatment.* Workshop at the conference of the Society for Neuronal Regulation, Scottsdale, AZ.

Gurnee, R. (2003, September). *Central 12–15 Hz activity in ADHD.* Paper presented at the conference of the International Society for Neuronal Regulation, Houston, TX.

Hammond, D. C. (1999). Roshi compared with the Rosenfeld depression protocol: A case report. *Journal of Neurotherapy*, 3(3–4), 63.

Hammond, D. C. (2000). The role of 40 Hz activity and training (question 1). *The Journal of Neurotherapy*, 4(2), 95–100.

Hammond, D. C. (2001a). Comprehensive neurofeedback bibliography. *Journal of Neurotherapy*, 5(1–2), 113–128.

Hammond, D. C. (2001b). Effects of antidepressant medications on the EEG. *Journal of Neurotherapy*, 5(4), 93–97.

Hammond, D. C. (2003a). QEEG-guided neurofeedback in the treatment of obsessive compulsive disorder. *The Journal of Neurotherapy*, 7(2), 25–52.

Hammond, D. C. (2003b). The effects of caffeine on the brain: A review. *The Journal of Neurotherapy*, 7(2), 79–89.

Hammond, D. C., & Gunkelman, J. (2001). *The art of artifacting.* Merino, CO: Society for Neuronal Regulation.

Harvard Medical School. (2004). The benefits of mindfulness. *Harvard Women's Health Watch*, 11(6), 1.

Herman, J. L. (1992). *Trauma and recovery.* New York: Basic.

Hodges, S. (2003). Borderline personality disorder and posttraumatic stress disorder: time for integration? *Journal of Counseling & Development*, 81(4), 409–417.

Hood, A. B., & Johnson, R. W. (1991). *Assessment in counseling: A guide to the use of psychological assessment procedures.* Alexandria, VA: American Association for Counseling and Development.

Horvat, J. (2004, August). *Coherence training.* Workshop presented at the International Society for Neuronal Regulation, Ft. Lauderdale, FL.

Hughes, J. R. (1994). *EEG in clinical practice* (2nd ed.). Boston: Butterworth-Heinemann.

Jasper, H. H., Solomon, P., & Bradley, C. (1938). Electroencephalographic analysis of behavior problems in children. *American Journal of Psychiatry*, 95, 641–658.

Johnstone, J., & Gunkelman, J. (2003). Use of databases in QEEG evaluation. *Journal of Neurotherapy*, 7(3–4), 31–52.

Joyce, M., & Siever, D. (2000). Audio-visual entrainment program as a treatment for behavior disorders in a school setting. *Journal of Neurotherapy*, 4(2), 9–25.

Katz, L. C., & Rubin, M. (1999). *Keep your brain alive: 83 neurobic exercises to help prevent memory loss and increase mental fitness.* New York: Workman.

Keeffe, E. B. (1999). *Know your body: The atlas of anatomy.* Berkeley, CA: Ulysses.

Kelley, M. J. (1997). Native Americans, neurofeedback, and substance abuse theory. Three year outcome of alpha/theta neurofeedback training in the treatment of problem drinking among Dine' (Navajo) people. *Journal of Neurotherapy*, 2(3), 24–60.

Kerson, C. (2002, September). *The benefits of measuring basal skin response during neurofeedback training.* Paper presented at the conference of the International Society for Neuronal Regulation, Scottsdale, AZ.

Keville, K. (1996). *Herbs for health and healing: A drug-free guide to prevention & cure.* New York: Rodale.

Krebs, D. (1995). Biofeedback in neuromuscular re-education and gait training. In M. S. Schwartz (Ed.), *Biofeedback: A practitioner's guide* (2nd ed., pp. 525–559). New York: Guilford Press.

Larson, G. (1989). *The prehisory of the far side: A 10th anniversary exhibit.* Kansas City, MO: Andrews McMeel.

Larson, G. (1984) *The far side gallery.* Kansas City, MO: Andrews McMeel.

Lee, J. R., & Hopkins, V. (1996) *What your doctor may not tell you about menopause: The breakthrough book on natural progesterone.* New York: Warner Books.

Linehan, M. M. (1993). *Skills training manual for treating borderline personality disorder.* New York: Guilford Press.

Lubar, J. F. (1995). Neurofeedback for the management of attention-deficit/hyperactivity disorders. In M. S. Schwartz (Ed.), *Biofeedback: A practitioner's guide* (2nd ed., pp. 493–523). New York: Guilford Press.

Lubar, J. F. (2001). Rationale for choosing bipolar verses referential training. *Journal of Neurotherapy,* 4(3), 94–97.

Lubar, J. F., Angelakis, E., Frederick, J., & Stathopoulou, S. (2001). The role of slow-wave electroencephalographic activity in reading. *Journal of Neurotherapy,* 5(3), 5–25.

Lubar, J. F., & Lubar, J. O. (1999). Neurofeedback assessment and treatment for attention deficit/hyperactivity disorders. In J. R. Evans & A. Arbarbanel (Eds.), *Introduction to quantitative EEG and neurofeedback* (pp. 103–143). San Diego, CA: Academic Press.

Lubar, J. F., & Lubar, J. O. (2002, February). Workshop at the meeting of the Future Health Winter Brain Conference, Miami, FL.

Lubar, J. F., Swartwood, M. O., Swartwood, J. N., & Timmermann, D. L. (1995). Quantitative EEG and auditory event-related potentials in the evaluation of attention-deficit/hyperactivity disorder: Effects of methyphenidate and implications for neurofeedback training. *Journal of Psychoeducational Assessment* (ADHD Special issue), 143–160.

Lukas, S. (1993). *Where to start and what to ask: An assessment handbook.* New York: Norton.

Luria, A. R. (1973). *The working brain: An introduction to neuropsychology* (B. Haigh, Trans.). New York: Basic.

Malchiodi, C. A. (1998). *Understanding children's drawings.* New York: Guilford Press.

Manchester, C., Allen, T., & Tachiki, K. (1998). Treatment of dissociative identity disorder with neurotherapy and group self-exploration. *Journal of Neurotherapy,* 2(4), 40–53.

Marieb, E. N. (1995). *Human anatomy and physiology* (3rd ed.). Redwood City: CA Benjamin/Cummings.

Martin, R., & Gerstung, D. C. (1998). *The estrogen alternative.* Rochester, VT: Healing Arts Press.

Mason, L. A., & Brownback, T. S. (2001). Optimal functioning training with EEG biofeedback for clinical populations: A case study. *Journal of Neurotherapy,* 5(1–2), 33–43.

McKnight, J. T., & Fehmi, L. G. (2001). Attention and neurofeedback synchrony training: clinical results and their significance. *Journal of Neurotherapy,* 5(1–2), 45–61.

Montgomery, D. D., Robb, J., Dwyer, V., & Gontkovsky, S. T. (1998). Single channel EEG amplitudes in a bright, normal, young adult sample. *Journal of Neurotherapy,* 2(4), 1–7.

Moore, J. P., Trudeau, D. L., Thuras, P. D., Rubin, Y., Stockley, H., & Dimond, T. (2000). Comparison of alpha-theta, alpha and EMG neurofeedback in the production of alpha-theta crossover and the occurrence of visualizations. *Journal of Neurotherapy,* 4(1), 29–42.

Norris, S. L., & Currieri, M. (1999). Performance enhancement training through neurofeedback. In J. R. Evans & A. Arbarbanel (Eds.), *Introduction to quantitative EEG and neurofeedback* (pp. 223–240). San Diego, CA: Academic Press.

Noton, D. (1997). PMS, EEG, and photic stimulation. *Journal of Neurotherapy*, 2(2), 8–13.

Nutt, A. E. (2003, November). The end of aging: breakthrough science may keep us from growing old. *Reader's Digest*, 70–75.

Othmer, S., & Othmer, S. F. (2000, June). *Beta/SMR training*. Presented at EEG-Spectrum, Philadelphia.

Othmer, S., Othmer, S. F., & Kaiser, D. A. (1999). EEG biofeedback: an emerging model for its global efficacy. In J. R. Evans & A. Arbarbanel (Eds.), *Introduction to quantitative EEG and neurofeedback* (pp. 243–310). San Diego, CA: Academic Press.

Papp, L. A., Coplan, J., & Gorman, J. M. (1992). Neurobiology of anxiety. In A. Tasman & M. B. Riba (Eds.), *American Psychiatric Press Review of Psychiatry* (vol. 11, pp. 307–322). Washington, DC: American Psychiatric Press.

Pease, B., & Pease, A. (2000). *Why men don't listen and women can't read maps*. New York: Broadway.

Peek, C. J. (1995). A primer of biofeedback instrumentation. In M. S. Schwartz (Ed.), *Biofeedback: A practitioner's guide* (2nd ed. pp. 45–95). New York: Guilford Press.

Peniston, E. G., & Kulkosky, P. J. (1991). Alpha-theta brainwave neuro-feedback for Vietnam veterans with combat-related post-traumatic stress disorder. *Medical Psychotherapy*, 4, 1–14.

Peniston, E. G., & Kulkosky, P. J. (1999). Neurofeedback in the treatment of addictive disorders. In J. R. Evans & A. Arbarbanel (Eds.), *Introduction to quantitative EEG and neurofeedback* (pp.157–179). San Diego, CA: Academic Press.

Pert, C. B. (1997). *Molecules of emotion: The science behind mind-body medicine*. New York: Simon & Schuster.

Peterson, J. M. (2000). Notes on the role of neurotherapy in the treatment of post-traumatic stress disorder. *Biofeedback*, 28(3), 10–12.

Pinel, J. P. J., & Edwards, M. (1998). *A colorful introduction to the anatomy of the brain*. Needham Heights, MA: Allyn & Bacon.

Posner, M. I., Rothbart, M. K., Vizueta, N., Levy, K. N., Evans, D. E., Thomas, K. M., & Clarkin, J. F. (2002). Attentional mechanisms of borderline personality disorder. *National Academy of Sciences*, 99(25), 16366–16370.

Preis, S., Jancke, L., Schmitz-Hillebrecht, J., & Steinmetz, H. (1999). Child age and planum temporale asymmetry. *Brain and Cognition*, 40, 441–452.

Putnam, F. W. (1989). *Diagnosis and treatment of multiple personality disorder*. New York: Guilford Press.

Ratey, J. J. (2001). *A user's guide to the brain: Perception, attention and the four theaters of the brain*. New York: Vintage.

Rector-Page, L. G. (1994). *Healthy healing: An alternative healing reference* (9th ed.). Carmel Valley, CA: Healthy Healing Publications.

Robbins, J. (2000a). *A symphony in the brain*. New York: Atlantic Monthly Press.

Robbins, J. (2000b, September 26). Some see hope in biofeedback for attention deficit disorder. *New York Times*, p. 7.

Rossiter, T. (2002). Neurofeedback for AD/HD: A ratio feedback case study and tutorial. *Journal of Neurotherapy*, 6(3), 9–35.

Rowan, A. J., & Tolunsky, E. (2003). *Primer of EEG with a mini-atlas*. Boston: Butterworth-Heinemann.

Ruuskanen-Uoti, H., & Salmi, T. (1994). Epileptic seizure induced by a product marketed as a "brainwave synchronizer." *Neurology*, 44, 181.

Sabo, M. J., & Giorgi, J. (1998, December). *EEG biofeedback: Applying the principles*. Workshop at Biofeedback Consultants, Inc., New York.

Sandford, J. A. (1995). *Intermediate Visual and Auditory continuous performance test administration manual*. Richmond, VA: Braintrain

Schnoll, R., Burshteyn, D., & Cea-Aravena, J. (1999). Nutrition and neurofeedback in the treatment of attention deficit hyperactivity disorder. *Biofeedback, 27*(4), 18–20.

Schnoll, R., Burshteyn, D., & Cea-Aravena, J. (2003). Nutrition in the treatment of attention-deficit hyperactivity disorder: A neglected but important aspect. *Applied Psychophysiology and Biofeedback, 28*(1), 63–75.

Schwartz, J., & Begley, S. (2002). *The mind and the brain: Neuroplasticity and the power of mental force*. New York: Regan.

Schwartz, J., & Beyette, B. (1996). *Brain lock: Free yourself from obsessive compulsive disorder*. New York: Regan.

Schwartz, M. S. (1995). Breathing therapies. In M. S. Schwartz (Ed.), *Biofeedback: A Practitioner's Guide* (2nd ed.; pp. 525–559). New York: Guilford Press.

Schwartz, M. S., & Olson, R. P. (1995). A historic perspective on the field of biofeedback and applied psychophysiology. In M. S. Schwartz (Ed.), *Biofeedback: A practitioner's guide* (2nd ed.; pp. 3–18). New York: Guilford Press.

Schwiebert, V. L., Sealander, K. A., & Dennison, J. L. (2002). Strategies for counselors working with high school students with attention-deficit/ hyperactivity disorder. *Journal of Counseling & Development, 80*(1), 3–10.

Scott, W. (2000, June). *Alpha/theta training*. Presented at EEG-Spectrum, Philadelphia.

Scott, W., Brod, T. M., Siderof, S., Kaiser, D., & Sagan, M. (2002, May). *Type-specific EEG biofeedback improves residential substance abuse treatment*. Poster presentation at the meeting of the American Psychiatric Association. Philadelphia. Also Available at http://members.aol.com/williamcscott/research.htm

Sears, W., & Thompson, L. (1998). *The ADD book: New understandings, new approaches to parenting your child*. New York: Little Brown.

Shannon, S. (2000, July). Alternative healing: What really works. *Reader's Digest*.

Shaphiro, F. (1995). *Eye movement and desensitization and reprocessing: Basic principles, protocols and procedures*. New York: Guilford Press.

Siever, D. (1999). *The rediscovery of audio-visual entrainment technology* (version 5). Edmonton, AB: Comptronic Devices Limited.

Siever, D. (2003). Audio-visual entrainment: I. History and physiological mechanisms *Biofeedback, 31*(2), 21–27.

Siever, D. (2004). Applying audio-visual entrainment technology for attention and learning – Part III. *Biofeedback, 31*(4), 24–29.

Sills, F. (2001). *Craniosacral biodynamics: The breath of life, biodynamics, and fundamental skills*. Berkeley, CA: North Atlantic Books.

Smith, K. (2000). The impossible child. *Family Therapy Networker, 24*(5), 46–57.

Soutar, R. (2004, August). *Linking the EEG of the anxious mind to behavior*. Workshop presented at the International Society for Neuronal Regulation, Ft. Lauderdale, FL.

Springer, S. P., & Deutsch, G. (1998). *Left brain, right brain: Perspectives from cognitive neuroscience* (5th ed.). New York: W. H. Freeman.

Stampi, C., Stone, P., & Michirnori, A. (1995). A new quantitative method for assessing sleepiness: The alpha attenuation test. *Work Stress, 9*, 368–376.

Stoll, A. (2002). *The omega-3 connection: The groundbreaking antidepression diet Program*. New York: Simon & Schuster.

Stordy, B. J. & Nicholl, M. J. (2000). The LCP solution: *The remarkable nutritional treatment for ADHD, dyslexia, and dyspraxia*. New York: Ballantine.

Striefel, S. (1999). Ethical, legal, and professional pitfalls associated with neurofeedback services. In J. R. Evans & A. Arbarbanel (Eds.), *Introduction to quantitative EEG and neurofeedback* (pp. 371–399). San Diego, CA: Academic Press.

Suldo, S. M., Olson, L. A., & Evans, J. R. (2001). Quantitative EEG evidence of Increased alpha peak frequency in children with precocious reading ability. *Journal of Neurotherapy*, 5(3), 39–50.

Swingle, P. G. (1996). Subthreshold 10-Hz sound suppresses EEG theta: Clinical application for the potentiation of neurotherapeutic treatment of ADD/ADHD. *Journal of Neurotherapy*, 2(1), 15–22.

Thatcher, R. W. (1999). EEG Database-Guided Neurotherapy. In J. R. Evans & A. Arbarbanel (Eds.), *Introduction to quantitative EEG and neurofeedback* (pp. 29–64). San Diego, CA: Academic Press.

Toomim, H. (2002). Neurofeedback with hemoencephalography (HEG). *Explore!, 11*(1), 19–21.

Toomim, H., & Carmen J. (1999). Hemoencephalography (HEG). *Biofeedback, 27*(4), 10–14.

United States Food and Drug Administration, *Biofeedback Devices-Draft Guidance for 510(k) Content*, August 1994-www.fda.gov/cdrh/ode/143.html

van der Kolk, B. A., McFarlane, A. C., & Weisaeth, L. (1996). *Traumatic stress: The effects of overwhelming experience on mind, body, and society*. New York: Guilford Press.

Vogt, B. A., Finch, D. M., & Olson, C. R. (1992). Functional heterogeneity in cingulate cortex; the anterior executive and posterior evaluative regions. *Cerebral Cortex*, 2(6), 435–443.

Walker, J. E., Norman, C. A., & Weber, R. K. (2002). Impact of qEEG-guided coherence training for patients with mild closed head injury. *Journal of Neurotherapy*, 6(2), 31–43.

Weiner, M. (1996). *The complete book of homeopathy*. New York: Avery.

White, N. E. (1999). Theories of the effectiveness of alpha-theta training for multiple disorders. In J. R. Evans & A. Arbarbanel (Eds.), *Introduction to quantitative EEG and neurofeedback* (pp. 341–367). San Diego, CA: Academic Press.

Wylie, M. S. (1996). Going for the cure. *The Family Therapy Networker*, 20(4), 20–37.

Wylie, M. S. (2004). The limits of talk. *Psychotherapy Networker*, 28(1), 30–36.

Wyricka, W., & Sterman, M. B. (1968). Instrumental conditioning of sensorimotor cortex EEG spindles in the waking cat. *Physiology & Behavior*, 3, 703–707.

Index